An Introduction to Public Administration

Second Edition

People, Politics, and Power

GW00702300

An Introduction to Public Administration

Second Edition

People, Politics, and Power

J. Denis Derbyshire

McGRAW-HILL Book Company (UK) Limited

London · New York · St Louis · San Francisco · Auckland · Bogotá
Guatemala · Hamburg · Johannesburg · Lisbon · Madrid · Mexico
Montreal · New Delhi · Panama · Paris · San Juan · São Paulo
Singapore · Sydney · Tokyo · Toronto

Published by McGRAW-HILL Book Company (UK) Limited
MAIDENHEAD · BERKSHIRE · ENGLAND

British Library Cataloguing in Publication Data

Derbyshire, J. Denis
   An introduction to public administration.
   —2nd ed.
   1. Great Britain—Politics and Government
   —1979–
   I. Title
   350'.000941   JN309

   ISBN 0-07-084866-1

12345 W.C. 8654

Filmset by Eta Services (Typesetters) Ltd, Beccles, Suffolk
Printed and bound in Great Britain by William Clowes Limited, Beccles, Suffolk

Contents

Preface

The first edition of *An Introduction to Public Administration* was written in the closing months of the government of James Callaghan and Mrs Thatcher moved into No. 10 Downing Street as the final proofs were being read. During the intervening five years there have been momentous changes in Westminster, Whitehall, and our local town and county halls, which have put a new complexion on politics and public administration.

The production of a second edition has provided an opportunity to bring the facts and figures up to date and has allowed me to reappraise some important concepts, such as the role of the Cabinet, the power of the Prime Minister, the accountability of government, and the degree of public participation in political activity. What still seems to be relevant and important in the original edition has been retained but substantial sections have been completely rewritten in the light of changed circumstances and attitudes.

The book will still be of value to students aiming for the B/TEC awards but will now be especially useful to 'A'-level students of government, politics, and public administration, as well as to first-year undergraduates of any discipline who require an introduction to politics and government.

Acknowledgements

David Patterson, who contributed the local government sections to the first edition, is absolved from any responsibility for errors or omissions in this book, although the value of his original work is again acknowledged.

In addition, I would like to thank the staffs of the library of the Royal Institute of Public Administration, the Central Management Library of the Cabinet Office, the library of Slough College of Higher Education, and the research staff of the British Institute of Management, for their help.

I am also grateful to the McGraw-Hill Book Company, and particularly Alastair Fyfe Holmes and Carolyn Ebbitt, for their encouragement and advice.

Finally, I am, again, greatly indebted to my wife, for her tolerance, and my sons, for their helpful comments.

J.D.D.

Part One   The political framework

The political setting

The nature of public administration

Government consists of two elements: the political and the non-political. The first is temporary and elected; the second is permanent and appointed. One could not exist without the other: theirs is essentially a partnership of mutual dependence.

When a Member of Parliament (MP) is asked to take charge of a government department he finds he has at his disposal a powerful machine capable of putting into effect any policies which he and his colleagues choose to adopt. It is a machine that will serve him well if he uses it wisely and it is one which has served his political opponents equally well in the past. A broadly similar situation exists at local level. The importance of the central and local machines is often underestimated; certainly their purpose is much misunderstood. Without civil servants and local government officers to implement their political decisions, ministers and councillors would be impotent. If they could not rely on the integrity of the people operating the machines, democratic government, as we have come to know it in this country, would be threatened.

The civil service and the local government service have the task of translating political objectives into practical realities and this process we call public administration. We shall be using the term public administration in a wider sense as well. We shall use it to describe the machines themselves: the departments of state and the local authority departments. We shall also use it at times to describe the people who operate the central and local machines. By public administration, then, we mean the machinery of central and local government, the process of implementing political decisions, and the body of people involved in that process.

Before we begin our study we must remind ourselves of the political context within which public administration operates.

The nature of political power

Politics might be described as something politicians do. We all know that politicians claim to represent our interests. They ask us to vote them into office so that they can do things on our behalf. They want to use the power of the state to do things which private individuals cannot or will not do on their own, such as building roads, libraries, hospitals, schools, and the like. At the same time most people are healthily sceptical about politics and politicians. They know promises made at election times are not always kept. They know that politicians have notoriously short memories. They recall the remark of a former Prime Minister that a week in politics is a long time.

We would probably all agree that politicians are concerned about the use of the power of the state. They seek election to Parliament or to a local council so that they may use public power, allegedly on our behalf. If they do not immediately get access to that power, in other words do not become part of the governing group, they range themselves in opposition to that group, hoping eventually to replace them and gain power themselves. Therefore, we might agree that politics is concerned with the securing of power and then the exercise of it: but is that understanding enough?

History records many examples of people, individually or in groups, gaining power and using it but acting in ways which the majority of people in this country would, at the present time, find objectionable. If pressed to explain their objections, they would probably say that they were not satisfied that the power had been gained legitimately. Or they might say that the power was not being used in the interests of the majority of people, but rather in the interests of the minority who had seized it. Some objectors might quote the dictum of Lord Acton that all power corrupts and absolute power corrupts absolutely. What the objectors to the use of power in this way are really saying is that there is a political way in which power can be secured and a non-political way. The political way is found in those states we usually call democracies and the non-political way has been demonstrated by dictators such as Hitler, Mussolini, the tsars of Russia, the autocratic kings of this country before the seventeenth century, and today by the rulers of those countries we describe as totalitarian.

In trying to identify and explain politics we have been forced to introduce other words and concepts such as democracy and totalitarianism. We will return to these in a moment: for the present let us stick to our search for an acceptable explanation of politics.

Politics as an evolutionary process

Aristotle, the Greek philosopher, in his second book *Politics*, gave the first clear indication of what politics was about. He was the first writer to realize that politics is an activity which recognizes the different interests and aspirations of people living together in the same community and tries to accommodate these differences within an acceptable system of government. A political way is only one method of governing a country. There have been, still are, and always will be other ways.

The political way has evolved over thousands of years as men and women have tried to survive in what has often been a hostile world. For long periods in the history of mankind basic survival has been the only objective and people have survived either by acts of individual self-preservation or by relying on one dominant person or group to protect them. As men came to master their environment so they were able to stand back a little and consider what they really wanted out of life beyond mere survival. It became evident that not everyone wanted the same things. Some people were more sociable than others; some placed great emphasis on material possessions, others on spiritual values. Peoples' tastes differed on food, music, literature, sport, and so on.

As long as one individual, or one group, was entirely dominant all these differences had to be subordinated to the wishes of that individual or group, and this subordination was the price people were prepared to pay for the protection provided. Even today, in undeveloped countries or in communities beset by external threats or dangers, this method of governing is still evident. At a time of crisis the willingness to accept the authority of the strong autocratic leader is always apparent. Politics provides an alternative. Many people would say it is a preferable alternative, not only in times of peace but in times of crisis as well.

Politics as a natural activity

The alternative politics provides is this. It is a method whereby people with differing interests can govern themselves by distributing power roughly in proportion to the importance of these interests to the wellbeing of the whole community. Politics operates on the basis that if a community is to survive, people with different views and aspirations must be prepared to compromise some of them for the benefit of all. A system of priorities must be determined so that the way the power of the state is used reflects the importance attached to a particular view or aspiration. Furthermore, these priorities are arrived at, not by imposition by one person or group, but by open discussion and a willingness to give and take.

Some people talk about the science or art of politics. Aristotle thought the activity which he called politics perfectly natural. The qualities which mankind possesses, he thought, make it natural that people should regulate their lives by moderation and tolerance: that was the hallmark of civilization. The extent, acceptance, and the preservation of political activity may be seen as a clear indication of the degree of civilized behaviour which a country has attained.

Economics and politics compared

Economists argue that the forces of supply and demand are natural. They provide an automatic means of determining how scarce resources should be distributed to meet virtually unlimited wants. The marketplace, through the price mechanism, is the natural regulator of competing economic demands. Politics may be viewed as the marketplace and price mechanism for competing social demands, but this analogy is not exact. In economic terms, in a free market you get as much out of the economy as you are able and willing to pay for. In the political marketplace what you get is largely determined by your ability to persuade your fellow men to agree to your taking it out.

Operating in the economic marketplace can be an individual or group activity; operating in the political marketplace is essentially a process conducted in groups. The size of the group has an important bearing on its ability to get what it wants, but there are other factors as well; its economic wealth is important, as are its degree of organization and its ability to persuade. Persuasion is at the heart of political activity; when a willingness to discuss and persuade is abandoned then politics is abandoned and replaced by something else.

Politics as an alternative to violence

The fact that free discussion and persuasion are at the heart of politics can best be demonstrated by reminding ourselves of how wars and violent disputes of that kind are eventually settled. Unless a policy of complete extermination is followed, wars are inevitably ended by some kind of political solution. This means that the parties to the dispute must eventually get together and agree on ways of co-existing peacefully: each side has to be persuaded to give something up to accommodate the wishes of the other. Obviously, in the case of war, the ability of the winning side to persuade is much greater than that of the losers, but most people agree that, in modern wars at any rate, there are no real winners or losers so that the willingness to compromise and find a solution is likely to be strong on both sides. A recent graphic example of this was the war in Vietnam.

The imperfections of politics

Because it is based on compromise and persuasion, politics is, inevitably, a 'messy' activity. It is more time consuming than direct, autocratic action; it is often irritating to someone who believes he knows what is best for the community and wants to get it done quickly. This is why in time of emergency some aspects of political activity are often suspended so that decisions can be taken more expeditiously. But let us not forget how throughout two world wars the Parliament at Westminster continued to sit and debate the nation's affairs, and that, although the wartime governments contained members from all the major political parties, there was still a Government on one side and an Opposition on the other.

Even in ancient Greece, where politics was born and flourished in the small city states, there were severe critics of it. Plato, Aristotle's mentor, disillusioned by the frailties of his fellow men and disturbed by the apparent failings of democracy in the city state of Athens, proposed in his book, *The Republic*, an alternative method of governing. He was willing to replace rule by the majority by rule by the enlightened few. It is an attractive idea. You find someone of supreme intelligence who is above the rough and tumble of daily living and is willing to devote himself entirely to the wellbeing of his fellow men. You then entrust all authority to him, knowing that his sense of right and wrong and what is good for you is better than yours. If such people existed on earth then perhaps the idea would work, but of course they do not and we are left with imperfect men and women living in an imperfect world. Politics recognizes and accepts these imperfections and tries to make the best of what there is rather than look for what will never be.

What politics is not

Politics then is the whole process of discussion, adjustment, and compromise which attempts to agree courses of action to follow; in other words, policies. These policies become the objectives which politicians, using the power of the state, attempt to seek. The activity we call politics is not confined to political parties. It involves interest groups, such as those representing workers or employers or professional people, and it also involves individuals seeking to use the power of the state on their own behalf.

There are, moreover, some activities closely resembling politics which are clearly removed from the actions of the state. Although they have many of the characteristics of politics it is misleading to think of them as political so we must exclude them from our definition. Let us look at an example. Someone in your department is due to retire at the end of the year and, as a result, a number of people hope for promotion. A is particularly keen and, unlike his colleagues, is not content to rely on the normal promotion procedures; behind the scenes he tries to influence people who he hopes will speak up for him when the moment for decision comes. Such behaviour inevitably irritates his colleagues who feel that his methods are unfair and underhand; some accuse him of playing politics. He is not: it is an abuse of the term.

Trying to get results by persuasion, argument, and intrigue has many of the characteristics of politics but, unless the intention eventually is to invoke the power and authority of government, then we should not describe that activity as political.

Politics and democracy

The great majority of countries in the world call themselves democracies. It is arguably the most misused word in the English language. These democracies range from systems which have evolved over hundreds of years, such as in this country, to those which were created overnight out of revolution, such as in Cuba or China. They range from systems where very little is written and much is implied, as in this country, to those where individual rights are clearly stated in a document, such as in the United States of America. They range from countries where there are strong liberal traditions of tolerance to those where the power of the state is exercised in such an autocratic way that it is difficult to distinguish them from the old-style rule of personal monarchs. Yet they all claim to be democracies. Why? One reason is that the word democracy has very respectable origins. In Greek it literally means government by the masses, or by the people; and direct democracy, whereby everyone was required to participate in the processes of government, flourished in Greece. Since those early days democracy, as a concept, has captured the imagination of men everywhere, as in the splendid words of Abraham Lincoln 'government of the people, by the people and for the people'.

Another reason for the popularity of the term democracy is that it is, to put it in commercial terms, a very attractive product to sell. It is encouraging for people to believe that they live in a democracy: it gives them a strong impression that they are in charge of their own affairs. A third reason for its popularity is that, as we have already seen, it is a word susceptible of many interpretations, thus enabling the unscrupulous person to manipulate the power of the state while hiding behind a smokescreen of legitimacy and respectability.

Democracy is therefore a word we should use with caution and we would be ill-advised to give it as precise a meaning as we have given to politics. Democracy is an ideal; politics is an activity. Democracy is what men would like to be; politics is what is actually taking place. Democracy is a concept; politics is a practicality. The one certain thing we can say about the two words is this. Democracy, in the sense of government for the people, may or may not be present in a community which does not practise politics. Where politics, as the activity we have already described, is clearly present then democracy must be present also.

Representative democracy

In the ancient Greek city states, with populations of about fifty thousand, it was possible to practise direct democracy. In other words everyone was expected to take an active part in the government of the state. There was a clear rotation of offices and popular assemblies to decide what laws to pass and what penalties people should pay for contravening these laws. Everyone was given an opportunity to participate. From the operation of direct democracy the word politics is derived, *polis* being Greek for state. As communities grew larger direct democracy became unrealistic, although vestiges of it have lingered in this country in the forms of juries and unpaid magistrates. The parish meeting retains some aspects of the popular assemblies of ancient Greece.

The practical successor to direct democracy was indirect, representative democracy, and this has become the most popular form of self-government in the world. It is

7

a practice with which we are now so familiar that it should not be necessary to describe it. How successful representative democracy is depends on a number of factors: methods of electing representatives, provisions for protecting the interests of minorities as well as majorities, the degree to which an elected government is kept responsive to the wishes of the electorate, and so on. The most obvious forms of representative democracy in the world today are the parliamentary systems of government, most of them derivations of the Westminster model which has evolved over hundreds of years.

The weakness of representative democracy is that we can erect all the structures, voting procedures and so on, and think we have thereby created government by the people. Yet we may not have succeeded in really involving the majority of citizens in the democratic process. The one clear assurance of genuine involvement is evidence of strong political activity: in other words the presence of politics.

Politics and public administration

The connection between politics and public administration is clear. Politics seeks to deal with controversial issues by looking at the arguments for and against, finding alternative solutions, and then, once a decision to act is taken, using authority and power of government through the administrative machine. In other words, public administration is the means whereby political decisions are implemented.

As part of the executive machine, public administrators should be politically neutral as far as their work is concerned. They will obviously have personal political views, which may or may not coincide with those of the politicians they serve, but these should not affect their ability to do their jobs effectively. If someone has such strong political convictions that he finds it impossible to suppress them when he is doing his daily work then it would be advisable for him not to consider a career as a higher civil servant or local government officer.

The politician and the administrator share a unique partnership. The politician relies upon the professional neutrality of the administrator and he, in turn, relies on the politician to accept responsibility for the political decisions he is required to implement. We shall look more closely at this relationship later.

Political power and authority

Power is the ability to get things done: authority is evidence of the possession of that power. Authority can be personal or impersonal; in other words, it can come out of an individual's personality or out of the position he holds. Personal authority disappears when the particular person possessing it disappears; impersonal authority is passed on from one individual to another.

Political power represents the wishes of the community to get things done and as a means to this end authority is formally invested in particular individuals or groups. Thus power and authority are legitimatized. That is the reason for making laws.

In a representative democracy, such as in this country, we elect MPs to discuss, on our behalf, current problems, in the hope that they will find solutions to them. When an issue has been debated and a course of action agreed, formal authority must be given for the use of the power of the state and this authority is evidenced in the making of laws. When we talk of the 'rule of law', as we shall later, we are really saying that in this country we expect political power to be used in a legitimate fashion. If a politician or a public administrator can demonstrate that he is acting in accordance with declared law we are prepared to accept his actions. If he is not then we are not.

Assignment

Governor to press Hong Kong case in Peking talks

Chinese optimism on Hong Kong

Thatcher rejects Falklands mediation

Falklands: US to back Argentina

Alfonsín pledges to seek peaceful solution to Falklands dispute

Influential Hong Kong firm set to desert

1. Compare and contrast the attitude of the British government to the sovereignty of the Falkland Islands and Hong Kong over the past five years.

Sources: Back copies of *The Economist*, *The Times*, and *The Guardian*. Anthony Sampson *The Changing Anatomy of Britain*, Coronet Books, 1983; use index.

2
The constitutional framework

The concept of a constitution

We have already distinguished between a political and a non-political way of resolving a dispute. We concluded that a country which claims to be a representative democracy will use political methods. It will use the power of the state to determine priorities and to settle rival claims of individuals and groups. It will give the state formal authority to use power by passing laws.

To make and enforce laws institutions are needed. A constitution provides a framework for these institutions and a set of broad guidelines within which they are expected to operate. If you were given the job of starting a local club, how would you go about it? First of all you would need to clarify certain things. What will be the club's objectives? What is it seeking to do? What sort of people are to be eligible for membership and how are they to be admitted? How is the club to be financed? Who is to be responsible for its day-to-day running? What authority are the people running it to have?

A constitution, in a broadly similar way, sets out how a country is to be governed. Just as the rules of a club represent, or should represent, the wishes of its members, so also should the constitution of a country. An obvious difference between the two is that there is the choice of joining or not joining a club whereas a person's place of birth, or the nationality of his parents, usually determines the country he is a citizen of, and hence the constitution he is affected by.

A constitution provides a blueprint for a system of government. It is rather like a set of architect's plans for a building. They give the overall dimensions and the shape and size of rooms. Even if they specify precisely the use to which each room is to be put, it is accepted that it will be up to the occupants of the building to change their uses from time to time and even to add extensions, although extending the building means modifying the master plans and will not be done lightly. A constitution will usually provide a similar flexibility within a broad framework, but a major change will need a special procedure.

The state as an institution

The institution which the master plan of the constitution creates we normally refer to collectively as the state. It is a word most people are familiar with but perhaps use too loosely at times. For example, what is the difference between a nation and a state?

The acquisition of nationhood is part of an evolutionary process. Most communities have their origins in family units. The family extends over the years and not only grows in size but also becomes more diversified as strangers move into the community and marry members of the original family. At some stage in the community's development a sense of belonging is established which reflects the concept of a family over a much wider area and a much more diverse collection of people. Even though they cannot always trace a direct relationship with each other through birth, the inhabitants of the area feel a sense of kinship and this sense is often carried with them even when they leave the original community and settle somewhere else. They feel they have roots in the community in which they were born.

Nationality and the nation state

This is really what we mean by being a member of a nation and acquiring nationality. The problem, in practice, is one of defining a nation and it is here that the concept of the state becomes important.

A man born in Wales may feel first Welsh and second British, or he may feel British first and Welsh in a secondary way, or not at all. Formally and externally he is British. When he travels abroad he carries a British passport. Even if he feels primarily Welsh this means, in a formal sense, no more than a man born in Devon feeling first Devonian, second English and third British. Like the man from Wales, he is officially British. This is because the institutions which govern both men and the constitution from which they are derived refer to the government of Great Britain and not Wales or England.

A nation becomes a state when it formally acquires the apparatus of government. In other words, when a set of institutions is established, to make laws, to administer the laws, and to determine disputes concerning them—what we have come to call the legislative, executive and judicial elements in a state. It is at this stage that a constitution becomes important.

All modern states have emerged from community origins and many are the result of the mergers of smaller states. The union of England and Scotland at the end of the seventeenth century is a good example. Germany did not become a state in its own right until the 1870s. Italy consisted of an assortment of small states each with its own prince until the late nineteenth century. Yugoslavia is a composite product of the Treaty of Versailles of 1919. Israel is perhaps the most recent example of a state deliberately created rather than naturally emerging. The world is so intermeshed today that it is virtually impossible for a community to exist as a recognized nation state. As a state it is accepted by other states, its citizens acquire an internationally acceptable nationality, and it usually has an opportunity to participate in diplomatic relations with other states. To be a stateless individual is to be considerably disadvantaged; indeed, a person without a passport denoting that he is a member of an internationally recognized state will find it difficult, if not impossible, to reside, except for temporary periods, in any established community in the world.

A constitution, then, provides a community with a framework of government which enables it to convert, as it were, a nation into a state.

Federal and unitary states

We have already seen that many states have evolved from the merging of smaller states. There are two basic forms these mergers can take. There may be a complete surrender of autonomy by the original states to the newly created one. In this case a unitary system of government is created; two clear examples are to be found in Britain and France. In both these countries the constitutions provide only for one parliament,

11

one executive, and one judicial system. The alternative to a unitary system is a federal one, and if we look around the world today we find that federal states are by far the most numerous. In a federal system there are, in effect, states within a state; the most obvious example is the United States of America.

A constitution, whether for a unitary or a federal state, usually sets out the composition, powers, and functions of the three main arms of government: the executive, the legislature, and the judicature. In a unitary state this is done for the single central government. In a federal state the constitution provides the blueprint for the federal government and each constituent state has a constitution of its own. Thus in the United States of America the federal executive, represented by the President, is reproduced in each of the 50 states by a governor. The federal legislature, consisting of the two houses of Congress, is reproduced in each state, although one state, Nebraska, has only one legislative body. Similarly, the federal judiciary, headed by the Supreme Court, has a broadly similar replica in each state.

The British Constitution

Most constitutions consist of a single, original, written document, which may have been added to over a period of time. The British Constitution is often described as unique because it is unwritten. This is not strictly true. What is really meant is that there is no single document which can be called the Constitution, such as there is in virtually every other state in the world. In the case of Britain there are several documents, mostly Acts of Parliament, which have a particular constitutional significance.

In strictly legal terms one Act of Parliament is no more significant than any other but there are some which have so influenced or determined the way in which the institutions of government have developed that they must be regarded as key elements in the constitution. Thus the Bill of Rights of 1688 set out fundamental powers of Parliament in contradistinction to those of the monarch. The Act of Settlement of 1701 carried this a stage further. The Parliament Act of 1911 determined relations between the House of Commons and the House of Lords and the Act of 1949 went further still.

It can be seen, therefore, that the British Constitution, in providing a framework within which the institution of government can operate, is concerned with the limitation of public power. It tries to ensure that no one person or group can achieve a position of absolute power. Most constitutions seek to do this; indeed, this aspect denotes the difference between constitutional government and dictatorship.

The flexibility of the British Constitution

Again, most constitutions contain provisions which make it difficult to effect fundamental changes in them. Usually special voting or consultative procedures have to be followed before a change can take place. The British Constitution is unique in that no special procedure has to be followed to make a fundamental change in the way government operates. In 1972, for example, Britain took the momentous step of becoming a member of the European Economic Community (EEC), merely by

12

passing an Act of Parliament in the usual way. Since most of the Constitution is contained in Acts of Parliament, and since in legal terms no one Act of Parliament is more significant than another, it is possible to amend or repeal any existing law which has a constitutional significance, and thereby change the Constitution. It is often claimed that the ability to do this gives the British Constitution great flexibility: but does it? There is a contrary view that because fundamental changes are so easy to make politicians are particularly cautious about doing so. The real source of flexibility is to be found in a number of unwritten understandings on how government should be conducted, known as constitutional conventions. It is these which, behind the formal façade of the institutions of government, really make it work.

In the latter part of the nineteenth century Walter Bagehot, who was at one time editor of *The Economist* and a very perceptive observer of the contemporary political scene, wrote a book called *The English Constitution*.[1] In it he described both the formal, or 'dignified', and the informal, or 'efficient', aspects of government. In formal terms, at that time, he saw the Queen as the head of government but he pointed out that in practical, dynamic terms, it was the Cabinet, led by the Prime Minister that governed the country. Bagehot's book represents a landmark in our understanding of British politics. It has a relevance even today.

Constitutional conventions

Bagehot recognized that all constitutions develop, alongside the written documents, a number of unwritten conventions. These informal understandings of how the formal machinery of government should operate and develop provide the flexibility which all constitutions need. An understanding becomes a convention when it is accepted and acted on by successive generations of politicians. If a particular practice adopted by one government is not followed by another, then it cannot be said to be a convention. On the other hand, if a practice has been followed for a number of years by a succession of governments it is likely to be regarded as a convention and if a new government seeks to ignore it, it is likely that its view will be challenged as being unconstitutional.

Most of the conventions in this country revolve around the relationship between the Crown as the formal head of the executive, and the Cabinet and Prime Minister as the effective head. The Cabinet itself is the product of convention. There was a time in history, before the second part of the eighteenth century, when the King resided over a committee of advisers of his own choosing and used them simply to obtain opinions before he took executive decisions. The balance of power progressively shifted from the monarch to Parliament until the committee of 'advisers' met without the King and became directly responsible to Parliament rather than the monarch. From these early meetings of the Cabinet the office of Prime Minister developed. None of this is contained in a constitutional document or even an Act of Parliament: it is all the product of convention.

Even in countries with formal written constitutions conventions flourish. In the United States, for example, the Cabinet is the personal instrument of the President. He chooses the members and they give advice and report to him and not to Congress. The ways in which the American Cabinet works are largely the product of conventions. There are also conventions which have developed to clarify relations between the President, the judiciary, and Congress.

The concept of a separation of powers

We have already said that constitutions are concerned with the limitation of public power. Some people would say that this should be the major concern of a constitution. The way most of them seek to do this is by balancing one arm of government against another in such a way that there is a limit to the extent to which one group of people can act alone and without the support of others. This approach is usually described as the separation, or balance, of powers.

It is probably most evident today in the constitution of the United States. The executive, in the person of the President, can do certain things alone but beyond a certain point must get the legislature, in the shape of Congress, to support executive action. Similarly, Congress depends on presidential support in certain things. If there is absolute conflict between the President and Congress then government will come virtually to a halt. The judiciary, as the third main element in the constitution, possesses an independence which allows it to 'hold the ring', as it were, between the executive and the legislature. In the United States this balance of powers is underlined by the fact that presidential elections are kept separate from those for members of Congress. The situation is quite different in this country.

The separation of powers in Britain

In Britain, although the functions of the three arms of government seem distinct and separate, in practice they are linked and interdependent. Members of the government, as the executive arm, are drawn from Parliament which is of course the legislative arm. Members of the highest court in the judiciary, the House of Lords, are also part of the legislature, at least in theory. Despite this common overlapping membership of the executive, legislature, and judiciary, there is, in a real, practical sense, a balance of powers. The government of the day can be dismissed by Parliament, on a vote of 'no confidence'; the House of Lords, as the supreme court of appeal, can rule that an action by the executive is illegal. In practice the balance is political rather than constitutional. As long as the government can command a majority of votes in the House of Commons it can make any laws and take any executive action it chooses. Even if the House of Lords, in its judicial capacity, rules that an action of the executive is illegal the government can use its parliamentary majority and pass legislation to legalize an otherwise illegal act.

Later we shall be looking more closely at politicians in action and we will see that democracy in this country is a fine balance between legal rules and practical politics. The willingness of politicians of all parties to work within the Constitution and follow the 'rules of the game' is the practical evidence of democratic government.

The fundamentals of constitutional government in Britain

Government is concerned with the use of power and a constitution indicates how that power should be distributed between the separate institutions of government. Thus the British Constitution today reflects both the history of this country, and the shifts of economic and political power which have contributed to that history, as well as the contemporary distribution of that power.

The House of Commons contains many more Members with middle-class and working-class backgrounds than it did a hundred years ago, and this is a reflection of the way economic power has shifted during that time. The House of Lords has much less political power than it had a century ago and its membership, largely through the creation of life peers, has also fundamentally changed. We have already said that the monarch has become much more of a figurehead and less of a political force during the present century. Despite these changes in the composition and operation of our main political institution, certain fundamental features of the Constitution have survived. They may perhaps be summarized as the Supremacy of Parliament, adherence of the Rule of Law, and the concept of responsible government.

The supremacy of Parliament

The idea of the supremacy of Parliament dates from the end of the seventeenth century; in simple terms, it states that only Parliament has the right to make laws and that this right is supreme and unlimited. This means that any Act of Parliament can, in theory at any rate, be passed and no one has the right to challenge it. The courts of law can interpret it but if Parliament does not like their interpretation it can override it by passing another Act to supersede that interpretation.

With a largely unwritten constitution it is obvious that opinions can vary about the right of one person or group to exercise power in relation to another. The supreme power of Parliament is unquestionable. Parliament can pass any law it wants, can amend or revoke the laws it has itself made, and cannot be overruled by anyone. It can even make laws which affect the citizens of other countries if it chooses. The two constraints on this unbridled power are whether it is practicable and whether it makes sound political sense. In other words, what are the likely consequences in practical and political terms?

The rule of law

The concept of the rule of law was most clearly stated by Professor A.V. Dicey, an eminent constitutional lawyer, at the end of the nineteenth century.[2] Dicey identified three features of the Constitution which he regarded as essential to the preservation of personal liberties in this country and which he felt were enshrined within what he called the rule of law.

First was the absence of arbitrary power. In other words, he argued, power could only be exercised within a legal framework. In practical terms this meant that if an official told a member of the public to do something, or not to do something, the person he was directing was entitled to ask him to cite his legal authority for doing so. The second feature of Dicey's rule of law was that no one, whatever his station or position in the community, was above the law: in other words, there should not be one law for the rich and another for the poor, or one for a civil servant and another for an ordinary member of the public. The third aspect, as enunciated by Dicey, was that individual rights are not guaranteed by a special kind of law, such as we would expect to find in a written constitution, but are contained within the ordinary law of the land.

Since Dicey first drew attention to these aspects of the British Constitution other constitutional lawyers have questioned whether, in a rapidly changing world, all that he claimed was still applicable. Certainly new types of courts and tribunals have grown up in the present century, and certainly ministers and civil servants take many discretionary decisions which seem to extend, rather than merely apply, existing law. Nevertheless, the three essentials which Dicey put forward still seem valid today, and the objection to someone in authority acting *ultra vires*, or beyond his legal powers, is pertinent and significant.

Responsible government

The concept of responsible government is the third fundamental feature of the British Constitution. It argues, in effect, that not only should government be representative of the people it serves but it should also be responsible to them. There are several ways in which this responsibility of government to the governed is achieved. The most obvious is that the government of the day is answerable for its actions to the House of Commons. The whole government is collectively answerable and if it irretrievably loses the support of the House it should resign. Individual ministers are regarded as being personally responsible for actions taken by civil servants on their behalf. In practice the situation is not quite as clearcut as it is stated here and this is discussed more fully later in this book. Nevertheless, the underlying principle of responsible government is valid. It is evidenced most obviously in the need for the government of the day to seek re-election at least every five years, and, in doing so, to hold itself responsible and accountable for the way it has governed during its period of office.

The importance of a constitutional framework

This book is about public administration. It is about central and local government institutions and how they and the people within them operate. It would be misleading to suggest that politicians and administrators are constantly checking whether or not the decisions they take are constitutionally correct. The constitutional framework is in the background rather than the foreground of their thinking but it cannot be ignored. In this country, where it is not possible to consult a single document, it is even more important to identify and understand the fundamental features of the Constitution. These essentials condition the whole atmosphere within which public administration operates.

A civil servant or local government officer may be working in an office far removed from the political atmosphere of Parliament or the Council Chamber. The tasks he is required to perform may seem routine and non-controversial. Nevertheless, whether he realizes it or not, he is part of a system of responsible government. Oblivious though he may be of it, he is acting within the constraints of the rule of law. As his career progresses he is bound to move nearer to the political firing line, and the closer he approaches it the more he will become aware of the constitutional framework within which he is working.

The average production floor worker in industry will only be obviously affected by economic forces when the next round of pay negotiations begins or when the rising cost of living causes his wife to complain that his earnings are insufficient for the family needs. The managing director of the firm, on the other hand, is constantly aware of competition from other firms, of the need to reduce production costs and increase profitability, and all the other economic aspects which provide the headaches and challenges of his job. Because the shop-floor worker is oblivious to them, does not mean that they do not exist.

Similarly, in public administration, the political and constitutional constraints are there whether we like them or not. An understanding of them is essential if the full implications of working in the public services are to be recognized.

References

1. Bagehot, W. *The English Constitution*, Watts, 1964.
2. Dicey, A.V. *Introduction to Study of Law and of Constitution*, Macmillan, 1961.

Assignments

2. Account for the reduced interest in the nationalist parties in Scotland and Wales over the past five years.

Sources: Back copies of *The Economist*, *The Times*, and *The Guardian*. Anthony Sampson *The Changing Anatomy of Britain*; use index.

3. Would the establishment of a federal state, with a written constitution, be the answer to the divisions between England, Wales, Scotland, Northern Ireland, and Eire? Give a reasoned answer.

3
Interest group politics

The representation of interests

Free communities are established on the basis of diversity. To say that all men are created equal is untrue; what we really mean is that their opportunities should be equal. People are innately unequal: some are bigger, stronger, more intelligent, calmer, more rational than others; indeed, it can be argued that the best way to provide equal opportunities is to recognize these inequalities. Saying people are unequal is another way of saying they are different, and the differences are not only seen in size, shape, and capabilities, they are reflected in people's interests.

Why do we have a choice of radio and television programmes, newspapers, films, and novels? Because people have differing interests. Not only do people's interests vary, but they tend to pursue them in different ways. Most of us have one or two fairly well-developed interests: sport, music, the cinema, reading, gardening, or whatever. When the interest is very strong it can be compulsive and time consuming; to be good at sport, for example, requires an enormous dedication of which few of us are capable. The majority of people are relatively passive even about their special interests; they are content to let others organize and run them for them. Virtually all organizations which claim to represent an interest or point of view are run by an active minority. Look at any organization you are a member of and you will find this is true.

We have already argued that political activity provides evidence of an active democracy and this is so even when only a minority of the community are themselves active. We also said that politics is an activity which thrives on recognizing and accepting people's different interests and aspirations, and seeks to determine priorities for satisfying them on the basis of discussion, persuasion, and compromise. There is a tendency to assume that politics is only found in organizations and institutions which have clearly defined political objectives, such as in political parties or Parliament. This is not so. Politics is much more pervasive and all-embracing than that. Whenever any person or group wishes to use the power of government to secure certain action on its behalf it has, whether it is aware of it or not, involved itself in politics. Our political spectrum must include, therefore, in addition to the organized political parties, the groups which represent sectional interests: the interest groups.

The nature of interest groups

The most obvious difference between an interest group and a political party is that the group's prime objectives are not political, and indeed it is possible for an interest group to function satisfactorily without involving itself in politics at all. If, on the other hand, an ostensibly non-political group became entirely involved in politics it would eventually become virtually indistinguishable from a political party. We might think, in certain cases, of an interest group as being a stage in the historical development of a political party.

Another important difference between an interest group and a political party is that the latter will consistently and continuously be concerned with using the power of government to secure its aims, while the former will only try to gain government support when it seems the most effective way of achieving a particular result. For example, an interest group such as the Consumers' Association obviously seeks to represent and promote the interests of consumers. It does this by giving advice to its members on the quality and value of consumer products and services and by identifying what it sees as the rights of consumers. It may also act on behalf of consumers in negotiations with producers. All this activity can take place without the Association having any direct contact with government or MPs. However, at certain times the Association will realize that it can only look after the interest of its members by persuading the government of the day actively to help it, perhaps by amending an existing law, or introducing a new one, or perhaps by changing its economic policies in favour of consumers. When this need for government help is recognized the Association temporarily enters the political arena to secure its aims.

This intermittent political activity highlights a third important difference between an interest group and a political party. It is that an interest group will be prepared to collaborate with, or at times oppose, the government of the day, whatever its complexion, whereas a political party will expect either to be in power, as the government, or in opposition to the government in power.

An interest group, then, is an organization, however formal or informal, which has been established to represent and look after the interests of a particular section of the community. Its membership can be restricted by rules of entry or subscription, or it can be quite open. Any benefits the group obtains can be restricted to its members or can have a wider, even universal, application.

Types of interest group

It has become fashionable to classify interest groups according to the claims they make on government. Thus we can speak of those with primarily economic interests, such as the Trades Union Congress (TUC) or the individual unions affiliated to it, or the Confederation of British Industry (CBI). Then there are those with social-cultural connections, such as professional bodies representing teachers, or groups with religious bases, such as Christian Aid, or those concerned with human rights, such as the National Council for Civil Liberty, Amnesty International, Justice, or the Howard League for Penal Reform. There are groups concerned with transport or communications, such as the Automobile Association, the Royal Automobile Club, or the Pedestrians' Association. Then there are those whose aims are to prevent the possibility of abuse of certain sections of the community, such as the Royal Society for the Prevention of Cruelty to Animals (RSPCA), the National Society for the Prevention of Cruelty to Children (NSPCC), or the League Against Cruel Sports.

It must already be evident that attempts at classification are fraught with difficulties. It would be comforting to think that interests and the groups representing them fall into neat, watertight compartments. They do not. A trade union, for example, may be thought of as being mainly concerned with economic matters but to think of this as its entire concern would ignore the social, 19 philanthropic, and political aspects of its work. An organization such as the Royal Society for the Prevention of Accidents is concerned about accidents to all kinds of people in a variety of circumstances. Many accidents will involve transport but they also occur at home and at work.

Sometimes the title of a group gives an obvious indication of its aims. The RSPCA and the NSPCC are two such cases, but how many people would have been able to distinguish between, Aims of Industry (renamed Aims for Freedom and Enterprise, and later, simply Aims) and the Industrial Society? The former is an organization well to the right in its political thinking and with a particular aversion to the public ownership of industry, while the latter represents both sides of industry, employers and employees, and seeks objectively to improve industrial relations through education and training. How many people would appreciate the different aims of the CBI, the British Institute of Management, and the Institute of Directors?

A thoroughgoing classification on the basis of aims could lead us into compiling lists with memberships which overlapped and might well, in the final analysis, confuse rather than clarify. An alternative classification could distinguish between groups which are primarily promotional and those which are primarily defensive. In practice the differences are not clearcut. An interest group will take a defensive stance when it feels the interests of its members are threatened and it will adopt an offensive, promotional attitude when it sees the need to do so.

A more reliable distinction between groups is to separate the permanent, or standing, from the *ad hoc*. Most national interest groups are permanent because they represent a particular, well-defined, section of the community. Professional associations such as the British Medical Association or the Royal Institute of British Architects are two examples. There are groups, however, which spring to life in a particular set of circumstances and which disappear when those circumstances have disappeared. Examples of these temporary, *ad hoc*, groups are those which fight the closure of a school or a hospital, or oppose the construction of an airport or a motorway. The need to organize and represent a concerted view about a particular event or proposed event suddenly arises and out of this need an interest group is formed. At some later date what is proposed is either carried out or abandoned: in other words the group is successful or unsuccessful. In either event the need for the group disappears and, with it, the group itself. Many temporary, *ad hoc* groups are, inevitably, local in character and we shall look at these characteristics later.

Pressure groups and political parties

When an interest group becomes active, either defending or promoting an interest, it tries to block a proposal or to initiate one, and in so doing, applies pressure, usually on government. It becomes a pressure group. What, then, distinguishes an interest group from a pressure group? They are basically the same. A pressure group is an interest group actively at work, and this almost invariably means applying pressure to government. The two most potentially powerful pressure groups in this country are, arguably, the TUC, representing organized workers, and the CBI, representing many of the employers of organized labour.

The TUC is a particularly interesting example of a pressure group and underlines the dangers of rigid classification. It is a major pressure group which is clearly identified with a political party and yet is not itself a political party. Over 80 per cent of the paid-up membership of the Labour Party consists of trade unionists and over 75 per cent of the Party's income comes from union sources. It is understandable that the TUC would normally expect a Labour government to be sympathetic to its views and that normally the CBI would expect to share a common outlook with a Conservative government, but it is not always as straightforward as this.

There have been periods when a Labour government was clearly out of step with the trade union movement: James Callaghan's 'winter of discontent' in 1978–9 is an example of this. There have also been times when Conservative governments found it easy to work harmoniously with the TUC and its affiliated unions.

Conversely, it would be wrong to suppose that the views and interests of a Labour government are always opposed to those of the CBI, or that the CBI has not at times been critical of Conservative governments.

The essential point is that pressure groups are not political parties, although they are part of the political process. They see their primary objectives as promoting and protecting the interests of their members whatever party happens to be in power. They will normally support that party's policies if they see them as reasonably coincident with their members' interests.

How pressure groups operate

In general terms it may be said that the main aim of a pressure group in its dealings with government is to influence policy in the interests of its members. The methods of doing this will vary, partly because of the membership of a particular group, particularly its leadership, and partly because of the character of the government in power. Some groups, although admittedly a minority of all groups, will apparently seek a confrontation with the government whether it is a right or left wing one. This is likely to happen if the group is convinced that what it wishes to do is so unlikely to have government support that the only way of securing its aims is to mobilize public opinion in the hope that the weight of sheer numbers will persuade the government to come into line with the group's views. The Campaign for Nuclear Disarmament (CND), which places great emphasis on rallies and other forms of public demonstration, is a classic example of this.

Most groups, however, hope eventually to persuade the government, at both politician and civil servant levels, to agree to their proposals, or objections, and are prepared, if necessary, to work with those in authority if this seems likely to produce a favourable result. Nor is this process entirely onesided. For many years now it has been the practice of successive governments to consult the most influential interest groups before embarking on a new policy or a change of policy which may affect them. Invariably it is in the government's own interests to have this consultation. There is little point in risking a confrontation with organized interests if by some compromise on both sides it can be avoided. On matters of firm party philosophy compromise would probably be unacceptable and so consultation with a group fundamentally opposed to the philosophy of the government of the day on doctrinal matters would be pointless. It should be remembered, however, that during its lifetime any government is going to have to take more decisions on which it is able and prepared to compromise than on which it feels obliged to take a firm, doctrinaire line.

Governments also want information and views. Although MPs may justifiably claim to represent thousands of citizens, it is very easy for politicians, and the civil servants who support them, to lose touch with current opinion. An interest group will be one of the richest sources of information and views on a specific area which concerns its members. By consulting groups it is possible to obtain what is in effect an immediate opinion poll result on an area of policy with which the government is currently concerned. Communications between pressure groups and government are therefore generally very much two-way affairs, with anticipated benefits on both sides.

Probably the most effective method of influencing public policy which a pressure group can adopt is to communicate with the government through departmental ministers and civil servants. Most government policy affecting a group will be formulated and/or implemented at departmental level and it is therefore useful to the group's leadership to have easy working relationships with ministers and the civil servants who advise them. The major national interest groups invariably have this sort of entrée into central government departments, and it is likely that the head of a major group, at director-general or general secretary level, will be on first name terms with his opposite number in a relevant government department. Much of this communication will be informal: by telephone, in correspondence, or at social-working meetings. It is useful for the civil servant to operate in this way because it provides him with flexibility and he is able to preserve his public anonymity. Thus the personalities of the permanent heads of the major interest groups are of considerable importance and it is significant that two Directors-General of the CBI have been men who had previously held senior appointments in the public sector, Sir Campbell Adamson in the Treasury, and Sir John Methven at the Office of Fair Trading.

Lobbying

When you visit the Houses of Parliament you will probably first find yourself in a large circular area right in the middle of the complex of buildings which collectively constitute the Palace of Westminster. This is the Central Lobby, and it is here that you will obtain your ticket to enter one of the two Houses. If you want to speak with your MP you will wait here while he or she is paged and brought to you. If you arrive in the early afternoon, just before the House of Commons begins its daily business, you will see the Speaker's procession move through the Central Lobby towards the House. To your left, as you enter the Central Lobby, a corridor leads to the Commons Lobby immediately outside the entrance to the House of Commons. The Peers' Lobby occupies a similar position to the right of the Central Lobby.

Making group representations to MPs is usually called lobbying. The reason for the use of the term should now be obvious. It is in the lobbies of the Houses of Parliament that Members and non-members can meet. The actual chambers of the two Houses are, of course, very restricted areas. Even senior civil servants are not permitted into the House of Commons beyond the Speaker's chair. During Question Time they are available physically within the chamber but technically outside the House, by the side of and behind the Speaker's chair, sitting in what is called 'the box'. On the occasions of the monarch's formal visits to Parliament the House of Commons chamber is out of bounds.

Lobbying, as we have already said, is a term used to describe the way in which pressure groups try to influence the government through Parliament. A deputation from, say, the National Union of Teachers, or the National Union of Students, will visit the Houses of Parliament to meet sympathetic MPs and convey to them a particular grievance or point of view. These visits may be coupled with a mass march or a demonstration near Westminster. Although it is a practice fairly frequently used in this country as a device for influencing policy, it is much more often and more effectively used in the United States of America. The reason for this lies in the differences between the two systems of government. In the United States members of the legislature, the Senate and House of Representatives, are very influential figures: much more so than backbench MPs in this country. Not only do they have much more control over legislation, through their Congressional committee system they also have considerable influence over the actions of the federal government. In this country lobbying, as a means of influencing policy, is inevitably a more circuitous and less promising method than direct contact with departmental ministers and civil servants. If you lobby a minister then, because of the openness of the method, you are probably going to give him less room to manoeuvre than if you approach him or his civil servants at departmental level, free from the publicity which is often attached to lobbying. If you lobby a backbench MP you are dependent on his finding the time and opportunity to make representations to a minister on your behalf. There is obviously a place for lobbying in British politics, particularly when it is part of a full programme of pressure applied to the government, but it is a less subtle and more cumbersome weapon than the departmental connections we have already examined.

Parliamentary representation of interest groups

As a variation on formal lobbying a number of interest groups have made arrangements with certain MPs or peers for them to represent them in Parliament. They act as advisers or consultants and are remunerated for it. The names of 'interested' MPs as they are called, can easily be obtained. They are published in *Dod's Parliamentary Companion* or in *The Times Book of the House of Commons*. Some MPs are, of course, completely sponsored. The most obvious examples are those sponsored by trade unions. Doubts have been expressed from time to time about the ethics of their being 'interested' MPs but whenever the matter has been raised in the House of Commons the reply from the Speaker has been that it was a long and well-established practice and Members were expected to use discretion and responsibility in the ways in which they went about advocating and supporting causes in which they had an obvious interest.

Interest groups and local government

Whereas central government is mainly concerned with providing a broad framework for the control of national affairs, local government is involved much more with actions which have direct and often immediate effects on individuals. This provides fertile ground for the establishment and growth of interest groups. For example, the issues involved in building a road or closing a local school are usually clearcut and the local council is readily identifiable as the responsible body to whom representations should be made. The kinds of local interest group and their activities often reflect this concern with immediate, practical action. Some groups will spring up almost overnight to fight local proposals for change, while others will be prepared to help

23

individuals tackle the council on matters specific to them, such as obtaining council accommodation or a rate rebate.

Another characteristic of some local interest groups is the often close contact between their members and the local council, sometimes to the extent that there is an overlap of membership. This leads to an informal system of relationships and to a decision-making process at local level which is diffuse and complex and in which interest groups will play an important part.

Types of local interest group

As at national level it is difficult to classify local interest groups into different types but a distinction can be drawn between *ad hoc*, temporary groups and those which occupy a permanent place in the local scene. For example, groups set up to fight or influence decisions on particular proposals, such as the demolition of an interesting local building or the merger of two schools, will probably not remain in being after the appropriate decision has been taken and implemented. Other groups may exist permanently to represent the views of a particular sector of the local community over a range of local government services and will maintain regular contact with the local council in a number of ways, such as written reports, formal and informal meetings, and contacts with officers as well as councillors.

A distinction can also be drawn between two kinds of local permanent groups: those which we might regard as genuinely local, such as a residents' association or a civic society, and those which are local branches of organizations that operate at national level, such as the Friends of the Earth, or the Council for the Advancement of State Education. The latter find they must combine their national activity to influence policy with local action in order to achieve their aims and to give practical help to their members and clients at the level where their interests are most directly affected.

As a final comment on our simple definition, we may note that many of the permanent groups which we called 'genuinely local' may start life as *ad hoc* groups set up to deal with a particular issue after which they will continue in being to watch over further proposals and plans drawn up by the local authorities and will gradually come to be accepted as consultees in the local decision-making process.

How local interest groups operate

The ways in which local interest groups operate, and the degree of success they enjoy will vary. *Ad hoc* groups tend to start life in response to what they often regard as an immediate and significant threat. This origin influences their activity, which is characterized by an initial flurry of support, lobbying of councillors, demonstrations, and so on. Typically, their stance is one of confrontation. Unless such groups quickly arrange to collect funds and recruit the expertise of professionals, such as lawyers, engineers, and town planners, their life is potentially very short and their effectiveness limited as the momentum from initial alarm and publicity dies away. This early phase can be critical as a major planning proposal, for example, may have to be fought for months as it passes through the lengthy decision machinery of the local planning authority and, perhaps, a local public inquiry.

24

The permanent groups, on the other hand, have either successfully completed the transition from *ad hoc* groups or possess a strong local organization and financial backing. They have probably convinced the local council that they are fulfilling a genuine need and that they represent the interests of a significant section of the local community. Normally they prefer involvement at a stage before proposals are crystallized and will therefore rely on contacts with officers and councillors and seek regular meetings and consultation. Since their activity is usually more subtle than that of the *ad hoc* groups, its success is more difficult to judge, but it is arguably greater since constant contact with the decision-making process and those at its centre must eventually lead to the creation of some community of interest, if only on the basis of compromise.

Despite widespread existence of pressure groups at the local level, it is still relatively unusual for councils to consult them in the same way that central government consults bodies such as the CBI or the TUC. This is probably partly because there remains in local government a strong tradition that the local councillor is the best representative of local views and that he does not need an interest group to keep him in touch with his constituents. However, with changes such as the right to public consultation afforded by town and country planning legislation, it is probable that the involvement of local interest groups with councils will develop as a two-way process with consultations being actively sought on both sides.

Assignments

Greenpeace fined £50,000 after failing to give pledge on pipeline

Greenpeace action pursued

The TUC calls for action by Lawson

4. Compare and contrast the structure and methods of Greenpeace and the Ecology Party.
5. Will the trade union movement ever regain the power and influence it enjoyed between 1974 and 1979?

Source: See Anthony Sampson *The Changing Anatomy of Britain*, particularly Chapter 4.

4
Party politics

Party politics in Britain

A political party can be described as an organization which brings together people who hold similar views about the country's social and economic objectives and are determined to secure these objectives by endeavouring to gain control of the machinery of government. We have already identified some important differences between interest groups and political parties: it will be useful to restate them in association with this definition of a political party.

We have said that the prime purpose of an interest group is not political whereas that of a political party obviously is. We also said that an interest group seeks to use the power of government only intermittently, whereas to gain power is the main aim of a political party. We said, thirdly, that an interest group would normally be prepared to cooperate with any government to secure its aims whereas a political party would expect to govern or be opposed to the government in power.

Our definition of a political party emphasizes these differences, but there is another important one which we should note. An interest group will always operate on a fairly well-defined front: the RSPCA is particularly concerned about the welfare of animals, the RAC the interests of motorists, the Caravan Club the interests of caravanners, and so on. A political party, on the other hand, will embrace a wide range of interests. Our definition speaks of a political party bringing together people with similar views about the social and economic objectives of the country: this is a very wide remit. A political party will have a policy about education, agriculture, defence, old people, children, transport, industrial relations, foreign affairs, and so on.

The enormously wide range of interests contained within a political party does, however, produce problems. It is unlikely that all members of a party will hold the same view about all the many aspects of society on which there is an official party policy. Indeed, this need to 'toe the party line' is too restrictive for many people who consequently find it impossible to commit themselves completely into membership of one party. They are not prepared to 'compromise their convictions', as they would probably put it. Yet, if they thought seriously for a moment, they would surely admit that the activity we call politics is essentially concerned with compromise. A loyal party member would say that when he remained silent and stifled his misgivings about an issue on which he disagreed with the official view of his party he was not discarding his convictions but merely being realistic and practical.

What happens when an active party member, perhaps an MP or a local councillor, fails to agree with the official line on a particular issue and is not prepared to remain silent about it? Should he stand his ground and leave the party? To do so each time such a situation arose would be unrealistic: no party could survive the practice of resignations whenever a difference of opinion on a particular point occurred. How, then, do parties manage to operate in the face of these problems?

A two-party system

For the past century and a half British politics has been dominated by the two-party system. Indeed, the political institutions themselves reflect this. HM Government is expected to be mirrored in HM Alternative Government, the official Opposition. The chamber of the House of Commons is designed only to accommodate two major parties: one in government and the other awaiting its turn to govern.

Through most of the nineteenth century this classic battle was waged between the Whigs and the Tories and later the Liberals and the Conservatives, as the two parties came to be termed. At the turn of the century this two-party domination was threatened by the emergence of the Labour movement which, after tentative beginnings, became a fully fledged party in 1906.

This interruption of the traditional two-party alignments was short-lived. Following a series of coalition governments during and immediately after the First World War, the once powerful Liberal Party dramatically split its ranks, some members favouring continuing links with the Conservatives and the rest a return to more independent policies. Matters were brought to a head at a momentous meeting of Conservative MPs at the Carlton Club in London on 19 October 1922 when, by a clear majority, the coalition with the Liberals was ended. The Conservatives won a decisive victory in the 1923 general election and the new Labour Party overtook the Liberals in parliamentary seats won and became the official Opposition.

Since 1923 the Conservative and Labour parties have continued the classic two-party struggle, with leaders of each party alternating as Prime Minister or leading the occasional coalition government. This swing of the political pendulum between the two major parties is depicted in Fig. 4.1.

The party-political spectrum

Earlier in this chapter we asked what a party member should do if he felt unable to accept the official party line on a particular issue. Should he compromise or should he leave the party? The nature of party politics in Britain has tended to make it possible for a dissenting member to compromise more often than resign. This is because each major party has contained within itself, in effect, a collection of sub-parties. Although it can be misleading at times, for the sake of simplification, we may speak of the centre and wings of a party. Thus the centre of the Labour Party comprises the solid, practical supporters who share what they would probably call moderate socialist beliefs based on a pragmatic view of what is politically possible. It is this moderate, middle group which is most likely to accept the compromises which political activity inevitably demands. To the left of the centre will be found people with what they themselves would describe as clearer socialist aims and less willingness to compromise them than those in the centre. Members at the extreme edge of the left wing would find something in common with the attitudes and objectives of an avowedly socialist party such as the Communists. To the right of the Labour Party centre will be found people whose socialist views are so moderate that, apart from disagreement on specific issues, they would not find it impossible to embrace the objectives of either the Liberal or Social Democratic Party (SDP).

A similar spread of attitudes has been evident in the Conservative Party, with a moderate centre and left and right wings.

27

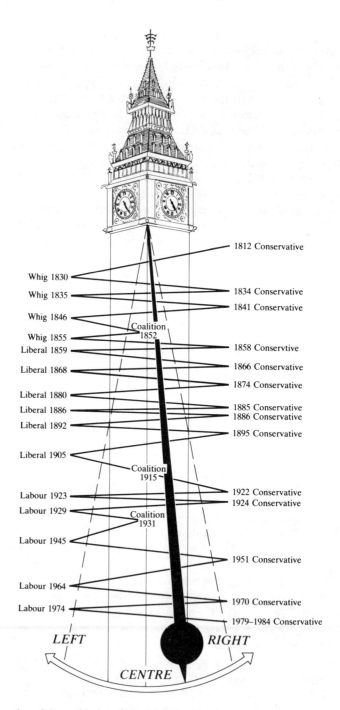

Fig. 4.1 The swing of the political pendulum 1812–1984

Breaking the mould

The leaderships of the major parties have, during the present century, tended to be drawn from the moderate centres. Indeed, it has been because of the 'centrist' nature of the leadership that each party has been successful in holding together a wide coalition of interests. The past five years or so have, however, provided evidence that the Conservative and Labour Parties cannot always be relied upon to produce moderate, centrist leaders, and, consequently, accommodate the wide spread of attitudes and beliefs which, traditionally, have been their strengths. On 26 March 1981 a new national party was launched, the Social Democrats. Its architects described its arrival as destined to 'break the mould' of British politics: the mould being the well-entrenched two-party system.

It can be argued that the Liberal Party has for many years offered a third choice to voters and consequently an opportunity to break the two-party stranglehold, but without significant success. In the 1979 general election, for example, Liberals won 4.3 million votes but were able to return only 11 MPs to the new Parliament. What prospect had the new SDP of doing any better?

Initially, it had a number of points in its favour. Firstly, it claimed to represent something completely new in that it owed no allegiance to the past. Secondly, it could justifiably claim independence from the two major party political paymasters: big business and the unions. Thirdly, unlike the Liberal Party, its leaders had all, within recent years, held high political office.

The story of the rise of the SDP, from the Limehouse Declaration to its alliance with the Liberals in the 1983 general election campaign, is now well known. Whether or not the two-party domination of British politics has been permanently ended is yet to be determined. In the 1983 general election the Conservative Party received 42.4 per cent of the total vote, 1.5 per cent less than in 1979, but increased its seats in the House of Commons by 37. The Labour Party received 27.6 per cent of the vote, its lowest since 1918, but obtained only 59 fewer seats than in 1979. The Liberal-SDP Alliance, on the other hand, received 25.5 per cent of the vote but only 23 seats: 12 more than the Liberals had obtained unaided in 1979.

As long as the present voting system remains it seems virtually impossible for a third party to gain sufficient seats to become a major parliamentary force. Indeed, the Alliance would have to persuade Tory or Labour voters to defect in significant numbers before a clear realignment occurred. An increase in the Alliance vote by at least 10 per cent would be necessary before it became a serious challenger to the two major parties. A popular vote of 37 per cent could make the Alliance the second largest party in Parliament, and hence the official Opposition. An increase in the vote to 39 per cent could put it into office. But this would have to be at the expense of the Conservative or Labour Party or both. The party political spectrum depicted in Fig. 4.2 illustrates how this could happen.

But merely increasing the size of the popular vote nationally might not be enough if that increase was more or less evenly spread. It would seem that the mould could only be broken certainly and permanently by a reform of the voting system.

Parties and the voting system

At the moment the simple majority vote ensures that in each constituency, of all candidates, the most popular person is elected. This does not mean that he is the least

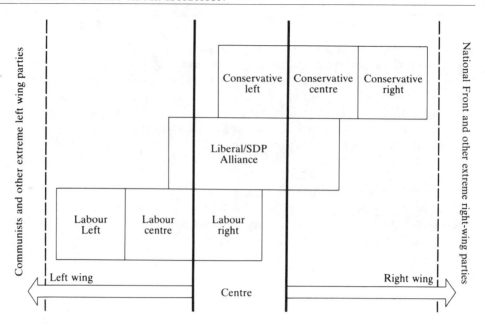

Fig. 4.2 The British party political spectrum

unpopular. It is possible to envisage a situation in which candidate A is the first choice of 40 per cent of the electors but the other 60 per cent would not be prepared to vote for him at all. Yet candidate B might be the first choice of only 30 per cent of the voters but half of the 70 per cent who did not make him their first choice would be prepared to give him their vote if their first choice candidate were eliminated. Under a system of proportional representation candidate B would win the election not because he was the most popular but because he was the least unpopular.

Proportional representation literally means securing a close relationship between votes cast and seats won. We have already seen how in the 1983 general election this relationship was by no means exact for any of the parties. On average, each Conservative MP was elected on the basis of less than 40 000 votes, each Labour MP on the basis of rather more than 40 000 votes, but each Liberal/SDP Alliance MP was backed by about 338 000 votes. Looked at objectively, this result seems grossly unfair: but is fairness the main criterion we should use in determining whether or not our electoral system is acceptable?

Before attempting to answer this question we should look at how proportional representation might operate in practice.

Forms of proportional representation

There are three major systems of voting that aim to achieve or approach proportional representation. They are the **alternative vote (AV)**, the **party list** device, which can be used with a variety of modifications, and the **single transferrable vote (STV)**.

Neither the alternative vote nor the use of the party list is theoretically a form of proportional representation in that neither is guaranteed to produce a close relationship between votes cast and seats won and, indeed, each can occasionally produce quite unpredictable results. They do, however, go some way towards rectifying the unfairness of the simple majority vote. At the same time, all systems of proportional representation are necessarily more complicated and hence more difficult for the elector to understand.

The AV is used in Australia and is the most straightforward of the three methods. It uses single-member constituencies and the voter is given a ballot paper containing the names of all the candidates and required to mark 1 against his first choice. He can indicate his second and subsequent choices by marking 2, 3, and so on but this is not compulsory. First preference votes are then counted and if any one candidate collects more than 50 per cent he is elected. If this does not happen the candidate with the least number of 1s is eliminated and the second preference of those voters who made him their first choice are distributed among the other candidates. If this does not result in one candidate obtaining more than 50 per cent the next last candidate is eliminated and his second preference votes redistributed. If during this process second preference votes for an eliminated candidate are revealed the third preferences on his ballot papers are redistributed. The process continues until one candidate emerges with a clear majority.

The main strength of the AV is its simplicity as far as the elector is concerned. It could be introduced more or less immediately into Britain without any need to alter the existing constituencies. Its defects are that it goes only part of the way towards guaranteeing fairer representation; it tends to favour middle, compromise candidates; and, as Australian experience has shown, it can produce startlingly unpredictable results. Its critics would argue that if we are to change our present, easily understood, system we might as well adopt a method that comes nearer to guaranteeing a close relationship between voting preferences and seats won.

The party list system is widely used in Western Europe for elections to national representative bodies. The first stage in the process is the production of lists by each of the political parties putting candidates forward for election. Each list comprises the names of candidates in a descending order of preference determined in advance by the party. A list can be national, regional, or refer to a quite small, multi-member constituency. At the election the voter merely votes for the party of his choice and seats are then distributed among the parties according to the proportion of total votes cast. Thus a party obtaining 40 per cent of the votes would be entitled to 40 per cent of the seats and sufficient candidates would be taken from the list in the party's own order of preference.

At first glance the party list system seems reasonably straightforward and understandable but practice has shown that it does not always result in the sort of proportional representation that theoretically it should. Also, in its undiluted form, it tends to be a rather impersonal system of electing members. Various formulae have, therefore, been devised and used to reduce the possibility of anomalies and to make the relationship between the voters and the candidates a little more direct. These formulae inevitably make the process more complicated.

Probably the most popular variation is the **additional-member system** used in Western Germany for elections to its federal parliament, the Bundestag. The voter is required to cast two votes, one for a candidate and one for a party of his choice. Half the Bundestag is elected just as is the House of Commons in Britain and the other

31

half, using the party lists, is elected in such a way as to ensure that the final composition of the parliament accurately reflects the national vote. In Western Germany, therefore, the party lists are used to correct the disproportionate results of the simple majority vote system.

The party list system has its supporters in this country and the authoritative Hansard Society, in a report of 1976, recommended a reform of the British electoral system on the lines of the additional member but with the 'balancing out' MPs coming not from party lists but from the defeated candidates in each party. The main strength of the additional-member method is that it allows for the retention of single-member constituencies while giving a guarantee of proportional representation.

The critics of the party list system, whether in its unadulterated form, or modified as in the additional member method, emphasize the cumbersome nature of its operation compared with the simplicity of existing voting methods. They also point out that an unmodified party list system prevents an MP from being a genuine representative of his constituents and shifts the choice of candidate from the voter to the party machine.

The STV is the 'purest' method of ensuring proportional representation and, in fact, is used by many professional bodies in this country and for district council elections in Northern Ireland.

The system requires multi-member constituencies but they can be quite small, returning, perhaps, three to five members. The ballot paper lists all the candidates, usually in alphabetical order, and the voter is required to place them in order of preference, from 1, 2 downwards. When the polls have been closed all the votes cast in the constituency are counted and the 'electoral quota' is calculated, in other words the minimum number of votes needed for election. This calculation is

$$\frac{\text{total number of votes}}{\text{number of seats} + 1} = \text{electoral quota.}$$

Thus in a three-member constituency with a total of 60 000 votes cast the electoral quota would be

$$\frac{60\,000}{3 + 1} = 15\,000,$$

and any candidate with 15 000 or more first preference votes would automatically be elected.

Let us suppose that of 12 candidates for the three seats only one obtained more than 15 000 first preference votes: in fact 16 000, a thousand more than the minimum required. All the second preferences of voters who gave their first preferences to the successful candidate would then be counted and their percentage distribution among the other candidates calculated. The 1000 'surplus' votes would then be redistributed on this percentage basis. If this redistribution brought another candidate up to or above the 15 000 vote quota he or she would be elected and the process would be continued until all three seats were filled. If during the process all the surplus second preference votes were used and there was still a seat to be filled then the bottom candidates would be progressively eliminated, the second preferences on their ballot forms being redistributed among the other candidates proportionately.

The prospects for electoral reform

If there is a reform in this country of the methods of voting in parliamentary, and perhaps local, elections STV is the most likely system to be chosen. Although in its 1976 Report, which we have already referred to, the Hansard Society stated a majority preference for the additional member system, it did not rule out STV. After considerable discussion, the Liberal/SDP Alliance agreed to back reform based on STV and in 1983 an all-party initiative 'The Campaign for Fair Votes' was launched.

The simple majority vote system clearly favours the two established major parties and it might seem odd, therefore, that a campaign for electoral reform, which would inevitably end this advantage, should receive support from members of the Conservative and Labour parties. However, a significant number of members of both parties, including some prominent trade unionists, acknowledge the inequities in the present system, which were so dramatically illustrated in the 1983 general election results, and believe it is no longer possible to justify the election of a government with a clear majority of seats in the House of Commons and yet with a clear minority of the popular vote.

The objectors to STV point to its drawbacks. Multi-member constituencies can confuse voters and make representation more impersonal. The method of voting is, inevitably, complicated. STV is less likely to result in clear parliamentary majorities, and, hence, allegedly, indecisive government.

Its supporters point to the widespread practice of proportional representation in other countries and argue that it is more democratic than our present system in that all voters are given a genuine opportunity to elect a candidate of their choice wherever they may live, rather than being permanently 'disenfranchised' because their constituency happens to be a 'safe' one for a party they do not wish to support.

The prospects for a third major party in British politics, whether it be the Liberals, the Social Democrats, or an alliance or fusion of the two, are closely related to the possibilities of a reform of the electoral system. If proportional representation were introduced the prospects would be good and we might well see an end to two-party politics as they operate today. But it is not in the interests of either the Conservative or Labour party to support such a change.

The surest way of reform occurring would be through some form of electoral pact. In other words, if at some point in the future a general election produced a 'hung' Parliament then the price of Liberal/SDP support for a minority Conservative or Labour government might be an undertaking to introduce proportional representation.

An alternative scenario is that the Campaign for Fair Votes, which already has a wide cross-section of supporters and sympathizers, might gather sufficient momentum as to be irresistible, even to a reluctant government, but it might take more than one general election for this to happen.

The characteristics of British parties

The names parties choose to adopt can be misleading. Is the Democratic Party in the United States strong on democracy while its opposition, the Republicans, are not? Is the Republican Party keen on a republican system of government while the Democrats favour something else? The answer to both questions is, certainly not.

Both parties believe in democratic, republican government. The differences between them are derived from historical, social, cultural, and economic forces. The Liberal Party in Canada is very different in many respects from its counterpart in Britain. European parties which have adopted titles such as Christian Democrats or Social Democrats are by no means as near to each other in outlook as their common names might suggest. Not only do parties with the same name or similar names differ in significant respects but most parties have over a period of time changed in outlook, in the social and economic bases of their support, and in their organization and methods of operating.

British political parties exemplify this. The first thing to note about them is that they have quite different pedigrees. The Conservatives can trace their origins through support by the landed gentry to an earlier espousing of the royal cause when other sections of the community favoured a republican system. The Liberals, who were until the 1920s the traditional opponents of the Conservatives, drew their support from the manufacturers of the eighteenth and nineteenth centuries, and before that they were the backers of Parliament in opposition to the royalists. The Labour Party was born at the beginning of this century by the coming together of moderate intellectual socialists and the emergent trade union movement. The SDP was formed by a group of dissentient Labour Party moderates hoping to attract people with similar views in the other parties, as well as those who had previously taken no active interest in party politics.

Today the Conservative, Labour and Liberal parties are vastly different in composition and outlook from their progenitors. When the right to vote depended on the possession of property the Tories, as the Conservatives then were, needed to rely only on a narrow, wealthy land-owning group. This wealth and its ability to manipulate elections was enough to secure seats in Parliament. The Whigs, as the Liberals were originally called, depended on the manufacturing community: the captains of industry with their newly created wealth. The Labour Party was a reflection of the third dimension in the community: the people who owned neither land nor manufacturing capacity but were dependent on those who did for their livelihood. If we look at the parties today it is possible to identify a hard-core minority in each whose backgrounds and attitudes still have a close affinity to these political origins, but each party now, if it is to win sufficient votes to get into office, has to appeal to a much broader band of electors.

Party images today

When people vote for a political party today they are mostly voting for an image or concept. Obviously, the finer points of the concept will vary in interpretation from individual to individual, but in general terms it is possible to make reasonably clear distinctions between the three parties.

The concept conjured up by the Conservative Party includes respect for tradition, and hence the monarchy; almost unqualified support for private enterprise; the view that, although the weak and underprivileged should be supported, in general people should be encouraged to fend for themselves and merit should be recognized and rewarded; a respect for law and order, nationally and internationally.

The concept which the Liberal Party brings to mind includes a less obvious support for tradition than the Conservatives and a willingness to accept radical change in order to solve problems caused by new circumstances; a fervent belief in freedom of trade at home and overseas; an even more fervent support for the rights of individuals and freedom of expression; a conviction that cooperation is possible and desirable between all sections of the community and particularly in industrial work situations; a belief in the idea of a united Europe with Britain playing a major role in its unification.

A concept of the Labour Party would include a belief in the need to create greater equality and a willingness to adopt economic and social policies to achieve this end; a consciousness of the class system and a wish to eliminate at least its excesses by creating greater and more equal educational opportunities; a recognition and acceptance of the need for trade unionism and a willingness to support the movement through legislation and economic and social policies; support for the public ownership of industry but more as a means to an end rather than an end in itself.

The concept which the SDP conjures up is one of radical moderation, if this is not a contradiction in terms. It shares much of the outlook of the Liberal Party but with a greater willingness to subordinate individual freedom to social needs. The obvious ease with which the Liberal and Social Democratic parties were able to share a common manifesto during the 1983 general election campaign illustrates how close their outlooks eventually became.

Party organization: the Leader

All the major political parties embody three main elements in their structures: an organization based on Parliament; another based on the permanent staff of the party; and a third based on grass roots support at constituency and ward levels. The structures of the party organizations are outlined in Fig. 4.3, in which their similarities and differences are highlighted. The comments about organization should be read in conjunction with that outline.

For a long time the Conservative Leader was selected by a process of discreet soundings of opinion within the Party. The last Leader chosen in this way was Lord Home, or Sir Alec Douglas-Home as he temporarily became, when he replaced Harold Macmillan. The method of selection was changed in 1965 and brought nearer to that of the Labour Party, so that until 1981 both parties gave authority to their parliamentary parties, in other words their elected MPs, to elect their Leaders.

After a long campaign within the Labour Party lasting nearly ten years, left-wing members, dissatisfied with the centrist policies of leaders such as Harold Wilson and James Callaghan, gained sufficient support for a change in the method of appointing the Leader. The 1979 annual conference agreed to set up a special commission to consider the Party Constitution and advise on how the Leader might be elected. By 1980 there was growing support in the Party for the establishment of an electoral college to do this and a special conference at Wembley, in January 1981, decided that in future the Leader would be elected by a college so comprised that 40 per cent of the votes would be cast by trade union representatives, 30 per cent by representatives of constituency parties, and 30 per cent by MPs. The leadership of the Party, including the National Executive Committee, had advocated equal votes for unions, constituencies, and MPs so the eventual decision must be seen as a victory for the left-wing activists.

35

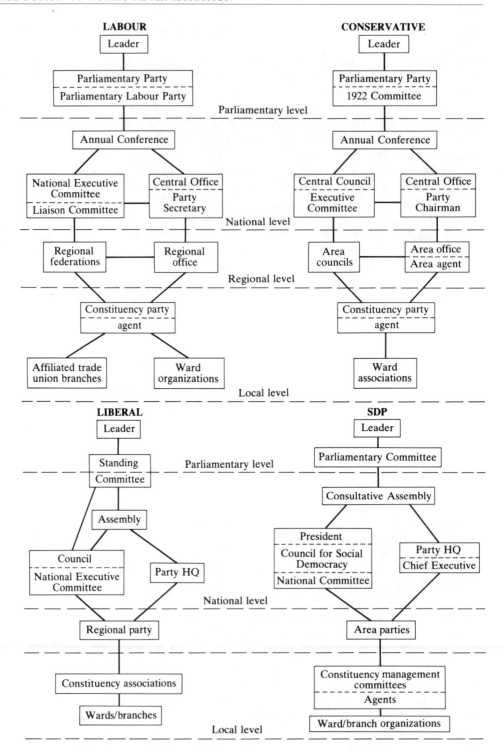

Fig. 4.3 Structures of the party organizations

The leaders of both the Liberal and Social Democratic parties must submit themselves to popular vote by all members of their parties.

The present methods of selecting leaders are to some extent indicative of the differences in composition, attitudes, and organization of the four parties. The Conservatives are accustomed to a Leader who 'leads from the front' and, although he or she is chosen more democratically than in the past, a considerable amount of almost autocratic authority still resides in the post. The Labour Party, on the other hand, has always been conscious of its democratic origins and composition and these are reflected in the way the Leader is selected. The electoral college is also, of course, a reminder that the Party owes much to the trade union movement both for its original creation and its continuing existence. The Liberal Party's approach to the election of its Leader is a reminder of the Party's traditional respect for representative government. The Social Democrats can claim, with some justification, to have the most democratic selection process of all, although some party members might feel that the replacement of Roy Jenkins as Leader by David Owen in 1983 was too precipitate to be called democratic.

Party organization in Parliament

All parties have parliamentary parties which are simply the sum totals of their respective MPs. There are, however, differences between the two parliamentary parties. In the case of the Labour Party the Parliamentary Party is more than just a collective name for all Labour MPs: it is the body which represents backbenchers. In its early years the Labour Party eschewed the title of leader and the Parliamentary Party elected a chairman. In the 1920s Ramsay MacDonald was given the title Chairman and Leader and then, in the post-war years, the role of Leader was finally and officially adopted. The effective organization of the Party in Parliament is now the Parliamentary Labour Party, or PLP as it is usually called; its chairman is the leading backbencher and regarded as an essential link between his fellow backbenchers and the Party leadership. The PLP meets regularly and its meetings are attended by ministers, including the Prime Minister when the Party is in office. The meetings are essentially for backbench Members, however, and senior members of the Party enjoy no special privileges. The PLP operates a number of subject groups which review and comment on aspects of Party policy or potential policy. It also has an influential Liaison Committee whose membership includes the chairman of the PLP, some key frontbenchers, such as the Chief Whip, and leading Party officials. Through the Liaison Committee, as the name implies, close contact is kept with other sections of the Party's organization.

The Conservative equivalent of the PLP is the 1922 Committee. They both perform similar functions although the 1922 Committee and its subcommittees, which correspond to the PLP's subject groups, are less formally built into the Party structure. The 1922 Committee takes its name from a famous meeting of Conservative MPs and peers following the 1922 general election, when it was decided to end the Liberal–Conservative coalition under Lloyd George. The Committee continued on a permanent basis so that it could keep an eye on the leadership of the Party which at the time was suspect because of its over-long association with the Liberals. The chairman of the 1922 Committee is, like his counterpart in the Labour Party, regarded as the Party's leading backbencher. Within the Conservative Party the

Committee is the primary body for liaison between backbenchers and the Party leadership and can, on occasions, be extremely influential.

In the Liberal Party, the Standing Committee coordinates policy inside and outside Parliament. It consists of 30 members, representative of all elements within the Party. It meets monthly and reports to the Council. The 'chain of command' in the Liberal Party is much more open and diffused than in the other parties so that a direct comparison at parliamentary level is not easy to make.

The Social Democrats have a Parliamentary Committee which comprises all MPs together with representatives of peers who have accepted the Party Whip. There is also a House of Lords Committee consisting of all party members in the House of Lords.

The National Conferences

Each of the main parties holds an annual conference at which policy and proposed policy is debated. Characteristically, the Conservative Party Conference tends to be more contrived and controlled by the leadership than the Labour Party equivalent. Again, however, in recent years the stark differences between the ways in which the two parties conduct their affairs have diminished significantly. At one time, for example, the attendance of the Conservative Party Leader was restricted to the last day's proceedings so that he could arrive more like a Messiah than a fellow member of the Party. Now, although the Leader still makes the final keynote speech, it is accepted that he or she will attend other sessions, as do the other party leaders.

How important and influential are the party conferences? Clause VI of 'The Constitution and Standing Orders of the Labour Party' says: 'The work of the Party shall be under the direction and control of the Party Conference, which shall itself be subject to the Constitution and Standing Orders of the Party.' In contrast, the 'Rules and Standing Orders of the National Union of Conservative and Unionist Associations' (the Conservative Party) merely set out, in strictly formal terms, who shall be entitled to attend the conference and when and how it will be convened. This contrast exemplifies the different attitudes of the two parties to their annual conferences. From the Conservative point of view it is a useful occasion on which the Party faithful can come together to meet the leading figures and air their points of view. The Party is generally very loath to wash its dirty linen in public so, in the knowledge that the Conference will take place in the full glare of the mass media, a lot of work is done behind the scenes beforehand so that the debates will suggest a reasonably united front across the Party. The Labour Party is less concerned about appearances of this kind. It has always prided itself on being an openly democratic party and can always argue, if a resolution is passed at Conference which the leadership finds embarrassing, that it is proof of the democratic nature of the Party.

The Liberal Party's annual conference, the Assembly, tends to typify the Party: democratic, outspoken, and attended by dedicated, sincere party workers. It is impossible to define a 'typical' Liberal since so many contrasting, and sometimes conflicting, strands are present within the Party and all of these are generally evident at meetings of the Assembly. Apart from making the keynote speech, the Leader usually participates on equal terms with his parliamentary colleagues.

The Social Democrats set out to change the style and organization of national conferences and have gone some way towards doing so. Their first, in 1981, was described as a 'rolling conference', with a special train taking party leaders and followers from Perth to Bradford and then to London. This first conference was judged successful by most observers and certainly attracted considerable media attention. Its two most notably novel features were, first, that it went out to its supporters, resulting in different compositions in attendances at each venue and, second, that a large number of people were attending a party conference for the first time: the 'political virgins' as they were popularly dubbed. Subsequent conferences have not been quite as innovative, but multiple, and often unfashionable, venues, such as Salford in 1983, have been chosen.

Having stated these differences in approach, the question of how important and influential conferences actually are can only be answered in a qualified way. The answer really depends on a number of factors. First, whether or not a party, Labour or Conservative, is in power at the time the conference is held. When a party is in office the leadership is in a much stronger position *vis-à-vis* the conference than when it is in opposition. It can always remind delegates that as the government of the day it has responsibilities wider than those to the party itself and hence reserves the right to govern even if the decisions it takes are not fully in accord with what conference would wish.

A second factor determining the power of conference is the position of the Leader within the party. If the Leader is strongly placed, not only within the party but in the nation as a whole, as reflected in opinion polls and coverage by the mass media, then he or she will be in a good position to influence and even dominate conference. Harold Wilson, as Leader of the Opposition, enjoyed this power in the early 1960s, Harold Macmillan, as Prime Minister, in the late 1950s, and Margaret Thatcher, as Prime Minister, in recent years.

The third factor is 'the state of Parliament', in other words whether or not a general election is imminent. If the life of Parliament is coming to an end and a general election is expected then each party will be keen to display a united front at conference. Differences are likely to be temporarily subordinated to the overriding need to win the next election. Open conflict is a luxury no party can afford at such a time. When Parliament is in the mid-stream, however, free debates are much more welcome.

Having stated all these qualifications, it can be said that the Labour Party attaches significantly more weight to the views and decisions of its conferences than do the Conservatives. Delegates to a Labour Party Conference tend to be much more powerful and independent personalities than their Conservative counterparts, union representatives being particularly influential. The role Conference can play is also much more clearly written into the constitution of the Labour Party.

The Liberal Party leadership normally gives considerable freedom to delegates to express their views and perhaps convert them into conference resolutions, but it reserves the right to adopt a pragmatic view about their acceptance. The Party's attitudes towards nuclear disarmament illustrate this.

The Social Democrats' national conference is described in the Party's Constitution as the Consultative Assembly whose purpose is 'to provide a forum for the discussion by members of the SDP of the policy and programme of the SDP and the conduct of its affairs'. Evidence so far suggests that this is largely what SDP conferences are about, with the leadership very much in the driving seat, despite the Party's democratic pretensions. This is perhaps to be expected in the early, growing years of a brand new party.

The central organizations

At national level outside Parliament the Conservative Party has a Central Council on which sit constituency representatives, adopted parliamentary candidates, party leaders, officials, and backbench MPs. It is an over-large and unwieldy body which appears to do little which is important or effective. It exists, it seems, mainly to present an appearance of democratic control. It has, however, an Executive Committee, which although numbering 150, is smaller and acts on behalf of the Central Council between its infrequent meetings.

Neither the Conservative Central Council nor its Executive Committee has the same power or influence of the Labour Party's equivalent, the National Executive Committee, the NEC. The NEC is a relatively small body which in membership is really a microcosm of the Party itself. Its 28 members include the Leader and Deputy Leader of the Party, 12 trade union representatives, seven constituency representatives, one representing the socialist and cooperative membership of the Party, five women representatives, and the Party Treasurer, who is usually a leading political figure and is elected annually by the Party Conference. The NEC controls party finance, is a disciplinary body, liaises with the PLP, and carries out an overall supervision of the organization centrally and locally.

The differences between the Conservative Central Council and the Labour NEC are a reflection of the contrasting approaches towards organization and policy making. Although some things have changed quite dramatically in recent years, the Conservative Party still adopts a much more autocratic line as far as the leadership and determination of policy are concerned. The Labour Party is historically and philosophically a more democratic organization. At the head of the Conservative organization is the Chairman of the Party who is the personal appointee of the Leader. He can be drawn from any source but is usually a prominent political figure. He has at his disposal a quite complex but efficient bureaucracy, under the day-to-day control of the Deputy Chairman, a career party officer.

The NEC controls the Labour Party organization through a career officer, the Party Secretary, who can be a very influential person if he chooses to use his position to its greatest effect. He runs a bureaucracy remarkably similar to that of the Conservative Central Office.

The Liberal Party equivalent of the Conservative Central Council is the Council, which normally meets quarterly. Its membership includes representatives from all sections of the Party: the Assembly, MPs, peers, the regional party, Women Liberals, Young Liberals, and members of the executive. Like the Conservative Central Council, it operates through the National Executive Committee (NEC), which meets bi-monthly. The Liberal NEC does not have quite the weight of its Labour Party equivalent. The relatively small full-time staff operate from Party headquarters.

The SDP's equivalent of the Conservative Central Council and the Liberal Council is the Council for Social Democracy, chaired by the President, who is elected by national, popular vote. The concept of a President in addition to the Leader is another SDP innovation. The post is a prestigious one within the Party. The first elected President was Shirley Williams. The Council for Social Democracy normally meets three times a year and delegates its day-to-day work to the National Committee, which meets monthly.

The headquarters of the Conservative and Labour parties used to face each other in Smith Square, which is only a short walk from the Houses of Parliament, Whitehall, and Downing Street. The Labour Party headquarters moved to a less fashionable address south of the Thames, in Walworth Road, near the Elephant and Castle, in March 1980. The Liberal Party headquarters in Whitehall Place are in the heart of Westminster, as are those of the SDP, in Cowley Street, near Westminster Hall and Westminster Abbey.

Organization at grass roots level

Although they all have area or regional organizations, the Conservative, Labour, and Liberal parties focus their local activities on the constituencies. The Conservative Party, largely through the efforts of middle-class women prepared to undertake responsibilities for fund raising and social activities within the constituency, generally has an efficient and effective local organization. The Labour Party is unable to rely on a similar reserve of voluntary help and is hence more dependent on its political activists who in recent years have tended to come from the left wing of the party, sometimes to the dismay of the centrist leaders.

The Liberal Party also places great reliance on the work of constituency associations, some of which have been very successful in what the Liberals call 'community politics'. Community politics involves attention to local as well as national issues so that, at constituency level, the line between local and national politics blurs. Much of the Liberal success in Parliament in recent years has been achieved through attention to local politics as a foundation for national activity.

From the outset the SDP made the Area Party its main local unit, largely because it was more convenient to communicate from headquarters with a manageable number of area officers than hundreds of constituencies. But areas can be very large, embracing several constituencies, and there has been some opposition to the area idea in favour of a constituency-based organization. If the Party's association with the Liberal Party becomes closer then, in the interests of uniformity, the SDP leadership might find the upgrading of constituencies unavoidable.

Party finance and control

The Conservative Party relies for its finance on donations from commercial and industrial sources, various front organizations, constituency contributions, individual donations, and investments. Spokesmen for the Party have, in recent years, claimed that business support amounts to no more than 15 per cent of its income, and a survey by the *Investors Chronicle* in 1978 went a long way towards confirming this figure. However, a number of groups with names which are overtly political sounding undoubtedly receive finance from industry and commerce and pass it on, through donations, to the Conservative Party.

The Labour Party is heavily dependent on the political levy paid by members of affiliated trade unions. As we have already noted, this source of finance probably amounts to over 75 per cent of the Party's total income. The Liberal Party's income,   41 modest by comparison, comes mainly from constituency contributions and personal donations.

The SDP relies upon a substantial personal subscription from each member, supported by fund raising at area and constituency levels. It believes that this is the only way in which its independence of big business and the unions can be assured.

It is difficult to judge with any accuracy the extent to which the Conservative and Labour parties demonstrate their indebtedness to their major sources of finance. An obvious way is through the honours system. Another is through appointments to the many quangos over which the government has control or influence. Much of this patronage is at the personal disposal of the Prime Minister of the day. Whether or not it is dispensed openly, the reality of this financial support is always in the background, of course, but the degree of cooperation between trade unions and the Labour Party on the one hand, or between business and the Conservatives on the other, has not been regular and consistent, and indeed both parties have found it necessary from time to time to introduce policies which their financial backers would not have wished them to have done.

The control of policy and organization within the two major parties has increasingly in recent years been concentrated in the hands of a relatively small élite based on the Leaders, their immediate parliamentary colleagues, and senior members of the parties' full-time staffs. The role of the Leader has been enhanced in recent years just as that of the Prime Minister has increased in stature. In office the two major parties look remarkably alike in their methods of operation. It is in opposition that the different origins and attitudes become more apparent.

Selecting parliamentary candidates

It is open to almost anyone to stand for election to Parliament. All that is needed is compliance with the nomination procedure, a minimum support for the nomination, and an ability to pay, and possibly forfeit, the deposit. On the other hand, it must be obvious that to have any real hope of being elected means enjoying the support of one of the major parties. How are parliamentary candidates chosen and adopted?

In all the major parties the responsibility for selecting candidates lies ultimately in the constituency. When a local branch of a party decides to adopt a candidate a selection committee is set up and applications are invited. Usually there is no shortage of applicants, particularly if the seat is 'safe' or marginally so. The world of active politics tends to be such a closed one that within hours of an announcement that a parliamentary seat is vacant or likely to become vacant there will be a flood of applications.

The headquarters of the parties become involved in the selection process in positive and negative ways. Each has lists of potential candidates which are made available to local branches. In some cases the central machine of the party will go further than merely suggesting candidates and will actively press for a particular name to be included in the selection committee's shortlist. On the negative side, each party head office reserves the right to veto a candidate whom the local organization may wish to adopt. The ultimate choice is that of the local branch and party headquarters would only wish to use its veto in exceptional circumstances. If it could not persuade the local organization to drop the unwanted candidate then its ultimate weapon would be to refuse to accept the local nominee as the official candidate and probably sponsor one of its own. Such clashes between the central and local offices are extremely rare, although they have occurred, of course, in recent years within the Labour Party. Eventually the local selection committee will draw up a shortlist of potential candidates, interview them, and make its final choice. At the selection interview or interviews the committee will obviously be looking for a potential winner and the successful candidate will need to convince his interviewers of his ability to win over the electors.

The backgrounds of parliamentary candidates

What are the routes to candidature? Service in local government as an elected representative is still the most obvious road to selection for parliamentary adoption. This is evident in all the major parties. In the Labour Party sponsorship by a trade union is a particular, and often certain, route to Westminster.

There are some pronounced differences in background between parliamentary candidates chosen by the three main parties but all seem to have one thing in common: they can in no way be described as being representative of the people they will eventually represent at Westminster. For example, the proportion of Conservative MPs with public school backgrounds is much greater than the proportion among Conservative voters. The proportion of Labour candidates elected to Parliament who are members of one of the professions is much greater than the proportion among Labour voters. In other words, parliamentary candidates tend to be drawn from a fairly select group of people. Even in the Labour Party the number of candidates who have enjoyed a university education is appreciably higher than the national average.

The backgrounds of Liberal and SDP candidates are not greatly dissimilar. This is not surprising. The road to national political office is highly competitive. To be successful demands a single-minded dedication which the majority of people would not be prepared to give: that the resultant participants form something of an élite is inevitable.

Fighting an election

The amount of money that can be spent during an election campaign is legally limited, but this applies only to the period of about three weeks between the time of the Proclamation summoning the new Parliament and the polling date. The run-up to a probable general election is often spread over months, even a year or so. During this pre-election period the main parties will try to influence voters through poster advertising, radio and television political broadcasts, public meetings in the constituencies, and, to a lesser extent, newspaper advertising. Leading members of each party will snatch at any opportunity to appear on television current affairs programmes or radio 'chat shows'. The time for official party political broadcasts is, by agreement between the parties and the broadcasting authorities, allocated in proportion to the number of MPs each party has at the time.

Obviously the two major parties will have greater resources than their smaller rivals to run an election campaign and will be able to spend vaster sums during the pre-election period. The Conservative Party will usually be better placed financially but, despite its relative wealth, it too has found it necessary in the past to launch a special fund-raising appeal in anticipation of a general election.

When the campaign is officially under way the tactics of the major political parties are fairly similar. In recent years great reliance has been placed on the personalities of the Leaders and, either at press conferences in London or through nationwide speaking engagements, or a mixture of both, each party has attempted to project a convincing image of its Leader.

In the final analysis, however, the purpose of a general election is to win as many seats as possible in Parliament and this means work at constituency level. Each party will, before the official start of the campaign, have published its manifesto, which is usually a statement of policy proposals which the party promises to implement if elected to form a government.

In the constituencies election campaigns are still mainly fought on traditional lines. House-to-house canvassing of voters is practised by most parties. This provides an opportunity to remind people of the need to vote, allows party literature to be distributed, and may provide some idea of voting intentions. Schools and local halls are rented for meetings at which the local candidate speaks, often assisted by one of the major personalities in the party. If the seat is marginal it is more likely that one of the political 'big guns' will come to give support.

Polling day itself is crucial, and it is then that the local organization of the party is shown at its best or worst. In constituencies there is evidence that seats have been won ultimately on the basis of a better constituency organization.

Party politics in local government

Many of the features of national party politics are reproduced at local level. Indeed, local government and parliamentary candidates use the same party organizations. However, traditionally, party politics at local government level have tended not to have quite the same air of legitimacy. This is partly because of the legal constitution of local authorities whereby the whole council is responsible for decisions taken rather than one party within it, and partly because local government is more concerned with implementation than central government: this can perhaps be summed up in the phrase 'there's no party-political way of building sewers'.

Party politicians play a similar role locally to that at national level. They provide an organization and set of policies which electors can readily identify. They also supply the discipline and direction which local authorities need. There are, however, important differences which we should note if we are to obtain a true evaluation of the role and importance of political parties in local government. Perhaps we should start with how the system works.

Within the council each major party will have its own party group comprising all the members belonging to that party. The party group system is of crucial importance in the running of a council's affairs. The majority party will act through its group to obtain the chairmanship, and thus leadership, of all or virtually all, the main committees while the minority parties will use their group to form an effective opposition. Party groups will meet before all major committees to agree their line on items for decision, and the majority party will monitor the activities of the committees through its group to ensure that party policy is being followed.

We have already noted that party politics forms a key link, between the electorate and candidates by providing a readily recognized policy stance for those seeking election under the banner of one of the major parties. Perhaps more important is their role in supporting candidates by providing finance, a body of willing helpers, and the services of a full-time party agent without which many local authority candidates, who are mostly part-time politicians, would be unable to fight a campaign.

Although local parties produce manifestos concerning local issues, it is doubtful whether many electors are aware of them, or of the performance of their local councillor, or even the local administration. There is strong evidence to suggest that a majority of people vote for the major parties in local elections on the basis of their current national standing rather than on local issues. Occasional massive nationwide local swings from one party to the other testify to this; this is not surprising since most party-political issues are more frequently identified and discussed in the media at national level, even those which are locally based, such as the sale of council houses or the provision of bus subsidies. This indifference to local conditions is reinforced by the difficulty of attributing local decisions to one party or the other when they are taken by a committee comprising members of all parties and when many local decisions are not obviously party policy anyway.

Central and local party politics compared

We should be careful about trying to find too many points of similarity in national and local party politics. There are some important differences: for example it is quite common to find a local authority dominated by one party. Election after election sees the return of the same party with only marginal changes in its majority. Whether this phenomenon of democratic one-party government is a serious disadvantage is difficult to tell. It can hardly be regarded as undemocratic for the voters of Durham continually to return Labour candidates even though some people might say it is foolish. It is also quite possible that debates within a one-party council will be just as effective over important local issues as those in councils with a better party-political balance.

At the other extreme, there is a strong tradition of independence among local councillors, especially in the more remote rural areas. Although independents probably express support for one of the major parties in national elections, it would be a mistake to assume that they are all Conservatives in disguise. There is a big difference between casting the occasional vote in a national election and publicly proclaiming support for a major party as a platform on which to fight all local issues. There are also those local organizations such as ratepayers' action groups, which return local councillors but do not feature at national level at all.

In the administrative field, there is no direct equivalent of the government or the Cabinet at local level, although in some authorities the central policy committee, composed entirely of majority party members and serviced by a team of officers, comes close to it. However, even though local parties can obtain effective control of an authority through their majority vote and their possession of the chairmanship of all the committees, the lack of a formal 'minister' and his link with the permanent head of a department is a significant weakness in forming a local party government. Therefore, while the party line on local issues may be clearly identified by the party group on the council, it often lacks the refinement necessary to convert it into effective administrative action. This is because the party group usually lacks the practical, and sometimes highly technical, information and analysis which is available to the permanent officers and their departments. This hiatus occurs because senior officers

45

are rarely, if ever, invited to party group meetings to give advice at the moment when crucial decisions are being taken. The result may be policies that founder at the implementation stage or which have to be reversed or fundamentally modified to fit actual circumstances.

Nevertheless, party politics is a growing force in local government and this is because it offers a number of solid advantages. As well as clarifying where individual councillors stand on issues and providing a mechanism for political organization to match the permanent administrative machine, it ensures some continuity of policy and protects individuals against criticism of unpopular, but perhaps essential, local actions. Its lack of integration with the administrative machine and its apparent lack of success in highlighting local as opposed to national issues may be gradually overcome as it is more openly recognized as a legitimate part of local government.

Assignments

6. Is the Social Democratic Party a temporary aberration or has 'the mould' of British politics been broken? Give a reasoned answer.

Sources: I. Bradley *Breaking the Mould*, Martin Robertson, 1981; Anthony Sampson *The Changing Anatomy of Britain*, particularly Chapters 5, 6, and 7.

7. Argue the case for and against the introduction of proportional representation into parliamentary elections in this country.

This can also be used as the subject of a debate with the motion: 'This House believes that proportional representation would enhance parliamentary democracy.'

5

Politics and the public

Popular political attitudes

It has already been argued that those countries which claim to be representative democracies are, in fact, run by a comparatively small élite, or a number of élite groups. It is also fair to say that these élites are able to run affairs because the majority of people are passive rather than active members of any organization to which they belong. Only about 20 per cent of the electorate in this country are actually members of a political party and this number would be very much smaller if we excluded those who automatically support the Labour Party because of their trade union membership. Probably no more than 7 per cent of the electorate, or less than three million people, can be regarded as being seriously interested in politics. Surveys have elicited this sort of pattern in recent years. What about the inactive 93 per cent?

The evidence is that they are generally sceptical of politics and politicians and most see voting as a duty rather than an opportunity. The majority will expect their particular individual interests to be protected and promoted by specific interest groups to which they belong. They are content to leave it to the judgement of the people who control the groups as to whether or not it is beneficial to enter the political arena to secure particular objectives. It is also probably fair to say that the majority of people get whatever minimal political information and education they acquire from the mass media, and particularly from television.

In the last century W.S. Gilbert, librettist of the Gilbert and Sullivan operatic partnership, wrote, in one of their songs, that every little girl or boy was born either a little Liberal or a little Conservative. People still do see themselves as voting 'naturally' for one party or another, and the underlying reason may be based on class, occupation, or family influences. Newer generations of voters are probably likely to be more open-minded but the evidence still is that the majority are either sceptical, apathetic, or both, or if moderately interested in politics, influenced more by the mass media than any other source.

Reporting politics

Reports of what goes on in Parliament come from two sources, official and unofficial. The official accounts are published in *Hansard*, the daily record of proceedings. The unofficial accounts are given in the newspapers and on radio and television, and are obtained by journalists who sit in the press galleries above the two debating chambers. There is another kind of journalist who does not try to obtain verbatim accounts of what goes on but relies on impressions he gets and information he gleans from politicians themselves. He is the lobby correspondent. Lobby correspondents of the national newspapers are often well known and influential. Adam Raphael of *The Observer* is a good example.

Rather like the government's relations with leaders of the major interest groups, minister's relations with lobby correspondents are usually regarded as beneficial by both parties. The journalist obviously wants material for his column. The minister, on the other hand, finds it useful to have a ready access to the media. The system of informal liaison between government representatives and journalists has grown, since the nineteenth century, into a well-regulated and sophisticated activity. There are now Lobby Rules known only to lobby correspondents and Lobby Meetings at which groups of journalists meet ministers. There is even an annual Lobby Lunch. Ministers use the Lobby for passing on information they want brought to the public's attention. It is a very useful way of amplifying formal statements of policy such as those set out in White Papers. It is also possible, through the Lobby, to leak information which the government does not wish to issue officially. The practice of leaking is used as a method of sounding public opinion. The government can try out a policy proposal to see what reaction there is to it without being officially committed to it.

Individual ministers who are in disagreement with their colleagues over some aspect of policy can also use the Lobby to express their disquiet without openly breaching the convention of collective responsibility and so embarrassing the government. Thus the lobby correspondent will use phrases such as 'I am reliably informed', or 'according to a government spokesman', or, if the matter is particularly delicate, he will merely publish the information as if it were entirely his own impression of what is taking place. How he handles the news or opinions will be determined by the Lobby Rules.

Lobby correspondents also have close, usually closer, contacts with backbench MPs. They are a rich source of information not only about what goes on in Parliament but also about proceedings at meetings of bodies such as the Conservative 1922 Committee or the Parliamentary Labour Party.

The importance of newspapers as a means of informing and educating the public about political affairs is doubtful. The papers with the largest circulations are highly selective in their accounts of parliamentary proceedings; their lobby correspondents are invariably looking for news of the 'man bites dog' category rather than accurately reporting everything that goes on. They cannot really be blamed for this: they know what their public wants and does not want.

Broadcasting and politics

In 1977 the House of Commons agreed to allow live transmissions of its daily Question Time on radio. There is little evidence that this innovation galvanized the man-in-the-street into taking a greater interest in politics. Indeed, some MPs felt that the microphones distorted the sounds of their proceedings, creating at times the impression of an unruly rabble rather than a responsible legislature. The experiment was not continued on a regular basis. Despite this, there have been, since that inconclusive experiment, some compelling, live, sound broadcasts from the Chamber. The debate immediately following the Argentinian invasion of the Falklands is one which made a considerable impact.

The exposure of Parliamentary proceedings to the television cameras has a much greater potential for success but MPs continue to resist it, and in 1981 a debate resulting in a motion to televise House of Commons activities was defeated by 176 votes to 156. In 1983, however, the House of Lords voted in favour. It will be interesting to see whether the Commons will eventually be courageous enough to follow suit. If it does then Ireland will be the only country in Western Europe which does not allow television cameras into its national debating chamber.

Leaders and followers

With the vast majority of the population sceptical or apathetic about politics what chance has democracy in this country? Probably as good as, and perhaps better than, in other parts of the world. Apathy or scepticism of the masses is not new. A minority of leaders and a majority of followers is usual. In most countries it is possible to identify a series of ruling groups who collectively can be called the Establishment. They are the modern equivalent of the royal courts which flourished in the eighteenth century and before. The Establishment in Britain seems more pronounced because part of it, at any rate, is still buttressed by royal connections, through the honours system, and because we are probably still the most class-conscious country in the Western world.

Most people are vaguely conscious, rather than acutely aware, of the Establishment. They see it as a 'them and us' situation. They instinctively recognize that there is a relatively small group of people who nationally, and to some degree locally, occupy positions of power and influence. Because the members of this group are in privileged positions and part of the established social and economic hierarchy of the country, it is legitimate to refer to them as the Establishment. They include leading politicians, leading members of interest groups, chairmen and chief executives of major companies and corporations, senior members of the professions, some leading academics, senior civil servants, and a limited number of senior local government officers. They form a fairly tight circle. They find themselves, in many cases, on national government or quasi-government organizations. They stand a better than average chance of appearing in the honours lists; OBEs and CBEs abound among them and they include many knights and peers.

On behalf of the government of the day, the civil service compiles and updates what is officially called the **central list** and more popularly known as the list of 'the good and the great'. The list consists of about 6000 names and it is the source of people to sit on public boards, committees of inquiry, royal commissions, and other government-sponsored organizations. The interesting thing about the 6000 or so people who collectively represent the Establishment is that, having reached a position of power and influence in their individual careers, they are yet further elevated through the system of government selection and patronage.

Virtually every country has an Establishment of one kind or another. The fact that one exists in this country should not be surprising. How does it fit into our pattern of democratic government?

A pluralist society

Two significant features have been revealed in this brief examination of politics in Britain. The first is that politics as an activity is not confined to political parties and other obviously political bodies. The second is that democracy does not necessarily mean that everyone, or even a significant majority, will be personally involved in politics. A representative democracy seems to mean what it says and the people who

49

represent our interests are very much a minority group. Indeed, it is possible to argue, as some political theorists have, that we live in a pluralist society. In other words, while political power is concentrated in the hands of a small number of people, it is at the same time distributed among a range of competing groups. Government, according to this view, operates on the basis of working agreements between the elected representatives of the people, in other words the politicians, and the leaders of the various groups representing particular interests. Thus a political party elected to office will have its policy programme, based on its view of society, which it hopes to implement. It realizes, however, that the practicability of implementing that programme depends on obtaining some working agreement with major interest groups, or risking a confrontation with them.

Some governments have in recent years been less willing to consult and compromise than others but all have been obliged to calculate the cost of pursuing policies which are opposed by major interest groups. Whether this is enough to justify the description of politics in this country as being pluralist is a matter of judgement. It is certain that politics is still, to a great extent, the 'art of the possible'. This means, inevitably, that any government must at least recognize the plurality of interests and hence the plurality of power in Britain.

Consensus politics

Let us conclude our survey of the political framework within which public administration operates by asking to what extent we have government by consent in this country. We have already noted the widespread apathy about politics but we have concluded that this does not necessarily indicate that people are dissatisfied. It seems as reasonable to assume that passivity can be an expression of satisfaction. Government by consent in a representative democracy will mean consent by the majority, but it ought, ideally, also to recognize and admit the needs of minorities. Does the British political system do this?

There are certainly no 'minority rights' as such built into the Constitution, but at the same time, in the absence of a written document, there is no list of individual rights either. The rights of individuals and of minority groups are built into the political culture and are the product of social and economic history. In a pluralist society minority groups have an opportunity to be represented in whatever way they wish, providing it is within the framework of established law. Thus persuasion and protest are allowed, even encouraged, within the bounds of law. The Young Socialists may demonstrate publicly against supporters of the National Front, and vice versa, provided they do so within the law. It is rare for any organization to be proscribed in this country, but it does occasionally happen when it uses open violence as an alternative to political action.

To explore the extent to which law, inevitably the product of the Establishment, protects and assists minorities is an exercise requiring much more space than the scope of this book allows. We can perhaps agree, however, that there is genuine evidence of consensus politics in this country if only on the basis that, although people can differ quite strongly in their individual views of what is best for society, the majority are in agreement about the way in which these different views should be pursued. In other words, there is a consensus that politics, as opposed to arbitrary or violent action, is an activity which should be nurtured and encouraged.

Assignment

8. Select a single political issue and follow its coverage in the press for one week, comparing the approaches of at least four daily newspapers.

Part Two The institutional framework

6
The central institutions

The monarchy

All politically governed states need a formal head to carry out what Bagehot described as the dignified duties of government. The formal head is able to represent the country abroad and to receive important visitors from overseas. The formal head also serves as a focal point through which people can express their patriotism and loyalty to the nation, regardless of which political party they support. The formal head also provides a continuity which party political leaders cannot since their authority rests on a fairly shortlived popularity with the electorate. In Britain the monarch is the formal, non-political, head of state.

The **Queen** now has few personal duties as formal head of government: the majority are ceremonial ones as head of state. Nevertheless, her role in government is not to be lightly dismissed. She must give her formal assent to laws. She is a vital part of the trinity of Parliament: the **House of Lords**, the **House of Commons** and the **Monarchy**. An Act of Parliament has no legal force until it has been formally approved by the monarch. She is responsible for appointing the Prime Minister. In most cases the contemporary political situation will have clearly determined whom it should be, but there have been isolated occasions, even in recent years, when the monarch has had to choose between nearly equal alternatives. She dissolves Parliament, thus creating the need for a general election. She will, of course, almost invariably do this at the request of the Prime Minister and there will be no question of her not acceding to that request. It is possible, however, to visualise a situation when an alternative to a dissolution presents itself: when the Queen could accept the resignation of the existing Prime Minister and call on another politician to take his or her place, thus avoiding the need for a general election. If the monarch felt that party-political support was so evenly balanced in the country that a general election would be unlikely to produce a party with a clear majority in Parliament and there was a possibility of a realignment of politicians within the existing Parliament, then she could invite someone to form a new government even if the Prime Minister sought a dissolution. She would not come to this decision unaided. She has her own personal advisers who themselves would take soundings discreetly among leading politicians. She might even consult living former prime ministers in the capacity of elder statesmen.

The Queen receives all the important government papers, including those produced for the Cabinet. The evidence is that this is not a mere formality and that she takes the trouble to read them. She receives the Prime Minister in audience, usually once a week, at which time she is briefed on the activities of the government. Bagehot argued that the monarch has three rights in her relationship with the Prime Minister, the right to be consulted, the right to encourage, and the right to warn. Much, of course, will depend on the actual circumstances but, again, the evidence is that the monarch *is* consulted, and that, from time to time, she *has* encouraged, and even warned. Our

55

first thoughts might be that any self-respecting prime minister would dutifully listen to such views and then promptly ignore them. After all, what can a monarch, isolated in a way of life, remote from the ordinary people, know of real political forces? Again, the evidence is that this is not so, and that most prime ministers have recorded their indebtedness to the monarch for the advice and encouragement they have received. This active involvement in political issues will not occur at every weekly meeting of the two, but only when particular circumstances arise. Nevertheless, we must remember that the continuity and experience in office which the monarch possesses can give enormous weight to the opinions she expresses.

The Royal Prerogative

Whereas the Queen herself has relatively few governing duties and a great many ceremonial ones, everything the government of the day does is done in the name of the Crown. The Crown is the external embodiment of government in this country and, in addition to providing a formal, dignified façade also provides a means of governing flexibly and effectively.

The means of achieving flexibility in government within a formal, legal framework is known as the **Royal Prerogative**, a term which describes the residue of personal powers in the hands of the monarch. Thus the Crown, within the Royal Prerogative, and without needing to obtain the sanction of Parliament or the courts, can enter into diplomatic relations with other states; conclude treaties with them; control the armed forces; declare war; conclude peace; appoint judges; initiate criminal proceedings; pardon offenders; summon and dissolve Parliament; appoint the Prime Minister and other ministers; confer honours; create peers; and appoint bishops to the Church of England. This is a formidable list of powers and one which any ruler would be grateful to have. Yet today these powers are virtually all exercised by the elected government of the day, and the monarch merely assents.

The conduct of foreign affairs and defence is in the hands of the Prime Minister and the Cabinet. Judges are appointed by the monarch on the advice of the Prime Minister, who in turn is advised by the Lord Chancellor. Ministers are appointed on the advice of the Prime Minister and it is only on rare occasions that the monarch is able to exercise discretion in the choice of the holder of this supreme office. The conferment of the great majority of honours and appointments to senior office in the State or Church are made on the advice of the Prime Minister.

The Privy Council

The normal method of exercising prerogative powers is by making an Order in Council and the body which formally approves an Order is the **Privy Council**. The Privy Council has its origins in the small group of personal advisers to the monarch, particularly during the Tudor and Stuart periods. Today, membership of the Council is bestowed partly as an honour and partly for convenience. As an honour it ranks high and is not lightly awarded. For convenience, all members of the Cabinet are sworn in as Privy Councillors and thus automatically take the oath of secrecy and allegiance to the Crown. The royal assent to legislation and the formal approval of executive acts, using the prerogative powers, are given in the name of the Crown by a small quorum of Privy Councillors drawn from the government in power. The Privy Council Office, in Whitehall, London, provides the administrative base.

The role of Parliament

Any attempt to analyse and explain a system of government must seek to answer the question of where the real source of political power lies. In an earlier discussion we explored the idea of Britain being a pluralist society and that concept is quite valid. But narrowing our examination to the institutions of government we can ask the question again.

We have already seen that most of the real power of the monarch has now passed to the Prime Minister and the Cabinet, but how much power resides in Parliament itself as the supreme law-making body? In theory Parliament is omnipotent: in practice it is mostly the servant of the political party or combination of parties in power. To put it in this way is a simplification, of course. The subtlety and sophistication of the British system is that Parliament is both the government of the day and the opposition to it. It has the power to make any laws it wishes but it can only exercise that power if a majority of members agree to do so.

Parliament, comprising the House of Commons and the House of Lords, is not really a legislating body. The government is the initiator of legislation: Parliament merely acquiesces to and smooths out the laws which the Cabinet puts before it. Its greatest role is still derived from its name. It is a talking place providing the country's principal debating chambers. Both the House of Lords and the House of Commons spend their time debating and, it is hoped, improving legislative proposals put before them, or debating non-legislative proposals or decisions which the government has announced.

In practice, then, Parliament is mainly a device to assist the Cabinet to govern. In theory it is also a device to ensure that the Cabinet governs in the interests of the people who are represented in Parliament. How effective it is in this second role we shall examine later.

The legislative process

Although Parliament is not really a frequent initiator of legislation, its role in considering, amending, and approving legislation is considerable.

An **Act of Parliament** starts life as a **Bill**, prepared by specialist draftsmen, and has to pass through five distinct stages before it can receive the royal assent. The **First Reading** state is a formal publication of a Bill. The **Second Reading** stage is when the principles behind the Bill are debated. The **Committee Stage** follows when the details are debated in one of the legislative standing committees or in the whole House of Commons or the House of Lords. The **Report Stage** comes next when the amendments agreed at the Committee Stage are reported back to the House. The **Third Reading** stage approves the Bill in its final form. A Bill can begin life in either House but must successfully pass all stages in both before the royal assent can be given. Financial Bills, or financial parts of Bills, are considered only by the House of Commons.

Parliament uses, at times, several devices for speeding up the progress of a Bill. The most familiar is the guillotine. As its name implies, this places a time limit on the consideration of certain parts of a Bill. A graphic example of the use of the guillotine was in the passing of the Industrial Relations Bill of 1970. Debate was restricted to only 50 of the 150 clauses the Bill contained. Understandably, guillotine motions are usually vehemently opposed by the Opposition and even governments with large majorities use them with great discrimination.

The **Royal Assent** converts a Bill into an Act and what were formerly clauses in the Bill become sections in the Act.

The judiciary

In our earlier discussion of the concept of the separation, or balance, of powers we identified the role of the judiciary as providing at least a temporary check on the possibly unbridled use of power by the executive. Thus, within the rule of law, the courts can declare any action of government *ultra vires*, or beyond its powers, and so ensure that arbitrary and totally unpredictable government is impossible. In practice, of course, any judicial decision can be overruled by Parliament, and since Parliament itself is largely subservient to the government in power it would seem that, in the final analysis, the judiciary is almost impotent. This would be a superficial and ingenuous view of what really happens.

The whole system of government is one of interdependence. The Cabinet needs the authority of Parliament to carry out its policies. Parliament needs the support of the courts and other law agencies to enforce the laws it makes. None of the three main organs of the constitution, the executive, the legislature, or the judiciary, is really free to act on its own. Each is, to some extent, dependent on the others.

It is also sensible to recognize that the line between legislation and adjudication is extremely thin. A significant proportion of law in Britain is, in reality, made not by Parliament, by itself or on behalf of the executive, but by judges. For example, a judge cannot rule that an Act of Parliament is invalid because he thinks it is immoral, but he can, and sometimes does, interpret an Act on the presumption that Parliament did not intend to violate 'the ordinary laws of morality'. This is another example of the way in which the concept of a strict separation of powers is unrealistic in this country.

The Prime Minister and the Cabinet

In recognition of the considerable potential powers and influence of the holder of the office of the Queen's chief minister, political theorists have, in recent years, debated the question of who is really in control: the Cabinet or the Prime Minister? John Mackintosh, in his book *The British Cabinet*,[1] drew attention to the power of the Cabinet committee system, and Richard Crossman, in his foreword to a new edition of Bagehot's *The English Constitution*,[2] took up some of Mackintosh's ideas and used them to argue that the Cabinet was now largely subservient to and controlled by the Prime Minister, and that really we should speak of Prime Ministerial rather than Cabinet government. The debate continues and probably will do so for many years yet, because there is no definitive answer to who really governs, Prime Minister or Cabinet. It is a matter of judgement and opinion.

When Bagehot analysed the nineteenth-century political scene he described the Prime Minister as being, within the Cabinet, the 'primus inter pares', the first among equals. The office must now be regarded as more than that. Although he or she is dependent to a great extent on Cabinet colleagues and permanent advisers, the Prime Minister is in a very privileged position.

There is at the Prime Minister's disposal a central machine operating through the

Cabinet Office, which provides more information about the whole of the government's responsibilities than any single minister can expect to have. Departmental ministers generally have more than enough to occupy their time in running their own ministries. If they are to challenge the Prime Minister's views in Cabinet on an issue outside their specific area of responsibility they must be prepared to devote a considerable amount of time and energy to reading the necessary Cabinet papers. The Prime Minister inevitably knows less than ministerial colleagues about their respective departments but more than any of them about the whole spectrum of government activity. The potential and actual powers of patronage are immense; each member of the Cabinet knows that he owes his position there to the Prime Minister. Any holder of the office of Prime Minister has enormous potential power. Exactly how that power is used will depend on his or her outlook and personality.

Britain's first post-war Prime Minister, Clement Attlee, reputedly controlled his Cabinet, which contained some very powerful political figures, unobtrusively and yet with consummate skill. Winston Churchill was already a legend by the time he formed his first peacetime administration in 1951 so that, despite his advancing years and irregular health, he could dominate it if he wanted to. His heir apparent and successor, Anthony Eden, had a short, unhappy premiership during which, assisted by ill health, he allowed his skill and experience in foreign affairs to dominate his thinking and eventually cloud his judgement so that, before he eventually resigned, he had isolated himself from the majority of his colleagues and tried, unsuccessfully, to operate as if the principle of collective responsibility did not exist. Harold Macmillan proved extremely adroit at both choosing and managing his team. Behind his smooth urbanity, he retained an ability to take hard, even ruthless, decisions, if he thought them necessary. Again, ill health forced his departure. Alec Douglas-Home was described by one minister who served in his short-lived Cabinet as 'the perfect chairman of committee', with a laudable willingness to delegate. If the fates had been kinder and he had been re-elected, he might well have become a very successful Prime Minister. During his eight years at 10 Downing Street Harold Wilson manoeuvred, rather than led, his Cabinet and what began as a well-developed managerial skill degenerated into an ability to compromise. He surrendered the office in mid-term, apparently tired and somewhat disillusioned by the experience. Edward Heath tended to dominate his Cabinet largely on the strength of his own personality and his ability to master a complex situation with surprising ease. He was, however, according to some colleagues, generally open to persuasion and might well, if he had won a second term of office, benefited from his earlier mistakes. James Callaghan came to the highest office at a time in his career when he must have thought that it had eluded him for ever. With a party showing increasing signs of division, he showed a remarkable ability to hold his Cabinet together with a mixture of reasonableness and toughness.

Margaret Thatcher has, perhaps, shown more than any other politician in the post-war period what enormous personal power can be extracted from the office of Prime Minister. After an uncertain start, when her national popularity fell sharply, she came to dominate her Cabinet in a way few, if any, of her predecessors had done. Her methods were obvious but effective. She gradually dismissed or excluded those members of her Party who did not share her personal vision of what she wanted Britain to become and then proceeded to establish her dominance by the forcefulness of her personality and her seemingly inexhaustible capacity for work. She was, of course, greatly assisted by the 'accident' of the Falklands invasion which made her a national heroine overnight. Whether or not she will maintain this dominance in more mundane circumstances remains to be seen.

What can be said, however, of all Prime Ministers since the office was established is that it is *they* who determine what it is to be. It can be a springboard to success or a trapdoor to failure. It can provide an opportunity for lasting fame or speedy oblivion. It is interesting that, of all the post-war Prime Ministers, probably only Attlee is still remembered, without qualification, as a success.

The British Prime Minister can never be a president, in the sense of a United States or French president, nor is it sensible to argue that, because of the dominance of one or more holders of the office, Cabinet government is being replaced by Prime Ministerial government. Within the confines of our flexible constitution, the Cabinet always retains the ultimate power to curb an unwelcome leader, but to exercise that power they would have to act in a totally concerted fashion and in recognition of the consequences of such action, for to bring the Prime Minister down would inevitably be to bring themselves down.

The role and functions of the Cabinet

Using a vivid metaphor, Bagehot described the Cabinet as a hyphen, or buckle, which linked together the legislative, or political, part of the state to the executive, or permanent, part. That description is still apt today. Some fifty years after the publication of the first edition of Bagehot's book a committee under Lord Haldane, as he was to become, was given the task of examining the machinery of government. In its report[3] the Haldane Committee identified the role and functions of the Cabinet. Although its methods have changed since then the functions and role are still virtually the same.

The Cabinet is a committee of the most senior politicians in the governing party or coalition of parties, and it has the task of taking the final policy decisions of the government. It is the Cabinet which collectively accepts responsibility for all actions of central government. If a member of the Cabinet is not prepared to accept his share of this collective responsibility then he has no alternative but to resign. If a dispute arises between two or more central departments which cannot be settled at civil servant level then it is the Cabinet which must act as the final arbiter.

Using the Haldane Committee's analysis, the main functions of the Cabinet, then, may be said to be:

1. the final determination of government policy;
2. the supreme control of the executive; and
3. the continuous coordination and delimitation of the activities of the separate departments of state.

The Cabinet has enormous potential and actual power. The source of this power lies, as Bagehot so rightly observed, in the fact that its membership includes not only leading politicians of the majority party but also the heads of the major central government departments. Collectively they control not only the civil servants who effectively run the departments but also the House of Commons which gives legal authority to the actions those civil servants take.

The Cabinet Office

Until 1917 the Cabinet did not have a Secretary let alone a Cabinet Office. The Prime Minister called meetings of the Cabinet himself. No written records of proceedings were kept and contemporary accounts suggest that the Prime Minister was the only member who could be said to have a clear recollection of what had been agreed, and since that recollection was his alone this put him at a considerable advantage compared with his fellow ministers. Now there is a fully-fledged Cabinet Office. It is run by the Secretary of the Cabinet, who, since the demise of the Civil Service Department in 1982, is also effectively head of the civil service, sharing its control with the Head of the Treasury. The Cabinet Office, located in Downing Street and physically attached to No. 10, includes the staff forming the Secretariat and a Statistical Office. Significantly, because of the Prime Minister's overall responsibility for national security, the Cabinet Office also houses the Joint Intelligence Committee, comprising civil servants and intelligence officers, which coordinates the activities of MI5 and MI6, and reports, through the Secretary of the Cabinet, directly to the Prime Minister. MI5 is, essentially, concerned with the United Kingdom's own security and the apprehension of foreign spies, whereas MI6, or the Secret Intelligence Service (SIS) to give it its proper name, is concerned with counter-espionage and intelligence abroad. Both are assisted by the monitoring facilities of SIGINT, or Signals Intelligence, housed at the Government Communications Headquarters (GCHQ) at Cheltenham.

The Cabinet Office has, therefore, in recent years assumed an increasingly important role in the centre of government and, despite its relatively small staff, is now, in association with the Treasury, the hub of the central government machine.

The Cabinet Secretariat draws up agendas for Cabinet meetings, on the instructions of the Prime Minister, and distributes minutes of these meetings. The Cabinet normally meets weekly in the Cabinet Room at No. 10 Downing Street. The seats around the Cabinet table are arranged in order of importance, the most influential ministers having places opposite or close to the Prime Minister. Non-Cabinet ministers are called in at appropriate moments if an item on the agenda requires their attendance.

Minutes and other papers are distributed to all Cabinet ministers as are the more important Foreign Office telegrams. The extent to which a departmental minister is able to find time to read all the documents which do not directly affect his own department is debatable. It is up to him to make time and take the necessary interest. In practice it means that discussions within the Cabinet are invariably confined to a minority of the members present: the minister or ministers directly concerned with a particular issue being discussed, the Prime Minister, and perhaps a small number of senior colleagues, who will probably include the Chancellor of the Exchequer, the Foreign Secretary and the Home Secretary.

Cabinet ministers are sworn to secrecy and completely reliable information of what actually takes place within the Cabinet room is difficult to obtain. In recent years, however, reliable leaks and writings of people such as the late Richard Crossman have given us what must be a reasonably accurate picture of what takes place.

The Cabinet committee system

The Cabinet now operates through an elaborate system of committees. Because the full Cabinet meets usually once a week for a period of a few hours, it is essential that the most productive use is made of this limited time. Therefore most agenda items are backed by papers prepared beforehand by one of the Cabinet Committees. A particular committee may have, itself, delegated more detailed work on a particular subject to a sub-committee. It is almost impossible for anyone outside the Cabinet to have complete and up-to-date information about the committees. A publication, *Organisation of Cabinet Committees*, is issued on a confidential basis to each central department but, because of frequent changes, it is seldom up to date.

There are two types of committee: standing, dealing on a fairly permanent basis with regular, continuing functions, and *ad hoc*, set up to deal with temporary matters. At any one time there are usually twenty to twenty-five standing committees. The number of *ad hoc* committees obviously depends on current activities. The most important current standing committees are Defence and Overseas Policy, chaired by the Prime Minister; Economic Strategy, also with the Prime Minister in the chair; Home and Social Affairs, chaired by the Home Secretary; and Legislation, chaired by the Lord President of the Council.

Prime Ministers and Cabinet committees

The Prime Minister, by chairing the main committees and by the selection of membership, and particularly chairmen, of others, can exert considerable influence over Cabinet committees. Determining chairmen of Cabinet committees is another example of the Prime Minister's powers of patronage. A Cabinet member can be 'rewarded' by being given a chair or 'disciplined' by being denied one. A striking example of this occurred during the Callaghan administration of 1977–9 when, although he was Secretary of State for Energy, the out-of-favour Tony Benn was denied the chairmanship of the committee on energy and the Industry Secretary, Eric Varley, preferred. The Prime Minister can also do a lot to determine the way a committee operates by the selection of membership. Thus the inclusion of a preponderance of left-wing or right-wing politicians, or those who are regarded as 'wet' or 'dry', will obviously affect the character of the committee.

The shadow cabinet

The role of the Opposition in Parliament is to examine and criticize, objectively, the policies of the government. It is also the available alternative government. It seems sensible that the public should have a corresponding group of politicians against which it can measure the effectiveness of the group in power. As a means of coordinating its operations and preparing for an opportunity to replace the existing government, the Leader of the Opposition chooses what has come to be called the shadow cabinet. In it virtually every minister in the existing Cabinet is 'shadowed' by a corresponding member in the Opposition 'cabinet'. Although it is not certain that all members of the shadow cabinet will occupy the same positions in the Cabinet itself if and when the Opposition return to office, it is a useful device for training future Cabinet ministers or keeping former Cabinet ministers in touch with current policies.

In theory the device of a shadow cabinet is a means of ensuring effective opposition. In practice, however, the dice are still heavily loaded in favour of the government of the day which has the entire civil service at its disposal whereas the Opposition is largely dependent on its own internal resources. In later chapters we will look in more detail at the ways in which Parliament attempts to control the executive and at its effectiveness. Formal recognition of the Leader of the Opposition and the payment of his salary from public funds has gone a little way towards remedying the imbalance of resources between government and opposition. Whether, in the interests of democratic government, this should be further extended is a subject for current debate.

Collective and individual responsibility

The whole Cabinet system operates on the basis of ministerial responsibility. Ministers individually accept responsibility for the work of their respective departments and collective responsibility for the work of the government as a whole. The acceptance of individual responsibility means that a minister should be prepared to accept the consequences of any act performed by a civil servant on his behalf, whether he is aware of it or not. Civil servants are traditionally anonymous and above politics: the minister is the man in the 'political firing line'.

The question of accepting responsibility is not in doubt: the consequences of this acceptance, however, depend on how embarrassing the issue is to the government. When a civil servant commits an error a minister will occasionally accept responsibility and offer the Prime Minister his resignation. On another occasion he will accept responsibility and carry on in office. In some cases the Prime Minister will sacrifice a colleague in the face of a public outcry. In many cases, however, it will be more embarrassing politically for a minister to resign than to stay on. The chances of a minister who has accepted responsibility for an error or misdemeanour by his civil servants actually resigning seem now fairly remote. In Chapter 18 we will examine in some detail the circumstances which resulted in the resignation of the Minister of Agriculture, over the so-called Crichel Down Affair, in 1954. This was, however, an unusual case. There are many instances, before and since 1954, when ministers and the government generally have decided to ride out the storm.

Sir Thomas Dugdale resigned, in 1954, on what he saw as a point of honour. Although he had personally not been aware of the maladministration of the civil servants in his department he believed he should have and, in consequence, accepted responsibility for their actions. Twenty-eight years later, in 1982, the man who had been Dugdale's Parliamentary Secretary, Lord Carrington, took a similar view about his personal responsibilities for allowing the dispute with Argentina over the Falkland Islands to drift into war and resigned, together with his junior ministers, Humphrey Atkins and Richard Luce.

In 1984, however, neither the Secretary of State for Northern Ireland, James Prior, nor his deputy, Nicholas Scott, thought it necessary to offer to resign in the light of the highly critical Hennessy Report on the breakout of Republican prisoners from the Maze Prison in Belfast, which resulted in 19 violent terrorists being at large. The Report found an amazing number of mistakes and failures at the Maze Prison but Mr Scott, although personally responsible for prisons, claimed that the deficiencies revealed were matters of implementation and not policy and, hence, beyond his direct control.

The evidence of ministers accepting or not accepting responsibility for the actions of their permanent officials suggests that the criteria now employed are political rather than administrative. In other words, when something for which a minister is ultimately responsible goes wrong the first question he is likely to ask himself is not was it my fault but rather, what are going to be the political consequences and can I live with them?

The consequences of collective responsibility are more clearcut. Unless there is an openly-stated agreement to differ, as was the case when the Wilson Cabinet was divided over the issue of membership of the EEC, then all members of the government must be prepared to stand by Cabinet decisions or resign. There have been several clear instances, in both the Conservative and Labour parties, of ministers resigning their offices rather than compromising their views. There have also been examples of Prime Ministers dismissing colleagues who have refused to accept publicly the doctrine of collective responsibility.

References

1. Mackintosh, J.P. *The British Cabinet*, Hutchinson, 1977.
2. Bagehot, W. *The English Constitution*, Fontana, 1963.
3. *Report of the Machinery of Government Committee*, Cmd. 9230, HMSO, 1918.

Assignments

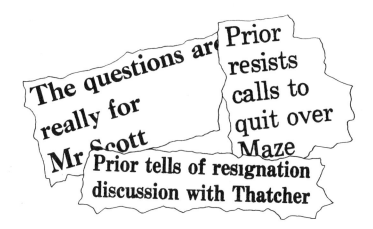

9. Compare the circumstances in which Lord Carrington resigned because of the invasion of the Falkland Islands in 1982 and those when James Prior did not resign in the wake of the Hennessy Report, of January 1984, on the escape of prisoners from the Maze Prison in Northern Ireland, and suggest which, if any, of the two actions was correct.

Sources: The Economist, The Times, and *The Guardian.* Anthony Sampson *The Changing Anatomy of Britain*, particularly Chapters 2 to 7.

10. 'Whatever the monarchy costs, it is money well spent.' Do you agree with this statement? Give your reasons.

7
The central government machine

The central departments

The main organizational unit of central government is the department or ministry. The number of departments is not constant; their size and names are also subject to change. There has been a more or less continuous attempt by successive governments in recent years to keep the number of departments down to a level where the majority could be directly represented by a minister in the Cabinet without making the Cabinet itself very large. In practice this has meant a target of about twenty departments: in the Thatcher government of 1983, for example, there were 16. They are listed in Table 7.1.

Only one of these departments was not represented in the Cabinet by its political head: the Law Officers' Department, which is not really a department or ministry as such. It comprises the Attorney-General and Solicitor-General and their associates as the chief legal advisers to the government.

The Treasury had more than one Cabinet minister, the Chancellor of the Exchequer and the Chief Secretary to the Treasury. As the Prime Minister is also nominally head of the Treasury, as First Lord, and head of the Civil Service Department, it can be said that the Treasury had three Cabinet representatives. The Thatcher 1983 Cabinet of 20 included, in addition to the Secretaries of State or Ministers in the departments already listed, the Lord President of the Council, the Lord Chancellor, who presided over the House of Lords, the Lord Privy Seal, who was also Leader of the House of Commons, and the Chancellor of the Duchy of Lancaster.

Table 7.1 The main central departments (Conservative government 1983)

Ministry of Agriculture, Fisheries and Food
Ministry of Defence
Department of Education and Science
Department of Employment
Department of Energy
Department of the Environment
Foreign and Commonwealth Office
Department of Health and Social Security
Home Office
Law Officers' Department
Northern Ireland Office
Scottish Office
Department of Trade and Industry
Department of Transport
Treasury
Welsh Office

The Lord President, the Lord Privy Seal and the Chancellor of the Duchy of Lancaster are, as their titles suggest, ancient offices of the Crown which have changed their original purposes and are now used to provide posts for senior ministers whose responsibilities can be switched to meet changing circumstances. In the 1983 Margaret Thatcher government, for example, Lord Cockfield, as Chancellor of the Duchy of Lancaster, was given responsibility for the civil service. When Harold Wilson was Prime Minister, Edward Short (as he then was) was given responsibility, as Lord President, for overseeing the drafting of proposals for devolution. Under Edward Heath, Geoffrey Rippon, as Chancellor of the Duchy of Lancaster, led the negotiations for our entry into EEC membership. The 1983 Cabinet of 20 was, in size and composition, broadly typical of other governments in recent years, Labour or Conservative.

What the departments do

If we take the departments listed in Table 7.1 as a model, and it is a reliable example, we can now look briefly at their responsibilities and activities and identify the changes they have experienced in recent years.

The title **Ministry of Agriculture, Fisheries and Food** is largely self-explanatory. It is the department which has probably been most involved in recent years with the European Commission in Brussels through the implementation of the Common Agricultural Policy.

The **Ministry of Defence** is a comparatively new creation. Prior to the 1970s the armed forces were controlled by three separate ministries, the Admiralty, the War Office, and the Air Ministry. They were then brought together under one senior minister, the Secretary of State for Defence, supported by three Under-Secretaries, for the Royal Navy, the Army, and the Royal Air Force respectively.

The **Department of Education and Science** is well known and its responsibilities are fairly obvious. The Secretary of State is concerned with all forms of public education outside the universities and for certain aspects of scientific research.

The **Department of Employment** used to have the title Department of Employment and Productivity, and before that was called the Ministry of Labour. Again, its major responsibilities are identified by its title. The old Ministry of Labour also operated the employment agencies with the rather Victorian title of labour exchanges. The job centres, as they were subsequently called, are run by the Manpower Services Commission which was extracted from the Department of Employment in 1973 to exist as a largely autonomous body.

The **Department of Energy** was also first created in the 1970s although it had a predecessor some years before in the shape of the Ministry of Fuel and Power. The Department is concerned with all kinds of energy: coal, gas, electricity, oil, and, to some extent, nuclear power. The large energy-producing public corporations, such as the National Coal Board, and the Electricity and Gas Councils, come ultimately under its control. It is also concerned, of course, with North Sea oil.

The **Department of the Environment** is another post-1970 creation. It was formed largely from the old Ministry of Housing and Local Government. In addition to overall responsibility for local government, the Department is concerned with other aspects of the environment. The duties of the old Ministry of Public Building and Works, which maintained the royal and other national and public buildings and

67

places, such as parks, have now been absorbed into the Department of the Environment.

The responsibilities of the **Foreign and Commonwealth Office** are largely explained by its title. Commonwealth relations and colonial affairs used to have separate ministries: they now fall within the ambit of the Foreign and Commonwealth Office, with the Foreign Secretary as its political chief. In the government of James Callaghan there was a separate Ministry of Overseas Development which concerned itself with the provision of technical, educational, and financial aid to the developing countries of the so-called third world. The functions remain but are now performed within the Foreign Office through a Minister of State.

The **Department of Health and Social Security**, as a direct supplier of services through its local offices, is a large employer of labour. It is represented in the Cabinet by the Secretary of State for Social Services. The Department is concerned with the administration of the National Health Service, the local authority community services, and the operation of the pensions and unemployment benefit schemes. The work of the old National Assistance Board has been taken over by the Department and it is also concerned with the needs of the handicapped and disabled.

The **Home Office**, once one of the 'big three' departments of state, the others being the Treasury and the Foreign Office, has in recent years tended to be the ministry of 'bits and pieces'. Its prime concern still is the administration of justice, and this includes overall supervision of the prison, probation, police, and fire services. Immigration control is also the Home Office's concern, as well as gambling, drugs control, theatre and cinema licensing, firearms control, and the supervision of charities. A full catalogue of the Home Secretary's responsibilities would occupy more space than these brief summaries allow.

The work of the **Law Officers' Department** has already been briefly explained. The Attorney-General and the Solicitor-General are the two chief legal advisers to the government, and the politicians who hold these offices are invariably lawyers with wide practising experience.

The **Northern Ireland**, **Scottish**, and **Welsh Offices** look after the affairs of these three parts of the United Kingdom. We will look at the differences and proposed differences in the relationships between these three regions and the government in London later in this book.

The **Department of Trade and Industry** was created in 1970 at a time when 'super' departments were in vogue. It was later split into the two constituent departments of Trade and and Industry and then reunited in 1983. At one time, it was thought that a single department was beyond the scope of one minister but the need to bring trade and industry policies nearer to each other has overruled this view. The Trade part of the department has an interest in most aspects of home and overseas trade, with an emphasis on its promotion. It operates an Export Credits Guarantee service to help exporters and has a special division to assist small firms. A Minister of State in the department has special responsibility for consumer affairs, including the maintenance of fair trading standards and the control of monopoly power. The Industry side is concerned with industry and industrial performance and in recent years has taken a keen interest in computers and information technology. Obviously, the work of the department impinges on that of several other central departments concerned with industrial production, including Employment, Energy, and Transport.

68   The **Department of Transport** has had a chequered life in recent years, existing

sometimes as a fully-fledged department and then, for a period, as part of a larger unit. It is concerned with most aspects of transport, land, air, and water. It is a provider and maintainer of motorways and major trunk roads, for the latter using local authorities as its agents. A number of public corporations are responsible to the Secretary of State, including British Rail, British Airways, the British Airports Authority, the National Freight Corporation, and the Civil Aviation Authority.

Despite several attempts to demote it, the **Treasury** has managed to retain its position as the senior central department. Between 1964 and 1969 it lost its responsibilities for the overall supervision of the economy to the newly-created Department of Economic Affairs but the transfer was temporary as functions of the department were re-absorbed by the Treasury. In 1968 the Treasury's responsibilities for recruitment, training, organization, and management in the civil service were given to another new creation, the Civil Service Department, but this, too, was closed in 1983 and these responsibilities have reverted to the Treasury, in conjunction with the Cabinet Office.

The Treasury's major function has always been the management of the nation's accounts, covering the whole field of public expenditure, and it is not surprising, therefore, that successive governments have tried to relieve the total burden of duties in one way or another. As we have seen, however, each experiment has been short-lived and the Treasury has remained, re-establishing its strength and even increasing it. The Prime Minister is, as we have already noted, formally its head, in the nominal role of the First Lord of the Treasury, and in recent years most Prime Ministers have taken a close interest in economic affairs. Its working head, the Chancellor of the Exchequer, not only occupies one of the oldest offices of state but is usually the most influential member of the Cabinet after the Prime Minister.

Types of central department

It must now be clear that the pattern of central departments is not static. Indeed, there has been more change in recent years in the distribution of functions between central departments than between those within local authorities. The Haldane Committee, which looked at the machinery of central government, in its 1918 Report discussed the various bases on which a department or ministry might be created. It suggested four:

1. according to the nature of its work, i.e., by functions;
2. according to the clientele served, e.g., a Children's Department or a Women's Department;
3. according to the processes employed, e.g., by putting scientists or engineers together; and
4. on a geographical or regional basis, e.g., the Scottish and Welsh Offices.

In practice most of the four principles have been used as a basis for determining the structure of departments at one time or another but it has been found that the functional one is most likely to avoid duplication and overlap. To use the clientele principle, for example, could mean having a department for young people, old people, deaf people, blind people, and so on, even though they shared many common needs in addition to those peculiar to their age and condition.

It is also possible to distinguish between departments which are largely executive

69

and those which are not. The former are primarily concerned with the administration of policies by the Cabinet whereas the latter, often called common service departments, are mainly concerned with providing services for the executive departments or ministries. In our list in Table 7.1 the Law Officers' Department and the Treasury would fit into the common service category whereas the other 14 would be regarded as primarily executive.

The organization of a department

It is impossible to speak of a 'typical' central department because such a thing does not exist. Each differs in some respects from the others. However, at the risk of some simplification, Fig. 7.1 attempts to identify the main organizational features which will be found in a major department represented in the Cabinet by a Minister or Secretary of State.

A department has two heads, the political, a Minister or Secretary of State, and the non-political, the Permanent Secretary. The Minister or Secretary of State is a politician, representing the department in Parliament, and probably in the Cabinet; the Permanent Secretary is a career civil servant.

Depending on the size of the department, the Secretary of State will be assisted by one or two Ministers of State. A Minister of State is a political office which has come very much into vogue in recent years. It is of immediate sub-cabinet rank and its holder usually has full responsibility, subject to the overall responsibility of the Secretary of State, for a major sector of the work of the department. Occasionally a Minister of State will be in complete charge of a small department.

The political office next in rank is that of Parliamentary Secretary. If the political head of the department is styled Secretary of State then, to avoid confusion, Parliamentary Secretaries are designated Parliamentary Under-Secretaries of State. If

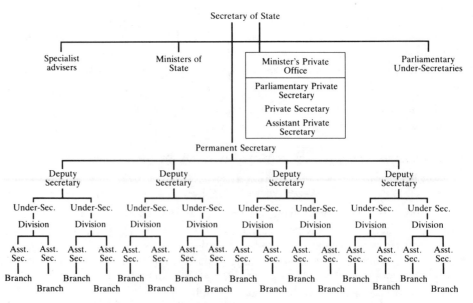

Fig. 7.1 Central department X: organization chart

the political head is styled Minister then the *under* prefix is dropped. One of the main jobs of the Parliamentary Secretary is to deputize for the Secretary of State in Parliament. Thus he will take on some of the burden of dealing with questions in the House of Commons, or will do much of the work of guiding a Bill through its committee stage. It is common for a department to be represented by at least two parliamentary secretaries: one in the House of Commons and one in the House of Lords.

Table 7.2 shows how the size of a department is reflected in its political weighting. The largest departments not only have more than one Minister of State but also 'sub-ministries', headed by a politician with the title of Minister, within them: Environment, the Foreign Office, Health and Social Security, and Trade and Industry are examples of this.

Table 7.2 The political composition of central departments (Conservative government 1983)

Agriculture, Fisheries and Food	Minister, two Ministers of State, one Parliamentary Secretary
Defence	Secretary of State, two Ministers of State, two Parliamentary Under-Secretaries
Education and Science	Secretary of State, two Parliamentary Under-Secretaries
Employment	Secretary of State, two Ministers of State, one Parliamentary Under-Secretary
Energy	Secretary of State, one Minister of State, two Parliamentary Under-Secretaries
Environment	Secretary of State, Minister for Local Government, Minister for Housing and Construction, three Parliamentary Under-Secretaries
Foreign and Commonwealth Office	Secretary of State, three Ministers of State, Minister for Overseas Development, one Parliamentary Under-Secretary
Health and Social Security	Secretary of State, Minister of Health, Minister of Social Security, three Parliamentary Under-Secretaries
Home Office	Secretary of State, two Ministers of State, two Parliamentary Under-Secretaries
Law Officers' Department	Attorney-General, Lord Advocate, Solicitor-General, one Minister of State, Solicitor-General (Scotland)
Northern Ireland Office	Secretary of State, two Ministers of State, two Parliamentary Under-Secretaries
Scottish Office	Secretary of State, one Minister of State, three Parliamentary Under-Secretaries
Trade and Industry	Secretary of State, Minister for Trade, Minister for Industry and Information Technology, one Minister of State, three Parliamentary Under-Secretaries
Transport	Secretary of State, one Minister of State, one Parliamentary Under-Secretary
Welsh Office	Secretary of State, one Minister of State, one Parliamentary Under-Secretary

Another feature of a 'typical' department is the Minister's Private Office. This is the Secretary of State's personal secretariat and normally comprises his civil servant secretary, styled Private Secretary, and a Parliamentary Private Secretary, who is an MP acting as the Secretary of State's unpaid 'dogsbody' in the House of Commons. At first sight a thankless task, the position of Parliamentary Private Secretary is usually accepted as a possible step on the ladder to higher political office. Similarly, civil servants acting as Private Secretaries to Ministers are often potential high fliers who see the post as a launching platform for a top job in the Service.

The Private Office is very much the Secretary of State's eyes and ears. His Private Secretary keeps him in touch with the permanent side of the department while his Parliamentary Private Secretary is his link with backbench opinion in Parliament. In France the concept of a Private Office has been elevated and expanded into what is called the Minister's *cabinet* (using the French pronunciation of the word) and consists of a high-powered staff of political and civil servant advisers. It has been argued that something like a minister's *cabinet* should be introduced into central government in this country. The forces of tradition and conservatism will probably inhibit such a development.

Most Secretaries of State will have the benefit of a specialist adviser or advisers, who may be scientists, economists or from some other discipline. These advisers are civil servants who form part of the departmental team on a permanent or semi-permanent basis. A more recent development is the appointment of political advisers. These are people chosen by the Minister to advise him on political aspects of policy. A political adviser is a temporary civil servant, often chosen from the academic field, and with a view of politics closely aligned to that of his chief. How these temporary additions to a department fit in, or sometimes fail to fit in, and how they are viewed by the permanent civil servants will be discussed later.

The permanent part of the central department machine is headed by the Permanent Secretary. This is the highest rank in the civil service and its holder is the most senior member of the department's permanent staff. He leads a hierarchical team of civil servants. Immediately below him in rank are Deputy Secretaries, each responsible for a division, or a number of divisions. The division is the major functional unit of a department and, if not headed by a deputy secretary is controlled by an Under-Secretary, who, in turn, is responsible for two or more Assistant Secretaries, each of whom normally heads a branch, or subdivision.

This, then, is the structure of a typical department, bearing in mind that there really is no such thing since each department has its own distinctive features. The structure we have outlined is, however, sufficiently general to be acceptable as an accurate reflection of central government organization.

The central political–permanent relationship

The relationship between a minister and his permanent secretary is the key to our understanding of how the central machine works. In theory the minister takes all the political decisions and his civil servants advise him on the most practical and effective means of implementing them. In reality it is not as simple and clearcut as this.

The minister is likely to spend only a few years as head of his department: five years would be well above average. The permanent secretary, on the other hand, is likely to be in charge of his department for a much longer period and, during that time will have worked with more than one minister. Moreover, the civil servant is following a long-term career in the course of which he will have had experience of several departments at varying levels. The relationship is, therefore, in several respects unbalanced. The permanent secretary is bound to be more knowledgeable about his department than the minister. The civil servant's ability to make full use of the complicated Whitehall machine is much greater. In many cases the permanent secretary will be more intelligent and better educated than the minister. How then does the minister cope? How can he be in control of his department? Is he in many cases a puppet dancing to the manipulations of his civil servants? The answer to the first question is that sometimes he does not cope: or at least not very well. The answer to the second question is that he *can* be in control of his department if he chooses to be and does the necessary homework. The answer to the third question is a qualified no.

Despite the writings of some political journalists, and particularly the views expressed in the posthumously published diaries of Richard Crossman,[1] it would be misleading to think of the minister–permanent secretary relationship as one of built-in conflict, with the politicians constantly trying to protect themselves from the schemings of civil servants, and the civil servants despairing of the amateurish decision-taking of the politicians. The vast majority of top civil servants are highly intelligent people, strongly motivated towards supporting their political bosses and to making their departments work efficiently. They are firmly in the second line of policy making and, whether they agree with it or not, they have to accept that the minister's political decision is eventually final. It is this largely anonymous secondary role that they have chosen to accept, with eyes open, at the start of their careers and most would freely admit that if, on the basis of experience, they have become in any way disenchanted they have only themselves to blame. Of course they will not always see eye to eye with their ministers. They will regard it as their duty to warn him of what would be, in their opinion, the unfortunate consequences of some particular decision and try to dissuade him from taking it. If, however, the minister has clearly made up his mind on a course of action, having been advised against it, he will expect his civil servants to support him and the evidence is that they invariably will.

The relationship, then, is a subtle one. It is dependent on the respective personalities of the two people involved and on the interactions of these personalities as much as anything else. If a minister knows his mind and is not so politically arrogant as not to be prepared to take advice and learn, then his relationship with his Permanent Secretary will undoubtedly be successful. If a personality clash occurs and cannot be resolved the minister has no choice other than that of asking the Prime Minister for a change of Permanent Secretary. That this happens only infrequently is an indication of this objectivity and impartiality normally displayed by our top civil servants.

The question of who determines policy and where policy ends and administration begins is another area of considerable interest and one which we shall explore later in this book.

The 'centre' of British government

Central government in Britain consists of twenty or so ministries or departments mostly situated in the SW1 postal district of London. At the heart of this 'machine' are two departments or units which may be described as the centre of British government: the Treasury and the Cabinet Office.

The term 'centre' was probably used for the first time by Sir Richard Clarke, a former Permanent Secretary to the Ministry of Technology, when he gave a series of lectures in 1971 at the civil service college, subsequently published under the title *New Trends in Government*.[2] In the second of his lectures, Sir Richard spoke of what he called the centre of government. It consisted, in his view, of the Cabinet, at the political level, and the Cabinet Office, the Treasury and the Civil Service Department, at the official level. He saw the Secretary to the Cabinet and the Permanent Secretaries to the Treasury and the Civil Service Department as the key civil servants and, in his opinion, the role of the centre was quite different from that of individual departments.

Sir Richard argued that the centre should have a coordinating, controlling, and forward-looking role, particularly in the area of financial provision. Its objectives should be to ensure that the overall policy of the government was accurately translated into departmental policies, and also that departmental views were represented in overall policy. From a financial viewpoint the centre's job was to ensure that departmental financial policies matched the overall financial/economic strategy of the government. The weakness in the organization of the centre, as Sir Richard saw it, lay in the fact that the three main central units were potentially likely to overlap or duplicate their functions. He saw two possible solutions: a federation at the centre, or the creation of a new central department or departments.

The problem of federation, like that of creating, super-ministries, was basically political: should you have one federal minister, or several ministers working closely together? An alternative to a federal solution would be, Sir Richard thought, to join the constituent parts together and then redivide them into separate departments: one he would call the Central Management Department and the other the National Economy and Finance Department.

Twelve years after Sir Richard Clarke's seminal lectures one part of the triumvirate he called the 'centre', the Civil Service Department, disappeared. The functions it used to perform remained, however, and became the responsibilities of the Cabinet Office and the Treasury. This has tended to strengthen, rather than weaken, the concept of a 'centre' and has had the effect of further concentrating power in that exclusive area of Whitehall in and around Downing Street, where the Prime Minister, the Chancellor of the Exchequer, and the Cabinet Office are located. If we add to the Treasury and the Cabinet Office the Prime Minister's personal Policy Unit at No. 10 Downing Street, we can see the significance of speaking of a centre in Sir Richard's terms.

We will look more closely at the role of central government in economic and financial management later. Let us end our examination of the central machine by taking our discussion of the coordination of central government policy a little further.

Coordination of central government policy

As Sir Richard Clarke pointed out in his lectures, coordinating the individual actions of each of the separate departments of state so that a coherent, overall policy is followed is probably the most difficult task facing central government. It is not a problem peculiar to governments: it confronts all large organizations and is mainly the consequence of size. When we remember the enormous spectrum of activities covered by the central departments it is obvious that in this case the problem is much greater.

74

The Haldane Committee, in 1918, identified one of the main functions of the Cabinet as that of coordinating the activities of the main central departments. In 1918 it was still barely possible to say that the Cabinet, through its newly created Secretariat, could do this. Since then, however, the scope of government has grown enormously and, as we have seen, the size of the Cabinet Secretariat has increased and a complex network of committees has grown up. The committees can undertake the detailed study of specific aspects of policy on behalf of the full Cabinet but the task of coordinating overall policy remains.

In 1970 the Conservative government of Edward Heath undertook a major review of the organization of central departments and published its proposals in a White Paper.[3] In the course of this restructuring new 'super departments', such as Environment and Trade and Industry, were created, in the hope that by bringing together the activities of smaller departments the span of responsibility of individual ministers would be increased but the number who would need to liaise and cooperate would decrease. The main practical problem has been that of finding 'super ministers' capable of heading the large departments. It was precisely because of this difficulty that Trade and Industry were eventually split. Their reunification in 1983 suggested that Margaret Thatcher believed that she now had colleagues of sufficient calibre to take on the task. Also, as Table 7.2 shows, the device of delegating to 'departments within departments' has been employed.

At the same time the Heath administration created a new vehicle for monitoring policy decisions, investigating the effects of policy implementation, and generally informing the Prime Minister whether or not the overall policies of his government were being implemented by the separate parts of the central machine in the way the Cabinet had intended. This vehicle was given the title of the Central Policy Review Staff.

The Central Policy Review Staff (CPRS) was established in 1970 under the chairmanship of Lord Rothschild. It consisted of about sixteen graduates, whose average age was thirty-seven, aided by a small supporting staff. It was located in the Cabinet Office, so as to be close to the centre of decision taking, and its job was to advise the Cabinet collectively and the Prime Minister personally on major issues of government policy. It undertook six-monthly reviews of the total strategy of the government and special studies of specific areas of policy on request. The high academic calibre of its members and the searching reports it produced soon attracted to it the popular name of 'Think Tank'.

In July 1983 the CPRS unit was disbanded. In announcing its demise in the House of Commons, Margaret Thatcher gave three main reasons for her decision. First, that since 1971 departments had established their own policy units for long-term planning; second, that the role of the Cabinet Secretariat had grown considerably; and third, that a Policy Unit had been established in the Prime Minister's Office.

Mrs Thatcher's arguments were, perhaps understandably, not universally supported. Her critics saw them as further evidence of her wish to concentrate more power in her own hands. Without attempting to judge whether or not these criticisms were justified, it is undeniable that most, if not all, post-war Prime Ministers have felt disadvantaged in that their Cabinet colleagues have known much more about at least one specific aspect of government than they have done. In government, as in most aspects of life, information is the key to power. The minister who is well briefed has a clear edge over his less-informed opponent. Admittedly, departmental ministers are only familiar with a limited number of trees whereas the Prime Minister surveys the whole wood, but even a strong-willed Leader might find it difficult to argue with a better-informed subordinate.

The end of the CPRS has been lamented by people from a wide variety of backgrounds. It was acknowledged that in the last few years of its existence it had seemed to drift away from its original purpose and had become involved in too many specific, and not necessarily long-term, issues. Nevertheless, many observers argued for a unit, detached from individual departments, and able to take a forward, 'global' view of policy, as an adviser to ministers collectively and not just a select few. The normal day-to-day workload of the Cabinet Office precluded it from assuming this role and a Policy Unit, acting solely for the Prime Minister, was not an adequate substitute.

The Downing Street 'centre'

Sir Richard Clarke's plea for better coordination of government departments at the centre is still valid and successive prime ministers have recognized it. They have, however, approached the problem in different ways.

Edward Heath saw the solution in super-ministries and a long-term think tank. Harold Wilson and James Callaghan, although less convinced about the ability of ministers to run large departments, accepted the need for the Central Policy Review Staff but they allowed its activities to degenerate so that it became increasingly concerned in short-term, specific issues. Perhaps, in the course of its studies, the Think Tank made too many enemies who were not prepared to defend it when the question of its continuing existence was raised. In 1977, for example, it produced a damning report on the Foreign Office and Britain's diplomatic service. The establishment immediately closed ranks and the report was virtually shelved.

Both Harold Wilson and James Callaghan had felt the need for support and advice from people of their own political persuasion and had strengthened the staff at 10 Downing Street with temporary political advisers. Margaret Thatcher continued the practice but in a more formalized way. After becoming Conservative Leader, in opposition, in 1975, she relied heavily on her mentor, Keith Joseph, who, in the year of her election, had set up the Centre for Policy Studies, as the Conservative Party's own, private think tank. On becoming Prime Minister, Mrs Thatcher created her own Policy Unit at 10 Downing Street, led by Sir John Hoskyns, with David Wolfson, a computer expert, and Sir Alan Walters, the economist, who had been lured back to this country from a professorship in the United States.

Sir John Hoskyns left the Unit in 1982 and was succeeded by Ferdinand Mount, the former political editor of *The Spectator*. In November 1983 the Unit had acquired a new head, John Redwood, a 32-year-old merchant banker, and was a team of eight people with one honorary adviser.

Margaret Thatcher also set up, soon after taking office, a 'cost-efficiency unit', reporting directly to her. It was established by Derek Rayner, later Sir Derek, and now Lord Rayner, who had been seconded by Marks and Spencer. Rayner had been one of several businessmen brought in to advise the government of Edward Heath, returning to their original jobs during the Wilson and Callaghan governments. Mrs

Thatcher recalled him and he steadily built up the Unit, which undertook a number of cost-cutting and efficiency studies in several central departments, revealing opportunities for making significant savings by avoiding excessive bureaucracy.

The 'Rayner Unit' was originally located in the Cabinet Office but later given an independent status. Lord Rayner returned to Marks and Spencer, as Chief Executive, in July 1983 and was replaced by Sir Robin Ibbs, a director of ICI.

The 'Downing Street Centre' now comprises a formidable combination of political, civil service, business, and academic talent in the Prime Minister herself, the Cabinet Office, with its network of committees, the Policy Unit, and the Rayner Unit. If we add to this the nearby strength of the Treasury we can see some semblance of the centre for which Sir Richard Clarke argued. In terms of numbers of people it is not large by the standards of the super-ministries such as Trade and Industry, but politically and administratively it has great potential strength. The significant aspect of the Downing Street Centre from Margaret Thatcher's point of view is that it is staffed by *her* people whom she feels she can trust and whose opinions she respects. As Secretary of the Cabinet and head of the civil service, Sir Robert Armstrong is, in effect, a unique super-civil servant, straddling the difficult demarcation line between politics and neutrality. The Policy Unit and the Rayner Unit are personally responsible to her and not advisers to the Cabinet as a whole.

Whether this accretion of power at No. 10 will be enough to remedy the imbalance between advice and information available to the Prime Minister and that available to cabinet ministers through their departments is a matter for debate. We shall look again at this and other aspects of policy making and coordination in our final chapter.

References

1. Crossman, R.H.S. *Diaries of a Cabinet Minister*, 3 vols, Cape/Hamilton, 1975–7.
2. Clarke, R. *New Trends in Government 1*, HMSO, 1971.
3. *Reorganization of Central Government*, Cmd. 4506, HMSO, 1970.

Assignments

11. Why was the Central Policy Review Staff established and why was it disbanded? Do you think it will ever be revived?

Sources: Anthony Sampson *The Changing Anatomy of Britain*, particularly Chapters 11 and 12. Read articles by Peter Hennessy in *The Times* on the CPRS.

12. 'A civil servant should be on tap, not on top.' Do you think this statement accurately describes the minister–permanent secretary relationship?

8

Decentralization and devolution

The need to decentralize

Decentralize is a word with a fairly obvious meaning. It implies that a decision has consciously been taken to operate away from the centre.

When the forerunners of the present job centres, the labour exchanges, were established under the control of the Board of Trade in 1909, they were located in towns of a reasonable size. The local exchanges formed part of an area and a number of areas constituted a division with a relatively senior civil servant supervising a division. The reason for local labour exchanges is immediately apparent. People seeking employment wanted something in the locality in which they lived.

We might say, then, that the prime purpose of decentralization is to bring the provision of a service nearer to the consumer, but there are other reasons. A large firm may decentralize its manufacturing operations so as to take advantage of different local labour forces. There may be a technical reason for decentralization. The optimum capacity of one unit might be such that to operate centrally would exceed that capacity and be uneconomic. Three decentralized units each of optimum size, would be more productive than one three times as large as the optimum. Whatever the reason, decentralization is a common phenomenon in virtually all organizations above a certain size.

In Britain we have two forms of decentralized government. First, we have central departments operating on a regional or local basis with field officers controlled by regional or local offices, which, in turn, are responsible to Whitehall and Westminster. Second, we have local authorities who for the most part implement national policies within their local areas. The difference between decentralized central government and local government lies mainly in the fact that the views of the receivers of services from local authorities are reflected in the elected politicians whose job it is to oversee local administrators. It is thus possible to interpret, through the elected members, national policies in a local way. A decentralized national service, on the other hand, merely applies national policies locally and does not consciously seek to give them a local interpretation. In other words, local government adds a second dimension to decentralization: it includes the decentralization of the political as well as the administrative element of government. It is, of course, too sweeping to describe the work of local authorities as being merely the local implementation of national policies; they have more autonomy and discretion than that, as we shall see in the next chapter.

The concept of devolution

Whereas decentralization is basically a practical operation, devolution, as many people try to interpret it today, is as much a concept as a reality. The word implies the devolving, or passing down, of responsibility and power, but exactly what is devolved and how much are matters of debate?

If we briefly remind ourselves of the main elements of government: the legislative, the executive, and the judicial, we can speculate on what forms devolution might take. We could devolve legislative power, thereby creating either complementary or subordinate legislatures to the Parliament in Westminster. We could devolve executive power to regional or local committees or cabinets. We could devolve judicial authority to a new stratum of courts. We could also devolve administrative powers or we could devolve political control.

To some extent judicial authority is already devolved in the sense that there are local and area courts, such as magistrates', county, and Crown courts, subject to the overall supervision of the Lord Chancellor and subject to rights of appeal to higher courts. Devolving administrative powers is really the same as decentralizing the implementation of political decisions and, as such, mostly a matter of convenience and economy. We are thus left with the prospect of devolving legislative, executive, or political power, or all three, and it is the extent to which these powers are devolved which has been the main topic of debate in recent years.

The 'lukewarm devolutionist' would wish to go no further than having a regionalized local government system with a regional assembly that was basically a deliberative body. In other words, he would be content with devolved power. The 'ardent nationalist', on the other hand, would be satisfied with nothing less than a separate state for his part of the United Kingdom, with a separate parliament, separate cabinet, separate prime minister, separate civil service, and separate judiciary. He would seek full national sovereignty.

Between these two extremes a number of intermediate positions can be assumed. Nearest to the nationalist might be the federalist who would argue for a federal government and state governments each with clearly defined powers. Someone holding views between the lukewarm devolutionist and the federalist would probably seek a regional assembly with some limited legislative powers and full deliberative powers. He would also expect to have a regional executive with freedom to act within the limits of the devolved legislative powers.

The possible range of relationships between central government and local areas within the country is illustrated in Fig. 8.1.

Devolution through regionalism

Although the United Kingdom is a unitary state it has enjoyed, and experimented with, over the years, several forms of regionalism.

During both World Wars the country was divided for defence purposes into administrative regions. Each region was to be rather like a watertight compartment in a ship: if one region was invaded and occupied the rest could continue to operate and support each other. In 1939 Regional Civil Defence Commissioners were appointed and although the ultimate emergency they were intended to deal with, invasion, did not occur, they provided a useful means of administering certain national policies on a regional basis. Although the regional commissioners were disbanded after 1945, a regional structure for central government continued, with all the major departments, apart from the Treasury, having regional or local offices, operating within regions which had been standardized by the Treasury in 1946.

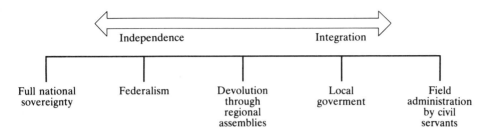

Fig. 8.1 The independence-integration spectrum

In the 1950s there was a movement away from decentralized central government in favour of stronger local authorities or of dealing directly with Whitehall, but the evidence of pockets of regional unemployment in the early 1960s revived the idea of strengthening the central government presence in the regions. Regional economic planning was encouraged by the establishment of economic planning councils, consisting of part-time regional representatives, and economic planning boards, consisting of civil servants operating on a regional basis. The economic planning boards have certainly done something to increase the awareness in Whitehall of the needs of the regions, but the councils, apart from the production of papers, have not made any very obvious impact.

Certain parts of the United Kingdom have for some time enjoyed a greater degree of administrative, executive, and even legislative, independence than others and it is understandable that there have been calls from time to time for an accelerated surrendering of powers by central government. This call for greater devolution was at its peak in the 1970s but, although there has been an apparent decline in interest since, it is inconceivable that it will not eventually revive.

Devolution in practice

The United Kingdom consists of four component parts, England, Wales, Scotland, and Northern Ireland and also includes the Orkney and Shetland Islands, the Inner and Outer Hebrides, the Isle of Wight, Isle of Anglesey, Isles of Scilly, and all the other small islands scattered around the coasts of England, Wales, and Scotland. The Channel Islands and the Isle of Man are Crown dependencies and not part of the United Kingdom. Each has its own legislative assembly, its own system of local administration and law, and its own courts. Within the United Kingdom various forms of devolution, each of which is more than mere decentralization, have been practised for some years. A comparison of the different relationships between London and the capital cities of Edinburgh, Belfast, and Cardiff will illustrate this.

The Secretary of State for Wales has full responsibility in Wales for child care, health, housing, local government, primary and secondary education, town and country planning, new towns, water and sewerage, roads, forestry, tourism, national parks, and historic buildings. In other words, he combines the functions of the English Secretaries of State for Education and Science, the Environment, Social Security, and Transport. Most of this is administered from the Welsh Office in

Cardiff, the Secretary of State having only a small ministerial office in London. The list of his responsibilities may read more like those of a major local authority than a major region, or even nation, but they should not be dismissed lightly. The fact that the Welsh Secretary has the power to apply policies with the needs of Wales specifically in mind is not insignificant.

Scotland enjoys an even greater degree of independence. It has, for example, a separate system of law which differs from that in England and Wales in several important respects. The Secretary of State for Scotland has similar responsibilities to those of the Welsh Secretary with, additionally, full responsibility for agriculture, fisheries, the police, and fire services. The Scottish Office in Edinburgh consists of five departments, the heads of which form a management group under the chairmanship of the Permanent Under-Secretary of State for Scotland. There is, therefore, in Edinburgh an even larger and stronger bureaucracy than in Cardiff: in fact, over 11 000 civil servants work from there.

Northern Ireland was given its own legislature by the Government of Ireland Act 1920. This preserved the supreme authority of the United Kingdom Parliament but transferred legislative powers in 'domestic' matters to a parliament, of a Senate and a House of Commons, at Stormont, near Belfast. Northern Ireland thus represented a situation as near to a federal system of government as we have experienced in this country, and this remained the case until a period of several years of political instability and sectarian violence resulted in the closure of Stormont and the introduction of direct rule from Westminster. Instead of domestic laws being passed by the Northern Ireland parliament they were made by the Secretary of State, using prerogative powers under Orders in Council.

In January 1974, a new constitution came into operation for the devolving of legislative powers from Westminster to the Northern Ireland Assembly and a power-sharing executive on which both Roman Catholics and Protestants were represented. There was immediate opposition in Northern Ireland to these arrangements and they came to an end within a few months; direct rule from London on an annual basis was renewed. The Northern Ireland Act 1982 established a new Assembly of 78 members, elected by the STV voting method. Whether or not the new Assembly will survive is problematical as not all parties took up their seats.

The situation in Northern Ireland in 1984 is that there are six departments of state in Belfast but all under the ultimate control of the Secretary of State who is, in turn, answerable to the United Kingdom Parliament in London. The departments are Agriculture, which has similar responsibilities to its equivalent in London; Economic Development, which, in effect, combines the functions of the Whitehall departments of Trade and Industry and Employment; Environment and Health and Social Services, which correspond broadly to their London equivalents; and Finance and Personnel, which has similar functions to and liaises closely with the United Kingdom Treasury.

The degree of devolution which existed in Northern Ireland before the introduction of direct rule has left the province with its own separate civil service, modelled on its counterpart in England, but recruited independently through its own Civil Service Commission.

Thus although the question of devolution has come to the forefront of political debate in recent years, as a reality it has been with us, in various forms, for quite a long time.

Evolutionary devolution in the United Kingdom

In an earlier chapter we explored the way in which a family unit can become a wider community, how that wider community might become a nation and how a nation would, at a certain stage in its development, wish to assume the title and acquire the institutions of a state. The United Kingdom as we know it today has passed through all these stages, and more. Wales was formally united with England in the sixteenth century and Scotland joined the union at the beginning of the eighteenth century. A united Ireland enlarged the union in the nineteenth century, with Southern Ireland regaining its independence in the 1920s. To speak now of devolving political power would seem, at first glance, a retrograde step and not in keeping with the 'natural' progression from a local community to an internationally recognized state. What, then, have been the forces behind this call for a greater degree of devolution?

Some we have already touched on. There have been economic indicators suggesting that too much wealth has been concentrated in England, and particularly in southern England. In the north and west of England, and in Scotland, Wales and Northern Ireland, there has been a growing feeling that government decision taking on economic matters does not give full weight to the non-metropolitan regions. The view that civilization stops immediately north of Watford has become less of a joke and more of an insult.

In the early 1960s criticisms of bias on the part of central government in London were growing in intensity. Whether or not they were justified was immaterial to many of the more vociferous critics: an 'us and them' attitude was developing. An article in *The Economist* at about that time echoed the concern of people in the regions and suggested that the government should build a motorway from London which ended abruptly in the middle of Yorkshire so as to encourage industrialists to establish new undertakings there.

For many years there has been a significant degree of dormant nationalism in Wales, associated particularly with a distinctive culture and language. To a lesser degree the same has been true of Scotland. This cultural nationalism began to ally itself with the economic nationalism, and politicians with clear nationalist labels began to win seats in local elections in Wales and Scotland. In July 1966 the Welsh Nationalists won a by-election at Carmarthen and in November 1967 the Scottish Nationalists turned a 16 000 Labour majority at Hamilton into a majority for their candidate. What had been of economic and administrative interest suddenly became politically important. Politicians of the two major parties realized that votes were to be won in Scotland and Wales on the basis not of Labour or Conservative policies applied throughout the United Kingdom but on the basis of policies which would have a direct effect on the interests of Scotland or Wales.

The Royal Commission on the Constitution

The politicians responded to this wave of national emotion by taking the most adroit political step available: appointing a Royal Commission. They could then say that something was being done in the knowledge that it would be at least two years before the Commission reported and action would be demanded. The composition of the government which set up the Commission is not important. It could have been Labour or Conservative. As it happened it was a Labour Home Secretary, James Callaghan, who appointed the Royal Commission,[1] under the chairmanship of Lord

Crowther. It took nearly four years to report by which time, in 1973, a Conservative Home Secretary, Robert Carr, was in office, and the original chairman had died and had been succeeded by Lord Kilbrandon.

The Commission's Report was not unanimous. A majority favoured some legislative devolution for Scotland and Wales but a strong Memorandum of Dissent, signed by two academics, Lord Crowther-Hunt and Professor Alan Peacock, argued for a complete regionalization of England, Wales, and Scotland, creating a middle tier of authorities between local and central government.

A political approach to devolution

During the two years following the publication of the Report governments were deeply preoccupied with Northern Ireland, industrial relations, and the question of whether Britain should remain a member of the EEC. Paradoxically, after the nation had, through a referendum in June 1975, said decisively that it wished to remain part of a larger community, in November of the same year the government, which was now Labour, under Harold Wilson, published a White Paper,[2] proposing a form of devolution for Scotland and Wales. Included in the proposals were an Assembly for Scotland with powers to legislate on social services, law, education, and the environment; an Assembly for Wales with no legislative powers; a Cabinet-style executive for Scotland, accountable to the Assembly; a Welsh executive based on Assembly committees, on local government lines; annual block grants voted by the United Kingdom Parliament to cover the costs of devolved functions; and the preservation of the sovereignty of the London Parliament by giving it an ultimate right of veto over either Assembly. Excluded from the devolved functions were industrial development, the control of university education, representation in the EEC, law and order, and the control of North Sea oil revenues.

The reaction of the Liberal Party to the White Paper was that it did not go far enough. The Conservative Party's reaction was that it went too far. The Leader of the Scottish Nationalists announced that his Party would support the proposals with 'grave doubts about its inadequacies'. In 1979 the government introduced a Bill based broadly on the White Paper. It was not enthusiastically received and passed its second reading in the House of Commons by only 292 votes to 247. An attempt to accelerate the committee stage by use of the guillotine failed and the Bill was withdrawn.

In 1977 legislative proposals for devolution were reintroduced. This time there were separate Bills for Scotland and Wales. Again, they followed the lines of the earlier proposals except that the legislative powers to be devolved were more clearly defined. Scotland was to have power to pass primary legislation, in other words Acts, in specific subjects. Wales would have power to pass only secondary legislation, in other words, regulations and other statutory instruments, under the authority of Acts of the United Kingdom Parliament. An additional feature of the two Bills was that, if passed, they would not come into effect until the people of Scotland and Wales had shown popular approval by voting in referenda. The Bills eventually passed through all their parliamentary stages and received the royal assent in the summer of 1978. The referenda were held on 1 March 1979 and resulted in a clear majority against the implementation of the devolution proposals as far as Wales was concerned and an inconclusive majority for an Assembly for Scotland. The Bills, consequently, never became law.

The future for devolution in the United Kingdom

It can be argued that the devolution of powers and responsibilities from central government to the regions is unnecessary in a country as small as the United Kingdom. It can also be criticized on the grounds of relevance. At a time when this country ought to be giving more serious thought to its long-term future in Europe, it should not be distracted by short-term, introspective considerations.

On the other hand, it can be argued that, despite its relative smallness, the United Kingdom does display strong regional differences based on economic, cultural, and social factors. South Wales is economically and socially closer to England as a result of improved communications, but mid- and North Wales are still remote and the number of people in the south-east of England who view the North as starting just outside Watford is real enough to be more than a joke. Scotland and Northern Ireland, of course, have a more valid claim for separate treatment and, as we have seen, this is partially recognized in the current arrangements: but do they go far enough?

With a Conservative government possessing a parliamentary majority large enough to keep it in office for another four years or so, the pressures on it for devolution are not strong. Indeed, in pursuit of their economic objectives, Margaret Thatcher and her Chancellor seem prepared to reduce the autonomy of local authorities rather than delegate more authority to them or to other regional bodies. Politics, however, is a very volatile process and changes in policy do occur—sometimes quite dramatically and sometimes over a period of time.

As we shall see in later chapters, the future of local government in this country is not clear or assured. The metropolitan counties are under threat and the financial base of all authorities is insecure and in need of reform. If another review of local government were sufficiently radical it could well reopen the question of how much power ought to be retained centrally and how much should be devolved.

References

1. *Report of the Royal Commission on the Constitution*, Cmd. 5460, HMSO, 1973.
2. *Our Changing Democracy*, Cmd. 6348, HMSO, 1975.

Assignment

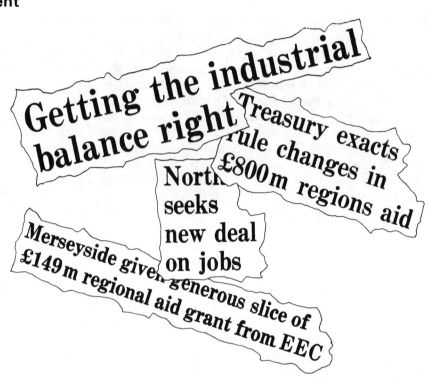

13. What are the essential differences, if any, between the devolution of powers to the regions and the regionalization of local government?

Sources: Chapter 13 of Anthony Sampson's *The Changing Anatomy of Britain* will be found particularly useful.

9

The local government machine

What local government is

Local government is a somewhat misleading term to apply to what is really decentralized government, since local authorities do not 'govern' as autonomous bodies and are always subject to the decisions of Parliament. They are what lawyers formally call 'creatures of statute'.

As we have already seen, the United Kingdom is a unitary state with all political authority ultimately centralized. It would be impossible, however, to perform all the many functions of government from London: at the very least, some administrative decentralization is inevitable. But local government involves more than just administrative decentralization: it embodies a degree of decentralization of policy making, representation, and accountability.

It is this combination that makes local government in this country so distinctive. Local authorities are locally representative and locally responsible, yet ultimately subject to central government direction and control. It is this sometimes uneasy marriage between the centre and the localities which is the key to the success or failure of local government, and it is something we shall examine more closely later in this chapter.

In summary, local government in the United Kingdom displays five main features which set it apart from other decentralized bodies or units: first, it is a well-defined system of individual local authorities; second, each authority is subject to democratic election by people who live in the locality; third, each authority is multi-purpose, in that it has responsibility for a range of functions and services; fourth, there is a limitation of the powers of each authority to a specific locality; fifth, each authority is ultimately subordinate to Parliament, and hence, in practice, to the government of the day.

An evolutionary system

Local government can be traced back to the feudal system and beyond but the present structure has largely evolved during the past century and a half.

The Municipal Corporations Act of 1835 made provision for democratically elected and controlled town councils. The Local Government Act of 1888 created county councils and county borough councils. The Act of 1894 introduced district councils and reformed borough councils, and an Act of 1899 brought in metropolitan boroughs within the county of London.

This evolutionary process has progressively reflected the features we have already noted, including the adoption of a uniform process of representation and the assumption of a multi-purpose role. Thus, over the years, single-purpose, *ad hoc* bodies were disbanded and their functions absorbed into the new local authorities.

These discarded bodies included the Turnpike Trusts, which had powers to build and maintain roads; the Boards of Guardians, who administered the Poor Laws; and the local Health and School Boards.

The reformed structure

The reforms of London government in 1965 and the rest of England and Wales in 1974 were not just the products of a fashionable restructuring zeal. It had become obvious in the 1950s and 1960s that the existing structure was no longer in step with economic, social, and demographic changes which had occurred.

The pre-1974 system outside London, as Fig. 9.1 shows, consisted essentially of a two-tier structure for 'non-urban' areas and a single tier for the larger towns and cities. The implied assumptions in this system were that counties and county boroughs were all large and capable of providing a range of major services, and non-county boroughs and districts were small. As a broad generalization it had some validity but there were obvious discrepancies. County boroughs such as Birmingham, Liverpool, and Manchester were unquestionably large but others, such as Chester and Canterbury, were not. Counties such as Lancashire and West Yorkshire were huge compared with others such as Rutland and Huntingdonshire.

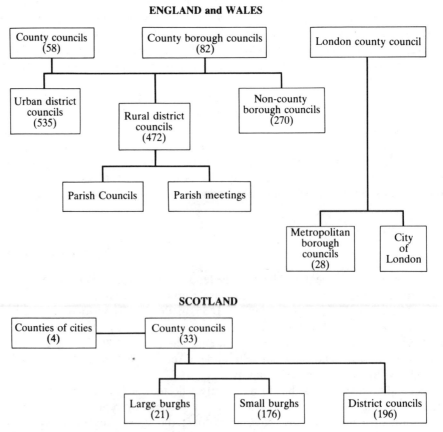

ENGLAND and WALES

SCOTLAND

Fig. 9.1 Local government structure before reorganization

There were additional difficulties. The boundaries of historic counties and the smaller towns were reasonably easy to delineate, but where should some of the major conurbations start and finish? The Royal Commission on Local Government in Greater London[1] had, with the backing of considerable applied research, recommended a two-tier structure and this, to a great extent, provided a model for the 'metropolitan' areas of the rest of England and Wales.

The need to secure effective coordination of education in the concentrated area of central London, formerly administered by the London County Council, was recognized by the government by making this service the responsibility of the Greater London Council through a special committee to be called the Inner London Education Authority (ILEA).

In the reformed structure the smallest unit is the parish council in England and the community council in Wales and Scotland. Not all districts contain parish councils: if they have 200 or more electors it is mandatory to elect one; below that number it is not necessary but one can be claimed if there are at least 150 electors in the parish. Parish councils are concerned essentially with local services, such as street lighting

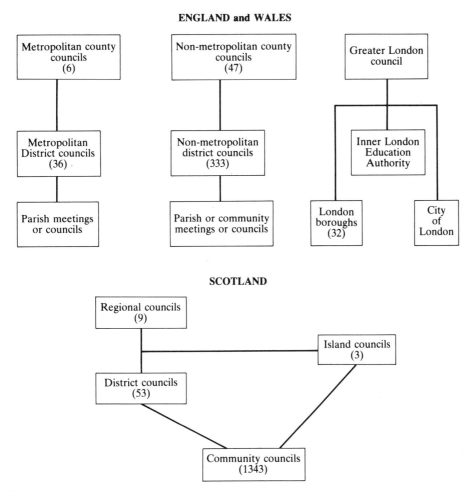

ENGLAND and WALES

SCOTLAND

Fig. 9.2 Local government structure after reorganization

and the provision of allotments. Some small towns which lost their borough status under reorganization and became parishes have retained the privilege of calling themselves town councils and naming their chairmen town mayors. These are merely courtesy titles and carry no additional powers.

Local government in Scotland was reformed by the Local Government (Scotland) Act of 1973, which followed the report of a royal commission chaired by Lord Wheatley.[2] The faults discerned in the Scottish system were similar to those found in England and Wales but the geography of Scotland posed additional problems. In its report, the Wheatley Commission advocated a radical restructuring based on four objectives of reform: power, effectiveness, local democracy, and local involvement. In identifying appropriate units, the Commission used three criteria: functional viability, in other words a size large enough to sustain a range of functions; correspondence with recognizable communities, which was especially important with such a dispersed population; and democratic viability, by which it meant that the control of the range of functions of an authority should be within the competence of the elected, part-time councillors. The Scottish reorganization was to be based on a two-tier structure of seven regional authorities, formed by amalgamations of existing counties, and 37 district authorities, derived from individual counties or enlarged counties of cities.

The Conservative government of Edward Heath, to whom the reports of both royal commissions were presented, opted for a two-tier structure for England and Wales as well as Scotland. Figure 9.2 shows the structure for Great Britain after reorganization. The system in Northern Ireland differs in several respects, including the use of proportional representation for electing councils.

What local authorities do

Local authorities responsibilities are essentially in two main areas: the regulation of certain activities within their localities and the provision of services. There are certain functions which they are required to perform by Parliament and others which they have the option to if they choose. These mandatory and optional powers are entrusted by normal legislation, through what is technically termed a **Public Act.** An authority can seek to extend its powers further by promoting a **Private Act**, whose jurisdiction extends only to a precise locality. For example, the Abingdon Market Place Act 1978 gives Abingdon Council the power to ban vehicles from the town market place.

The normal range of functions is wide: indeed larger than those performed by any other public body. They are distributed among the various types of local authority largely according to their size, with the bigger councils concerned more with coordination, regulation, and planning, and the smaller with actual provision. A summary of these responsibilities is given in Table 9.1. For convenience, they may be classified into five main groups: **personal**, **environmental**, **amenity**, **trading**, and **protective** services.

The personal services

The main functions within this category are **education**, **careers advice and assistance**, **personal social services**, **health services**, and **housing.**

Education is local government's most costly service and the basic responsibilities still stem from the Education Acts of 1944, for England and Wales, and 1945, for

Scotland. This legislation requires local authorities to provide, free of charge, adequate primary and secondary education for everyone between the ages of five and sixteen. This means the provision of schools, teachers, supporting staff, and facilities, including such things as transport and maintenance grants in certain cases.

The local authorities charged with these responsibilities are styled local education authorities (LEAs). LEAs are also required to provide resources and facilities for part-time and full-time education beyond the age of 16, in tertiary colleges or colleges of further education. They also contribute to the provision of higher education in the form of polytechnics and colleges of higher education and the awarding of grants to students in their localities who wish to follow courses of higher education.

The Employment and Training Act of 1973 requires LEAs to provide **careers advice and information** for pupils and students attending educational institutions, other than universities, in their localities and an **employment service** for young people leaving or having recently left school or college. There are some 2000 careers officers operating this service, which is additional to those provided within schools or colleges or by bodies such as the Manpower Services Commission.

Personal social services are concerned with peoples' social welfare, with particular emphasis on the needs of the handicapped and less privileged, such as old people, children, and those with a physical or mental disablity. The facilities local authorities provide include residential homes and hostels, and occupation and training centres, but the emphasis in recent years has been on 'community care', through home helps, home facilities and adaptations, recreational facilities, and assistance with travelling. As part of this provision, the work of local authority social workers is of particular importance.

Another aspect of the community care programme is the contribution which local authorities make to the **National Health Service** by the provision of health centres, home nursing, health visiting, maternity and child clinics, family planning services, school medical services, vaccination, and the ambulance service.

Housing is the second most costly local authority service. A series of Housing Acts requires authorities to provide, conserve, maintain, and improve housing for people requiring accommodation in their localities. The provision of housing has become a lively party political issue in recent years, with Labour governments encouraging the building and letting of houses and flats by local authorities and Conservative governments placing emphasis on private house building and the sale of rented council accommodation to the occupiers.

The environmental services

The main services within this group are **environmental health, highways, traffic and transport**, **planning**, and **emergency services**.

The **environmental health service** is one of the longest-established local authority functions. The titles of the officials operating this service have changed over the years. At one time they were called Sanitary Inspectors, then Public Health Inspectors. Their current, perhaps rather more impressive, name is Environmental Health Officer. Environmental Health Officers are concerned with the control of nuisances (such as waste tips or insanitary or overcrowded premises), offensive trades (such as glue making), the enforcement of building regulations, and the control of vermin. Within the same category of service, local authorities collect refuse and provide public toilets, cemeteries, and crematoria.

Services concerned with **highways, traffic and transport** are the responsibilities of a number of types of authority. Motorways are the concern of central government as are trunk roads, but it is usual for the latter to be built and maintained by local authorities as agents of central government. All other roads are the direct responsibility of local government. The local authorities with major road responsibilities are designated highway authorities and their functions include traffic management, road safety, and the prevention of accidents. Local authorities may also provide passenger transport services or assist in their provision through grants.

The **Town and Country Planning Act** of 1947 brought something of a revolution to the British way of life. It required local authorities to carry out surveys of their localities and to prepare development plans for the future use of land. It also required anyone wishing to carry out a development, such as the building or alteration of premises, to obtain the permission of the local authority beforehand. In this way most of the excesses of development and exploitation which occurred in the nineteenth century and between the two World Wars have been prevented.

Emergency services are those activities which used to be termed 'civil defence', and are mainly concerned with the possibility of this country being involved in war. Since the next major war that the United Kingdom might experience would probably involve the use of nuclear weapons, there are understandably, strong differences of opinion among ordinary citizens and their representatives about the value of trying to 'prevent the unpreventable'. In consequence, as far as can be judged in such a sensitive area, the provision of emergency services across the country is likely to be patchy.

The amenity services

Amenity services have grown enormously in scope and size during recent years. This growth has been commensurate with the increased leisure time available to people and the more highly developed tastes which they have acquired. The facilities include leisure and sports centres, swimming baths, libraries, concert halls, theatres, and the sponsoring or subsidizing of cultural, social, or sporting events.

The trading services

Some trading services are close to those classified as amenities but it is rare for a pure amenity service to make a profit, or even break even, which some trading services do. Many of them are subsidized by the rates but there are also some innovative and highly successful exceptions. Notable examples of local authority trading include the racecourse at Doncaster, airports at some of the major cities, Hull's telephone system, and Birmingham's bank. Local authorities in holiday resorts, of course, can operate extensive and profitable services for visitors.

The protective services

The main protective services are **police, fire,** and **trading standards.**

The **police service** has, with the exception of London, been locally appointed and locally controlled since the middle of the nineteenth century. Since 1946 it has been less locally based and less locally controlled. The Metropolitan Police is the responsibility of the Home Secretary; other forces are responsible to police authorities, which are committees consisting of two-thirds councillors and one-third magistrates. The average police force is now quite large and its operational area may well cover that of several local authorities. The police committee's powers are now more or less limited to maintaining a police force and appointing a chief constable, and even here there is a need to obtain the approval of the Home Secretary. The police service in the United Kingdom has always enjoyed a unique position compared to its equivalents in other countries. For example, a policeman legally has little more authority than the common law affords him and he sees his ultimate responsibility to 'the law'. But in practical terms, what is 'the law'?: in common parlance it is the police service itself. Some aspects of the questions surrounding the accountability of police forces will be discussed, among other current issues, in our final chapter.

It was not obligatory for a local authority to provide a **fire service** until 1938. Since 1972 local authorities responsible for fire services, the fire authorities, have been required to cooperate with and assist one another and it is possible for several fire brigades to amalgamate under a single chief fire officer. Although the Home Secretary has some control over its fire brigades, through inspection and the issuing of regulations, a fire authority has much more autonomy and control over its fire service than a police authority has over its police force.

The **trading standards service** was once known as the weights and measures service but, as it expanded its role and became more concerned with consumer protection in its widest sense, most local authorities gave their service a more positive title, some selecting the consumer protection service but more, and increasingly, the trading standards service. Trading standards officers are responsible for ensuring fair trading through honest weights and measures, minima qualities for foods and drugs, the detection and prosecution of traders employing false or misleading practices, as well as assistance and advice to consumers and suppliers on all aspects of fair trading. Locally they liaise with the voluntary citizen's advice bureaux and nationally their 'parent' organizations are the Department of Trade and Industry and the Office of Fair Trading.

Table 9.1 provides a summary of the responsibilities of local authorities.

How local authorities operate

The political machine

Each local authority has an ultimate decision-taking body in the shape of the council, comprising anything from forty to one hundred members. Nowadays, each council reflects its party political composition, with a majority party, or coalition of parties, able to determine overall policy.

An individual councillor has no personal executive power: this is retained by the council as a corporate body but, for administrative convenience and efficiency, a council will delegate authority to its committees. The chairman of a committee consequently wields considerable power because of his delegated role. Party political control of a council, therefore, is exercised through committee membership, and particularly committee chairmanships, as well as through the full council. A 'typical' committee system is illustrated in Fig. 9.3. In this example the committees reporting directly to the council are policy, education, planning, social services, amenities, housing, and environmental health. The policy committee's main role is that of coordinating overall policy and it has sub-committees covering the main aspects of resources: finance, personnel, and property. The others are service committees, responsible for the range of services we have already outlined, and each will have one or more sub-committees to deal with specific functions or services.

93

Table 9.1   The distribution of functions between local authorities

Function	London		England and Wales				Scotland	
			Metropolitan areas		Non-metropolitan areas		Region and/or	
	GLC	Boroughs	Counties	Districts	Counties	Districts	island	District
Education	1 see below	X		X	X		X	
Careers advice	1 see below	X		X	X		X	
Social services		X		X	X		X	
Community health services		X		X	X		X	
Housing	X	X		X		X	X	X
Environmental health		X		X		X	X	X
Highways	X	X	X	X	X	X	X	
Traffic and transport	X		X		X		X	
Planning	X	X	X	X	X	X	X	X
Emergency services	X	X	X	X	X	X	X	X
Amenity services	X	X	X	X	X	X	X	X
Trading services		X	X	X	X	X	X	
Police			X		X		X	
Fire	X		X		X		X	
Trading standards		X	X		X		X	X

Note 1: These are provided in central London through the ILEA.

The committees and sub-committees, like the council, consist of councillors. The full-time officials are in attendance and service the committees.

The administrative machine

Day-to-day administration is carried out on a departmental basis, each major department, or group of departments, being responsible to a specific committee and, ultimately, to the council itself. A 'typical' administrative structure is shown in Fig. 9.4. The management team is the administrative equivalent of the policy committee, with the task of coordinating the work of all the departments in the local authority. It will comprise, therefore, the leading department heads.

Studies of local government organization and management, such as the Maud[3] and Mallaby[4] Reports of 1967, the Bains Report[5] of 1972, and the Paterson Report[6] of 1973 suggested various solutions to the problems of the coordination of policy implementation and many of them have been adopted. It would be foolish to suggest,

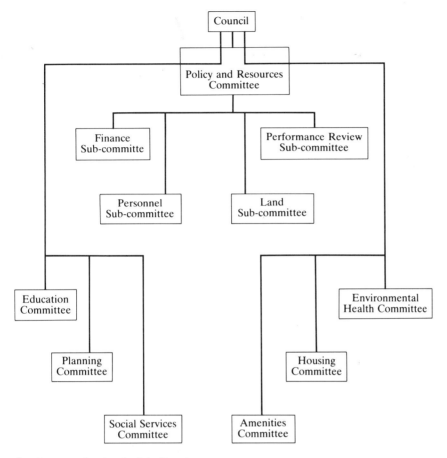

Sample structure based on the Bains Report

Fig. 9.3 A local authority committee structure

however, that difficulties no longer exist. The sometimes competing objectives and needs of individual service departments often make the task of what the Bains and Paterson reports refer to as 'corporate management' a daunting challenge.

The political–administrative interface

The theory of how local government works, which also applies to central government, is that temporary politicians make the policy decisions and that permanent officials carry them out. If this is an over-simplification as far as central government is concerned, it is even more so at the local level.

Even though they are often responsible for huge departments, and consequently have to delegate extensively to the permanent officials, at least ministers are engaged in a full-time occupation. Local councillors, on the other hand, apart from a minority in the major authorities, operate on a part-time basis. It should be obvious, therefore, that they must be even more heavily dependent on the views and advice of the officers.

The chief officers in local authorities have much more overt discretion than their

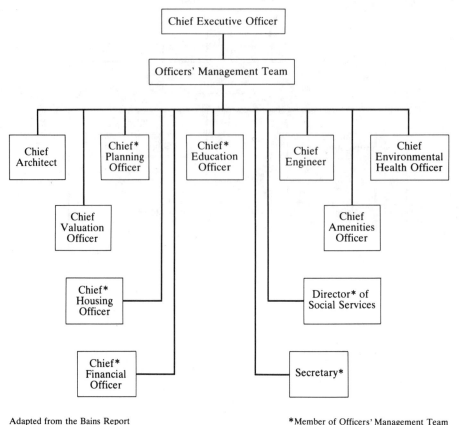

Adapted from the Bains Report   *Member of Officers' Management Team

Fig. 9.4 A local authority administrative structure

civil service counterparts. For example, whereas civil servants are largely excluded from Parliament, local government heads can speak in open meetings of their authorities and the relationship between a committee chairman and a chief officer can be closer, franker, and more personal than that between a minister and his permanent secretary.

Conflicts will arise but they are rare and the sensible councillors trust and rely on the integrity of their chief officers. They, in turn, if they are equally sensible, recognize where the sometimes unclear boundary between advice and decision is drawn. In any event, both know that ultimately they are responsible to the laws that Parliament makes.

The central–local interface

The relationship between central government and local authorities is, inevitably, an unbalanced one. Each side recognizes that, through its majority in Parliament, central government ultimately has the last say. Nevertheless, there is a basic interdependence because ministers know that a large part of the public provision of services in this country would collapse if they could not rely on the activities of local government. Local councillors and officials, on their part, are realistic enough to recognize their

96

financial dependence on central government, and it is in the area of finance that many potential conflicts are likely to occur.

Because of this dependence there will always be some element of tension, but it has been heightened in recent years by an apparent tendency towards greater centralization. Ever since democratically elected councils have been in existence successive governments have proclaimed the virtues and benefits of an independent system of local government, but their deeds have rarely matched their words.

Since 1979, when the Conservative government of Margaret Thatcher came into power, a difference in outlook has developed and clashes between the centre and the localities have seemed almost inevitable. This has been more than the 'we know best' attitude which has always tended to percolate from Whitehall. It has gradually focused itself on two main aspects: the control of public spending, and an apparent distrust by ministers of the motives and sense of responsibility of the leaders of some of the major local authorities. Ken Livingstone, of the Greater London Council, epitomizes this but he is not alone.

Traditionally, left-wing governments have been the proponents of greater centralization and parties to the right and centre have extolled the virtues of local independence. The Conservative government of Mrs Thatcher, however, through its determination to tackle inflation by keeping a tight grip on public sector spending, has found itself the greatest centralizer of them all. Clashes with local authorities over what Whitehall has seen as their spendthrift habits have been exacerbated by the fact that many of the bigger authorities which have been categorized as the 'big spenders', and often legitimately because of the social and economic problems in their localities, have been party-political opponents. If we add to this the fact that Mrs Thatcher's zeal to 'privatize' is bound eventually to bear upon some of the services which local authorities have traditionally provided, then the ingredients for potential conflict are all there.

Thus we have witnessed in recent years increased control of local government revenue sources and spending and even proposals to abolish the Greater London Council and the other metropolitan county councils in England and to transfer their functions to smaller authorities and new *ad hoc* bodies. We shall be looking at both of these manifestations of increased central control in more detail in later chapters.

Despite this evidence of growing friction, the business of government, centrally and locally, must go on. To balance the record, therefore, it should be said that there is still a great deal of cooperation, at both political and administrative levels, if only because, uneasy bedfellows though they may be, each needs the other.

An evaluation of local government

Local government has always been the Cinderella of politics in this country and it probably always will be. Turnouts at local elections are rarely greater than 40 per cent and the work which councillors perform is, on the surface at any rate, unglamorous. They are unpaid and even the daily attendance allowance of under £15 cannot be said to be generous.

Yet, as we have seen, the services they provide are essential for the maintenance of a civilized society. Indeed, if a stark choice had to be made, we could, as a nation, more comfortably dispense with central than local government.

The scale of local operations is large by any standards. Local authorities spend on

97

goods and services nearly 10 per cent of the gross national product. They employ far more people than central government. In many localities they are the biggest single employers.

And yet this nondescript, negative image persists. Why? Many local authorities are themselves to blame: the standard of their public relations is often appalling. Some of the shire counties, for example, seem to have chosen locations for their headquarters so remote as to give the impression that they want to avoid contact with the public rather than increase it. Our town and county halls are often typified by long, anonymous corridors and unattractive lobbies and offices. Much the same can be said of central government, of course, but Whitehall is understandably and inevitably remote for many people whereas local authorities are on our doorstep.

Some local authority members might well object to this gloomy description and argue that local government is bound to lose whatever it does. If it is outward-going, ambitious, and inventive, like the Greater London Council, supporting minority groups and fringe cultural activities, central government criticizes it for being irresponsible and spendthrift. It is reasonable to predict that should a normally quiescent authority start spending on improving its public image ratepayers would protest about the waste of public money.

What, then, is the solution if there is one? First, central government needs to know much more about local government than it does. Certainly Whitehall and the ministers have all the figures at their disposal but how many of them have any intimate knowledge? Some MPs, of course, have arrived at Westminster via the town hall route but they tend to be in a minority. The Liberal Party has the best record of 'community politics' but this may be because the national voting system has forced many potential MPs to set their sights lower if they are to be politically active.

There should, ideally, be much more movement between Westminster and town hall and between the civil service and the local government service. In most other countries in Western Europe this interchange is taken for granted.

Above all, Parliament and central government should start taking local government seriously. They should match the rhetoric about independent local authorities with deeds. If, as is sometimes claimed, local authorities act irresponsibly it is often because they are treated irresponsibly: by central government, by Parliament, by the media, and even by their own electors.

References

1. *Report of the Royal Commission on Local Government in England, 1966–9*, Cmd. 4040, HMSO, 1969.
2. *Report of the Royal Commission on Local Government in Scotland, 1966–9*, Cmd. 4150, HMSO, 1969.
3. *Report of the Committee on Management of Local Government*, HMSO, 1967.
4. *Report of the Committee on the Staffing of Local Government*, HMSO, 1967.
5. *The New Authorities: Management and Structure*, HMSO, 1972.
6. *The New Scottish Local Authorities: Organization and Management Structures*, HMSO, 1973.

Assignments

14. Contact your representatives at each level of local government, parish, district, and county and ask them to explain what their respective roles are.

    This assignment could operate as a class exercise, with each representative being invited to address the class.

15. Discuss the case for and against the abolition of the Greater London Council and the other metropolitan county councils.

    This could also be conducted as a debate, with the motion: 'This House believes that the proposal to abolish metropolitan counties is a retrograde step.'

10
The quasi-government sector

The 'fringe' of government

Outside the formal structure of central government in this country is a large number of semi-autonomous bodies set up by the government and dependent on it for all or a major part of their finance. They are sometimes described as the '**quangos**': quasi-autonomous national-governmental organizations. In official circles they are referred to as the 'fringe bodies'. In academic circles a distinction is sometimes made between quasi-autonomous government bodies (QGs) and quasi-autonomous non-governmental bodies (QNGs). The difference represents the degree of direct government involvement.

The Civil Service Department reported in 1978 that there were 252 such bodies, compared with 196 in 1971, 103 in 1959 and only 10 before 1900.[1] Their number has grown in step with the government's increasing interest in and supervision of the nation's economic and social affairs. Some political commentators would argue that the number of 252 represents only the visible part of an iceberg and that the actual total is nearer 800: the exact number is obviously dependent on how you choose to define a fringe body or quango. The definition the Civil Service Department used for the purposes of its survey was 'organizations which have been set up or adopted by Departments and provided with funds to perform some function which the Government wish to have performed but which it did not wish to be the direct responsibility of a Minister or of a Department'. The authors of the survey graphically described the role of many fringe bodies as 'government at arm's length'. Excluded from this definition are any bodies which are not clearly permanent, as well as advisory committees or working parties. We have included in this chapter some bodies falling outside this rather restrictive definition so that it is not difficult to consider a total far greater than that used for the survey.

Using only the Civil Service Department's 1978 list, these 252 organizations had a combined annual expenditure of £2376m, and employed 184 000 people, equivalent to a quarter of the total manpower of the civil service. They are therefore too significant to be ignored, and in recent years they have been the subject of much public discussion.

The debate about fringe bodies, or quangos, has centred on four things. First, they represent an increasing, and to some people unwelcome, expansion of government intervention in economic and, in many cases, industrial affairs. Second, people are concerned about the cost of maintaining such bodies. Third, there is concern about the immense amount of political patronage which their existence gives to governments. Fourth, people are disturbed about the lack of public accountability associated with them. Whether government intervention in industry, as evidenced by the growth of fringe bodies, is beneficial or harmful is largely a matter of political attitude and judgement. We will never really know whether it would have been better to have had more or less state involvement in some part of the economy because 'ifs' cannot be measured. We cannot evaluate something which did not happen, we can only speculate. Nevertheless, we shall be looking more closely at state activity in the industrial and business world in a later chapter.

The cost of maintaining some 252 national bodies of this sort is obviously not insignificant: probably about 3 per cent of the Gross National Product. Whether or not it is excessive depends on whether we think we are getting value for money. Included in the £2000m+ which the quangos cost in 1978 was £476m for the University Grants Committee, £350m for the Manpower Services Commission, £284m for the Housing Corporation, £205m for the BBC and Independent Broadcasting Authority (IBA), £195m for the several research councils, and £106m for the Atomic Energy Authority. It would be a rash person who would say that all, or even some, of the services these bodies provide are unnecessary: indeed, it can be argued that well over 50 per cent of the money spent by the listed quangos is a form of investment and, as such, essential to the long-term prosperity of the country.

Political patronage

The amount of political patronage their existence creates is certainly something which should concern us. It can be said that a successful political career is a good qualification for public office but it can also be said that this alone is seldom enough. Rewarding old colleagues for faithful service is not the best criterion for selection. Indeed, it was nepotism and patronage in the civil service which was so sharply criticized in the Northcote–Trevelyan Report of 1853,[2] and which led to sweeping reforms in subsequent years.

In 1978 the Civil Service Department produced a scheme for consideration by a Cabinet committee which would have made some fundamental changes in the ways in which men and women are selected to sit on public boards, commissions, and committees. At the moment, apart from people personally selected by ministers, names are taken from the 'central list', or the list of the 'good and the great', as it is popularly called, to which we have already referred in an earlier chapter. The Civil Service Department proposed that people should be able to write in and nominate themselves for consideration for appointment, and that a publicity campaign should be launched, particularly in the regions, to encourage people to come forward. The scheme also suggested that there should be a standard form for completion by those people who were either nominated or put themselves forward. The proposals apparently met with opposition from some Cabinet ministers and were shelved.

In a critique of the practice of awarding paid and unpaid appointments to former political colleagues or supporters, Conservative MP Philip Holland argued, in 1978, that quangos should be more accountable, that there should be better regulation of appointments to them, and that more thought should be given to their purposes.[3] Jack Jones, the former General Secretary of the Transport and General Workers' Union, had been singled out as the holder of eight quango appointments. Whereas it is reasonable to question obvious nepotism, the case of Mr Jones should be viewed more cautiously. Not all appointments are paid and a man who has successfully led the biggest trade union in the country must surely, when considered objectively, have qualities which the nation would be wrong prematurely to cast aside. Nor is it true that Labour government appointees are always present or former Party supporters or

101

Conservative government appointees always to the right in politics. Two notable appointments come to mind which at the time they were made caused some surprise. Labour MP, Alfred Robens, as he then was, was appointed Chairman of the National Coal Board by a Conservative government, and Conservative MP, Aubrey Jones, chairman of the Prices and Incomes Commission by a Labour government.

Types of quasi-governmental body

As with interest groups, any attempt to classify quangos into types is bound to be an arbitrary exercise. The Civil Service Department, in the Survey to which we have already referred, used a fivefold classification: those which were educational in character; those concerned with social welfare; those which had financial or economic characteristics; those concerned with industry; and those concerned with agriculture. Such a classification has obvious limitations in that it neither tells us much about their purposes nor advances our understanding of their origins.

If we shift the emphasis more towards purpose and origins a more helpful classification emerges. We can divide the bodies into four main groups:

1. those intended to promote some activity, area, or group;
2. those designed to regulate some activity, area, or group;
3. those designed to coordinate activities and possibly arbitrate in disputes between parties whose activities they are coordinating; and
4. those intended to advise governments on some aspects of policy.

Applying this classification to individual fringe bodies, or quangos, we find that only occasionally will a body fit neatly into *one* category. More often than not it will find a place in more than one. This should not worry us unduly: things may fall into neat groupings in theory but in practice it is seldom the case. Providing our classification helps us better to understand the purposes and origins of the bodies we should be satisfied.

We may now attempt to list some of the most significant fringe bodies under the first three headings of our classification. Advisory bodies have not been included and will be considered in a later chapter when we examine the policy-making process. Fifty-eight selected bodies are listed in Table 10.1: all are significant and national in character. Whether the category into which a body falls represents a major or minor interest is indicated, as well as the name of the sponsoring central department. It is interesting to note that, of the 58 listed bodies, 45 can be said to have the promotion of some activity as their prime concern, whereas only 9 have a primarily regulatory function. The lesson which might be learned from this is that, although in recent years governments have become more and more involved in social and economic affairs, their prime purpose seems to be to help rather than hinder.

Forms of quasi-governmental body

Fringe bodies, or quangos, are found in a variety of forms. The six main kinds are: committee, commission, council, association, authority, or corporation. They all have one feature in common: the highest unit of decision taking is in the shape of a committee. Thus the University Grants Committee is what it says it is, a committee from the academic world, supported by an administrative staff. The Manpower

Table 10.1 Fringe bodies: a threefold classification

| Name of body | Scope of interest | | | Sponsoring department |
	Promotional	regulatory	coordinating	
Advisory, Conciliation, and Arbitration Service (ACAS)	3	1	2	Employment
Agricultural Research Council	1	3	2	Education and Science
Arts Council of Great Britain	1	3	2	Education and Science
British Broadcasting Corporation	1	–	–	Home Office
British Council	1	3	2	Foreign and Commonwealth
British Film Institute	1	–	–	Education and Science
British Tourist Authority	1	–	2	Trade and Industry
British Wool Marketing Board	1	3	2	Agriculture
Central Bureau for Educational Visits and Exchanges	1	–	2	Education and Science
Central Council for Education and Training in Social Work	1	3	2	Health and Social Security
Central Midwives Board	2	3	1	Health and Social Security
Central Transport Consultative Committee	3	1	2	Trade and Industry
Civil Aviation Authority	3	1	2	Trade and Industry
Commonwealth Development Corporation	1	3	2	Foreign and Commonwealth
Commonwealth Institute	1	–	2	Foreign and Commonwealth
Community Relations Commission	1	3	2	Home Office
Council for Education and Training of Health Visitors	1	3	2	Health and Social Security
Council for Small Industries in Rural Areas	1	–	2	Environment
Countryside Commission	1	2	3	Environment
Criminal Injuries Compensation Board	1	3	2	Home Office

Table 10.1 (contd.)

Name of body	Scope of interest			Sponsoring department
	Promotional	regulatory	coordinating	
Crown Agents for Overseas Governments and Administrators	1	3	2	Foreign and Commonwealth
Design Council	1	–	2	Trade and Industry
Eggs Authority	1	3	2	Agriculture
Equal Opportunities Commission	1	2	3	Home Office
Forestry Commission	1	3	2	Scottish Office
Gaming Board for Great Britain	2	1	3	Home Office
Health Education Council	1	3	2	Health and Social Security
Health and Safety Commission	2	1	3	Employment
Health and Safety Executive	2	1	3	Employment
Herring Industry Board	1	3	2	Scottish Office
Horserace Betting Levy Board	1	2	3	Home Office
Housing Corporation	1	–	2	Environment
Independent Broadcasting Authority	2	1	3	Home Office
Manpower Services Commission	1	–	2	Employment
Meat and Livestock Commission	1	3	2	Agriculture
Medical Research Council	1	–	2	Education and Science
Milk Marketing Board	1	3	2	Agriculture
Monopolies and Mergers Commission	–	1	–	Trade and Industry
National Computing Centre Limited	1	–	2	Trade and Industry
National Consumer Council	1	3	2	Trade and Industry
National Council of Social Service	1	–	2	Home Office
National Economic Development Office	1	–	2	Treasury
National Film Finance Corporation	1	–	2	Trade and Industry
National Marriage Guidance Council	1	–	2	Home Office

Table 10.1 (contd.)

Name of body	Scope of interest Promotional regulatory coordinating			Sponsoring department
National Research Development Corporation	1	–	2	Trade and Industry
National Savings Committee	1	–	2	National Savings
National Water Council	3	2	1	Environment
Post Office Users' National Council	3	1	2	Trade and Industry
Potato Marketing Board	1	3	2	Agriculture
Race Relations Board	1	2	3	Home Office
Royal Fine Art Commission	1	–	2	Education and Science
Schools Council	2	3	1	Education and Science
Science Research Council	1	–	2	Education and Science
Social Science Research Council	1	–	2	Education and Science
Sports Council	1	–	2	Environment
United Kingdom Atomic Energy Authority	1	3	2	Energy
University Grants Committee	–	2	1	Education and Science
White Fish Authority and Herring Industry Board	1	3	2	Agriculture

Services Commission is a large organization with several constituent parts but, at the top, it has a body of people forming a Commission and taking ultimate responsibility for its activities; the Science Research Council and the Social Science Research Council are committees; the Scottish Special Housing Association has administrative and clerical staff but is essentially a committee; the Independent Broadcasting Authority is, again, a committee, and the various bodies with the title corporation are headed by boards or committees.

This structure is not, of course, remarkable. Virtually all decision taking within the governmental sphere is undertaken collectively through some form of committee. An important essay on the British Constitution by Professor K.C. Wheare, first published in the 1950s took this aspect of government as its basic theme.[4] Decision taking by committee is not exclusive to the public sector. Most large national and international privately owned companies and corporations are riddled with committees from the boards of directors downwards.

Although in some cases it is not strictly accurate, it is probably a fair generalization

105

to say that the form in which a body has been set up gives some clue to the extent of its independence of the government. Thus a commission is likely to have marginally more freedom of action than a committee: compare a departmental committee of inquiry with a royal commission, as we do later. An authority is likely to have rather more autonomy than a council or an association. A corporation, as evidenced by public corporations such as the BBC and those controlling the nationalized industries, is likely to have the greatest degree of autonomy of all. It should be stressed that this analysis is a very broad generalization and will not fit every individual case.

The concept of 'hiving off'

Although it was not an entirely original concept at the time, the Report of the Fulton Committee on the Civil Service,[5] in 1968, strongly advocated 'hiving off' as a means of improving the effectiveness of central government. It argued for better management within the civil service and particularly for more 'accountable management'. By this it meant that it should be made more evident who was responsible for what in a department so that the person or persons concerned could be held accountable for any deficiencies or inadequacies in provision or performance.

In advocating this the Fulton Committee was applying what it considered to be good industrial and business management methods to the central government departments. In a large industrial organization, for example, it is important to know the costs of production in the various operational areas and manufacturing units. One way of doing this is to create 'cost centres' and 'profit centres'. It is then possible for accountants to calculate and inform management whether department X or shop Y is making a profit or a loss compared with its performance a year, or less, ago. It may seem incredible but large companies which have been profitable in overall terms have not always known from which parts of their businesses the profits have come and whether losses in some areas have been disguised by profits in others. Without this knowledge it is clearly impossible to know whether it is sound policy to expand a particular section or contract it. The use of management accounting techniques, allied to better information collection by means of computers, have largely solved this potential weakness in well-managed companies.

The Fulton Committee detected that in large central departments it was difficult, if not impossible, to measure the effectiveness of the constituent parts, and it recommended a policy of hiving-off in certain cases. In other words, it suggested that certain functions or units within departments might be extracted and set up outside in a semi-autonomous role so that the limits of their responsibilities would be clearly defined and their effectiveness more easily measured. In this way, the Committee argued, a separate, semi-autonomous unit could enjoy and demonstrate accountable management.

Another argument for hiving-off, and this precedes the Fulton Committee, is to take a governmental function away from close political control: in other words, to 'depoliticize' it. This was one reason, for example, why the Post Office was made a public corporation instead of a government department in 1969.

A third reason for hiving-off is to free a function or unit from the normal close administrative supervision to which central departments are subjected. The most important and obvious form this supervision takes is Treasury control, and it involves compliance with strict rules, particularly concerning the preparation and submission of financial estimates and the control of expenditure. Before it became a public corporation the Post Office had been exempted from the most stringent aspects of Treasury control; when it lost its departmental status it was completely free. We will examine other aspects of Treasury control later in this book.

An example of hiving-off: the Manpower Services Commission

The process of hiving-off has added to the number of fringe bodies, or quangos, in recent years. The most significant example is the Manpower Services Commission. It was established in 1973 by the government of Edward Heath and its main purposes were to take over and develop the 'employment exchange' function of the Department of Employment and ally this to an identification of national training needs and the provision of vocational training. It began with a staff of about 19 000 civil servants, taken out of the Department of Employment, and was established with two main wings, the Employment Services Agency (ESA) and the Training Services Agency (TSA). The Commission itself was to exercise a planning and coordinating role. The work of the Commission has developed on these broad lines, although since 1978 a certain amount of restructuring has taken place in the course of which the titles ESA and TSA have disappeared.

Although it is staffed by civil servants the Commission enjoys a high degree of autonomy. During its brief lifetime unemployment has grown significantly and it is understandable, if ironic, that a rise in the number of jobless people has created more jobs in the Manpower Services Commission. The original staff of 19 000 had grown to over 25 000 in 1978 and was expected to increase by at least another 1000. Its remarkable growth (over 6 per cent per annum in staffing, and over 35 per cent per annum in total expenditure) and its comparative freedom from the normal control and accountability of a government department has drawn criticism from several quarters. Despite this criticism its record is generally impressive.

It has shown considerable imagination and powers of innovation and enterprise. The old labour exchanges have been transformed into attractive job centres, located in prime urban sites, and people at all levels, including managers and members of the professions looking for highly paid word, have turned to them. It has also devised a number of novel training and job-creation schemes, the success of which has sometimes proved embarrassing. Some of these schemes are examined in Chapter 15.

It is certain that many of the innovatory activities of the Commission, and its ability to respond quickly to changing needs in the labour market, would not have been possible if it had remained just a division of the Department of Employment. Its work has, undoubtedly, placed great demands on the civil servants who staff it, particularly as their work has frequently been in the political firing line. Some measure of its success may, perhaps, be gleaned from the fact that its role in vocational education, as well as training, has grown significantly, often at the expense of the longer established institutions overseen by the Department of Education and Science.

The future of the fringe

In the absence of evidence that politicians in the future are going to be significantly less interested in social and economic affairs, we must assume that the fringe of government will continue and may even grow. Political parties have different views about the proper relationship between government and industry and whereas the Conservatives might claim that they would like to 'set the people free' there is so much established involvement in economic affairs that it would be extremely difficult, if not impossible, for any government to stand aside and let individual initiative have total freedom of expression.

The main areas of activity we have defined as 'quango territory' are now a permanent feature of our society. There will always be a need to promote some government-sponsored objectives. There will always be a need to regulate areas of economic and social activity. There will always be a need to coordinate the work of national organizations in the public interest, as the government of the day identifies it. The government will always be seeking advice on policy. We may accept, then, that fringe bodies, or quangos, are here to stay. We should therefore address ourselves not to the unrealistic task of abolishing them but to the constructive task of improving them. The questions we might profitably ask are these.

First, do we need them all? Are some perhaps expendable because the original purpose for their creation has disappeared, or because their work could be done by some corresponding body? In other words, we need a regular, periodic review of their objectives.

The second question we should ask concerns their membership. Are the best qualified and experienced people chosen to serve on them, or are there too many 'jobs for the boys'? In other words, we need an impartial, objective review of their membership.

Our third question should be whether they are adequately accountable for their actions and the decisions they take. Because of their nature they should not be subject to the close, detailed control applied to a government department but, on the other hand, dispensing the money and power that they do, they should not be completely free from responsibility and accountability to the nation. In other words, some means of measuring their effectiveness and holding them accountable for their actions, which does not unduly inhibit their freedom of operation, should be devised.

In 1980 an investigation into fringe bodies was conducted by a senior civil servant, Sir Leo Pliatzky. In his report,[6] published in 1980, he made certain recommendations which he believed would improve their efficiency and accountability. He argued for regular reviews of their purpose and justification for operating, and recommended that their activities should be monitored by the House of Commons specialist select committees.

References

1. See *Survey of Fringe Bodies*, Civil Service Department, 1978.
2. *The Organisation of the Permanent Civil Service: together with a letter from the Rev. B. Jowett*, Parliamentary Papers, 1854, vol. 27.
3. Holland, P. *The Quango Explosion*, Conservative Political Centre, 1978. Incidentally, Mr Holland describes a quango as a quasi-autonomous national governmental organization. The definition of 'quasi-autonomous non-governmental organization' is American in origin.
4. Wheare, K.C. *Government by Committee*, Oxford University Press, 1955.
5. *Report of the Committee on the Civil Service*, Cmnd. 3638, HMSO, 1968.
6. *Report on Non-Departmental Public Bodies*, Cmnd. 7797, HMSO, 1980.

16. Investigate three recent industrial disputes in which ACAS has been involved and assess the importance of its contribution.

Sources: The Economist, The Times, The Guardian, or *The Daily Telegraph.*

17. Do you think it would be beneficial if the local careers advisory service were transferred from local government to the Manpower Services Commission? Give a reasoned answer.

109

11
The international scene

Commonwealth to Common Market: Britain's inevitable realignment

Forty years ago a glance at a map of the world would have shown vast areas coloured red which constituted the greatest Empire ever created; it embraced a quarter of the world's population, a quarter of the world's land area, covered every continent, and included every race. It was the British Empire.

In 1945 this Empire was controlled by three departments of state in London. The Dominions Office looked after the white-settled self-governing dominions of Canada, Australia, New Zealand, South Africa, and Newfoundland. Collectively, they had emerged as the nucleus of what was to be known as the British Commonwealth. The India Office controlled the subcontinent of India, a land of 400 million people and as yet not subdivided. The Colonial Office administered the rest of the Empire, which included large parts of Black Africa, Malaysia, Burma, territories in the Far East, South America, and other possessions scattered throughout the world. In 1945, at the end of the Second World War, Britain still headed this enormous combination of peoples and territories whose potential wealth and power were incalculable but she did so at a time when her own resources were at their lowest ebb.

The Labour government which came into power under Clement Attlee took over a country which was virtually insolvent. The war effort had used up a quarter of the nation's wealth, including a large slice of assets which had been invested in all parts of the world. Britain had been victorious in arms but in economic terms was not far short of being the defeated. It is possible to argue that this descent from being the first world power in the second half of the nineteenth century to being a power of the second grade a century later was inevitable. It can be said that the super powers of the United States, USSR, and China would inevitably have developed or emerged. This may be so. The 1939–45 war, nevertheless, greatly accelerated the process.

The economic facts of life in 1945 meant that Britain had somehow to come to terms with her new condition. It was rather like a millionaire finding overnight that he was bankrupt. It took a long time for attitudes to adjust. Governments, looking at the 'balance sheets', absorbed the message rather more quickly than the man-in-the-street, but even leading experienced politicians were clinging to Britain's world role a decade after the war had ended. The abortive Suez adventure of the Eden government in 1956 represented the time when most politicians recognized the reality of the situation and began to settle for an international role which was no longer that of one of the great powers. For many people outside politics the myth of greatness persisted. For them Britain was not just a group of islands off the mainland of Europe: she was still the hub of a huge international wheel of power and influence.

The disparity in wealth between the United States and her major Western ally, Britain, in 1945 was enormous: whereas Britain had been forced to dissipate at least a quarter of her total resources, the United States had been able to maintain what was virtually a peacetime domestic economy while still being the major provider of war resources for the Allies. In 1941 a Lend-Lease Agreement had been arranged between the two countries through which strategic supplies had generously flowed into Britain from across the Atlantic. With the end of hostilities the Agreement was ended without consultation with the British government. Recovering from the shock, a delegation was sent to Washington to negotiate a loan. This was eventually agreed, on relatively harsh terms, in December 1945, but it proved to be a very temporary palliative.

The post-war economic recovery of Europe

By the end of 1946 it was evident that the economies of the Western European countries, including Britain and Germany, would only revive if generously primed by a wealthy outsider. The one obvious, indeed only, wealthy outsider was the United States and in a speech at Harvard University on 5 June 1947, the American Secretary of State, George Marshall, outlined a plan for injecting wealth into Europe through a four-year recovery programme which was to acquire the popular name of the Marshall Plan. There was more than an element of self-interest in the proposal, in that the United States, as an international trading nation, would expect in the long run to benefit from trade with the revived countries of Europe.

The original scheme had intended to include the USSR but the Russians shied away from such a close association with a capitalist country, and a conference was arranged in Paris, under the chairmanship of the British Foreign Secretary, Ernest Bevin, to draw up a plan for European Economic reconstruction. At the conference, held on 12 July 1947, a Committee for European Economic Cooperation was set up comprising, in addition to Britain and France, Austria, Belgium, Denmark, Greece, Iceland, Ireland, Italy, Luxemburg, the Netherlands, Norway, Portugal, Sweden, Switzerland, and Turkey. Britain and France assumed responsibility for Western Germany's participation.

The success of the recovery programme is now well known. Not only did it largely achieve what it was intended to do, revive the shattered economies of Western Europe, but it also produced two other results. The Committee set up for distributing Marshall Aid funds became the **Organization for European Economic Cooperation** (OEEC) and the forerunner of closer and more permanent links between nations in Western Europe. The other result was the creation in Eastern Europe, at the instigation of the USSR, of a corresponding, opposing block, the **Cominform**. The scene was thus set for a new pattern of European groupings: on one side of what Winston Churchill called the Iron Curtain was the East European, communist block, and on the other side the West European, capitalist block.

At the time when the Marshall Plan was coming into operation Winston Churchill, now leader of the Opposition, was canvassing the idea of creating something approaching a United States of Europe, with aims of political as well as economic integration. The government of the day, however, through the Foreign Secretary, Ernest Bevin, favoured a series of bilateral non-aggression pacts with West European countries. There was still in Britain, as we have seen, a hope that at least some of the international status and power associated with the leadership of a world empire could be retained. It was genuinely believed by many people that Britain could have the best of several worlds. She was seen as existing in three distinct, but

111

overlapping, circles: the Commonwealth, as the British Empire had now become; the Atlantic Community, which meant retaining and enhancing the 'special relationship' with the United States; and Europe, by establishing free trade and reciprocal defence agreements.

In the later 1940s and early 1950s it is undoubtedly true that Britain could have, had she chosen, been the clear, unchallenged leader of Europe. She had the prestige and, in relative terms, the power. Ernest Bevin did go some way towards leading his European neighbours towards a closer relationship but shied away from a full-blooded, long-term commitment. The old imperial links were still strong. Thus, on his initiative, a treaty was signed in Brussels in 1948 between Britain, France, the Netherlands, Belgium, and Luxemburg which provided for collective self-defence and economic, social, and cultural cooperation. In the following year the Brussels Treaty Powers, as they were known, with Denmark, Iceland, Italy, Norway, Portugal, Canada, and the United States, signed the North Atlantic Treaty which set up the mutual defence arrangements of **NATO**. In 1950 it was agreed in principle that West Germany should also be included.

With the injection of Marshall Aid, the economies of the Western European nations began to recover quickly. By 1950 many of them had passed their pre-war levels of production. In 1948 the Netherlands, Belgium and Luxemburg had agreed to set up a **Benelux Customs Union** to help the development of trade between them. Statesmen in other countries were seeking ways of closer cooperation with their neighbours.

The genesis of the European Community

In 1950 Robert Schuman, the French Foreign Minister, proposed the creation of a Community to share the coal and steel resources of France, Germany, and any other European countries willing to join them. His aims were partly economic and partly political; it was his hope that by pooling the 'weapons of war' a future European conflict would be averted. In 1951 a treaty founding the **European Coal and Steel Community (ESC)** was signed in Paris by France, West Germany, Italy, Belgium, the Netherlands, and Luxemburg. 'The Six', as they were soon to be called, had taken their first major step towards European integration. Britain stood aside, still reluctant to exchange her imperial role for a wholehearted commitment to Europe.

In June 1955, following an initiative by the three Benelux countries, the Foreign Ministers of the Six met at Messina, in Sicily, to discuss further steps towards European integration. The meeting identified four areas in which, in the view of the six Foreign Ministers, further cooperation could profitably take place: atomic energy; establishing a common market to foster trade between them; setting up a **European Investment Fund**; and harmonizing pay and working conditions across all six countries.

There followed nearly two years of intensive negotiations between the governments of the Six, with Britain attending some of the earlier discussions as an observer. Then on 25 March 1957 treaties were signed in Rome setting up the **European Economic Community** (the Common Market) and the **European Atomic Energy Community (Euratom)**. The preamble to the **Treaty of Rome** establishing the EEC stated its basic objectives as being: the establishment of the foundations for an ever closer union among European peoples; the improvement of their working and living conditions;

the progressive abolition of restrictions on trade; and the development of the prosperity of overseas countries. The main economic aim was to create a customs union by the abolition of internal tariffs and other barriers to trade, and the establishment of a common external tariff; the development of a common policy for agriculture; and the introduction of measures to ensure the free movement of labour, capital, and services. The target date for establishing a common external tariff was 1970: it was attained in July 1968, a year and a half ahead of schedule.

Britain's decision to join the Community

Britain's reaction to the Rome Treaties was to propose a free trade area between the EEC and other members of the OEEC, including herself. The French view was that this was impracticable in the absence of a common external tariff for everyone and harmonization of other matters, such as working conditions and social security systems. Under Britain's leadership, the seven OEEC countries which were not members of the EEC, Austria, Britain, Norway, Portugal, Sweden, and Switzerland, formed a **European Free Trade Area (EFTA)**. They were later joined by Finland and Iceland. EFTA was, however, a long way short of the economic, and eventual political, integration which the founders of the EEC envisaged, and hopes of joining it to the Community progressively dwindled.

During the long drawn-out EFTA/EEC negotiations, conducted on Britain's behalf largely by Reginald Maudling, it was becoming apparent that, both economically and politically, this country's future lay in Europe and not in her old imperial territories or even in closer association with the United States. A process of decolonization had begun soon after 1945 and the loosening of links with former dominions and colonies was accompanied by changes in our pattern of international trading. Although it was by no means a unanimous view, there was a growing feeling that Britain's economic future lay in having access to the large common market which the EEC had created. Some politicians, Edward Heath notable among them, were prepared to commit Britain to much more than economic union: they were prepared for eventual political fusion as well.

On 31 July 1961 the Prime Minister, Harold Macmillan, announced in the House of Commons that Britain had decided to make a formal application for negotiations with a view to joining the EEC. Edward Heath was chosen to lead the British delegation at the negotiations. From the Prime Minister's point of view he was an ideal choice: Heath was a committed European, had travelled extensively in Europe, and knew many politicians there; he also had an enviable capacity to master a difficult and complicated brief. No one in Britain at that time was more likely to have success in the negotiations than he. By the end of 1962 provisional agreement had been reached on a number of major points but, on 3 January 1963, General de Gaulle, the French President, announced to the press his opposition to the British application. Negotiations were broken off. This was clearly a bitter blow to the Macmillan government and to Edward Heath in particular.

In 1961, when negotiations had first begun, the Labour Party in opposition had expressed great reservations about EEC membership. There were several staunch pro-Europeans in the Party but there were as many, if not more, against the idea of joining. The new Leader of the Party, Harold Wilson, was thought to be at best lukewarm. His deputy, George Brown, was a fervent European. After two years'

113

experience as Prime Minister it was evident that Wilson, too, was convinced that the economic arguments for joining the EEC were too strong to resist. In April 1966 he announced that provided 'essential British and Commonwealth interests are safe-guarded', the government was prepared to consider starting negotiations for a second application to join.

On 2 May 1967 Harold Wilson told the House of Commons that formal negotiations for membership would begin. Again, France proved to be the stumbling block. In October 1967 the French Foreign Minister, Couve de Murville, clearly on instructions from President de Gaulle, told his fellow EEC ministers that, although France had never in principle opposed the admission of new members, he saw great difficulties in the applications of Britain and Ireland, Denmark, and Norway, who had decided to seek membership as well. Efforts to resume negotiations met with no success and it seemed obvious that as long as de Gaulle was President of France Britain's application would be blocked.

President de Gaulle resigned in April 1969 and was succeeded by Georges Pompidou, whose attitude towards enlarging the Community seemed more helpful and flexible. In June 1970 the Conservatives returned to power under Edward Heath, and negotiations for membership were resumed almost immediately. During 1971 the British delegation, led by Geoffrey Rippon, made rapid progress and in July a White Paper was published describing the terms which had been agreed; in October both Houses of Parliament voted in favour of entry and the **Treaty of Accession** was signed on 22 January 1972. Britain had been joined in her application by Denmark, Ireland, and Norway but, as a result of a referendum held in the following year, Norway withdrew.

On 1 January 1973 the United Kingdom, Ireland, and Denmark formally entered into membership. The Six had become Nine. The last obstacle to permanent membership was crossed in June 1975 when Harold Wilson's Labour government held a referendum to determine whether or not EEC membership should be retained. A two to one majority voted to stay.

After years of negotiation, Greece became the tenth member of the Community on 1 January 1981. Discussions were already under way for the possible membership of Spain and Portugal at some future date. Meanwhile Greenland had achieved full independence from Denmark on 1 May 1979 and decided to review its Community membership, which had originated through Denmark's application. Following a referendum in February 1982, 52 per cent of Greenland's voters decided to leave. Although the population of Greenland is small, her departure reduced the territorial area of the Community by more than half.

The European Community of Ten

The Community of Ten has a total population of nearly 270 million, over 80 per cent of whom live in the four largest member countries, Germany, the United Kingdom, Italy, and France. It is understandable, therefore, that all the institutions reflect, in their membership and powers, this unbalanced distribution. The structure of the Community is relatively simple, as Fig. 11.1 shows.

The Council of Ministers is the supreme decision-taking body and consists of representatives from each of the 10 member countries. The representatives vary according to the subject under discussion: if it concerns economic policy then the

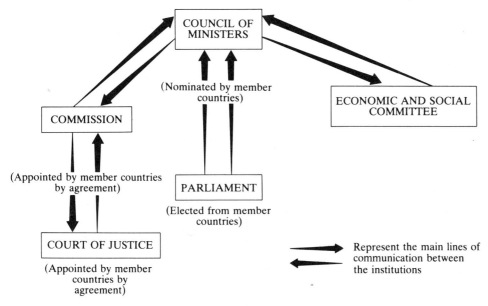

Fig. 11.1 Main institutions of the European Community

Finance Ministers will take part; if it is a matter of external policy the Foreign Ministers will participate; if it is agricultural policy the Ministers of Agriculture will attend. The Presidency of the Council changes at six-monthly intervals, each member state taking its turn.

Most decisions by the Council are taken on the basis of proposals made to it by the Commission. Until 1974 it was agreed that these decisions should always be unanimous, in other words, it was possible for any one member state to veto any decision. At a meeting in Paris in December 1974 the heads of government of the member states agreed to alter the unanimity rule and distinguish between issues which:

(a) affected member states' vital interests;
(b) were of prime importance but not vital; and
(c) were of secondary importance.

In the case of (a) grade decisions the unanimity rule still applies; in (b) grade cases a 'qualified majority' must be obtained; in (c) grade cases a simple majority is all that is needed.

To cater for decisions where a 'qualified majority' is prescribed, the votes of member states are weighted as follows:

Germany	10	Greece	5
Italy	10	Ireland	3
France	10	Denmark	3
United Kingdom	10	Luxemburg	2
Belgium	5		—
Netherlands	5		63

115

For qualified majority cases at least 45 votes must be cast for a decision to be effective. This means in practice that if there is a disagreement between the 'big four', three can only outvote the fourth if they have the support of at least three of the smaller states. Even with provisions for a qualified majority, ministers still tend to seek unanimity on the basis of compromise.

Once a policy decision has been taken by the Council it will assume one of two forms: a regulation or a directive. Both are legally binding, the difference between them being that regulations are binding on all member states whereas directives are binding only on specific countries to whom they apply. The Council also issues recommendations from time to time which have no binding force.

The **Commission** is rather like a mixture of a Cabinet and civil service Permanent Secretaries. It is composed of 14 members: two each from Germany, France, Italy, and the United Kingdom, and one each from Belgium, the Netherlands, Ireland, Greece, Denmark, and Luxemburg. The members are nominated by each member state for a four-year, renewable, term of office. One member acts as President and five others as Vice-Presidents, each for two years. The position of President is an influential, and highly prized, appointment.

The Commission is responsible for drafting policies in the interests of the Community as a whole so that, although members are drawn from different countries, during their periods of office they are expected to subordinate any national feelings in deference to a Community view. Proposals are sent to the Council of Ministers for acceptance; if they are not accepted they are returned to the Commission for redrafting. It also acts as the guardian of the Community treaties and it can refer a member state to the **Court of Justice** for breaking a treaty or failing to comply with a regulation or directive.

The Commission executes the decisions of the Council of Ministers and has a substantial civil service at its disposal in Brussels, supplied by the member states.

The Court of Justice is responsible under the EEC Treaty for ensuring 'the observance of law and justice in the interpretation and application of the Treaty'. This means that it has the authority to decide whether or not the Council of Ministers or the Commission or a member state has fulfilled its obligations under the Treaty. Cases can be brought to the Court by one of the Community institutions, by a government, by a firm, or by an individual. In theory one member state could complain to the Court about another member state, but so far this has not happened. Cases range from infringements of the anti-monopoly rules, through complaints by employees of the Community institutions about their conditions of service, to those concerned with the application of the Common Agricultural Policy or the Community's social policies. The composition and methods of the Court are based on continental practice, the judges and officials being appointed by member states usually for six-year terms. Since the Community has no enforcement machinery of its own, decisions of the Court have to be implemented by national courts. Its status really rests on two foundations: respect for the rule of law by member states and a wish to preserve the essential principles of the European Community. The Court operates from Luxemburg and should not be confused with the International Court of Justice, based in The Hague, or the European Court of Human Rights, based in Strasbourg, each of which has a wider jurisdiction and is supported by a much larger group of countries than the EEC members states.

The **Economic and Social Committee** is a consultative body consisting of representatives from the member states covering a wide spectrum of interests including employers, trade unions, the professions, and farmers. The Committee's primary aim is to give advice to the Council of Ministers and the Commission. In accordance with the Community treaties, it must be consulted before certain decisions can be taken.

The **European Parliament** consists of 434 representatives elected by the 10 member states in proportion to populations. France, Germany, Italy, and the United Kingdom each has 81 members, Holland 25, Greece and Belgium 24, Denmark 16, Ireland 15, and Luxemburg 6. This means that, for the United Kingdom, there are 66 English, 8 Scottish, 4 Welsh, and 3 Northern Ireland 'Euro-constituencies'. Each one approximates to eight domestic constituencies and has roughly half a million voters.

Distribution of power in the Community

As we have seen, the Council of Ministers is the supreme decision-taking body. Most policy is initiated by the Commission, submitted to the European Parliament and the Economic and Social Committee for consideration, adopted or rejected by the Council, and, if adopted, executed directly by the Commission, or by the Council, or by the member states themselves. The European Parliament uses a network of committees to consider policy proposals. If it is unhappy about any item it can suggest an amendment which the Council can accept or reject. If the Parliament and Council fail to agree the implementation of legislation can be delayed for a period of up to three months.

By most objective standards the Community is not a particularly democratic organization. Indeed, its apparent lack of democracy is the target for many of its critics. Members of the two most powerful institutions, the Council of Ministers and the Commission, are nominated, not elected, by member states. The only truly representative body is the European Parliament and, understandably therefore, many people see the democratic future of the Community in its hands.

As a fully directly-elected body it is only into its second term of four years so that its full potential has yet to be revealed. Already, however, it has shown evidence of a willingness to question and challenge the decisions of the less democratic organs of the Community. Its powers and responsibilities lie in three main areas: the adoption of the Community budget; the oversight of Community legislation; and the general supervision of the activities of the Community's many institutions. It agrees the budget with the Council of Ministers, can suggest amendments, and, as an ultimate power, can reject it. It has exercised its power of rejection on at least two occasions and when this happens the budget has to be reconsidered by the Council and the Commission and submitted to the Parliament again. It debates proposed legislation and from time to time will pass observations on it to the Council, suggesting amendments. Its debates also cover the activities of the many Community institutions and their general supervision is delegated to the Parliament's 18 specialist committees.

The formal powers of the European Parliament are perhaps not very great: its potential strength lies in the fact that it can claim to be genuinely representative of the member states. It is encouraging to note that it now operates in much the same fashion as national parliaments, with a clearly defined spectrum of parties. They split into six main groupings, as Fig. 11.2 shows, with the Socialists and the Christian Democrats being the most numerous. United Kingdom representatives are distributed

117

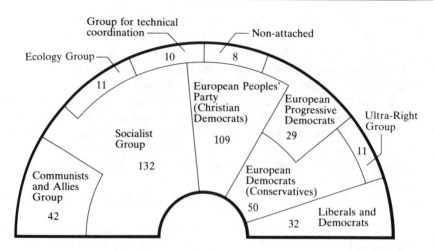

Fig. 11.2 Political groups in the European Parliament

among four of the party groupings: the Conservatives dominate the European Democrats, Labour members form part of the Socialist group, and the minor parties have joined similar minority groupings in Europe. The June 1984 elections increased the number of minority groups, as Figure 11.2 indicates.

As a European Parliament, aligned in political groupings, begins to feel a genuine identity of its own it is inevitable that it will want to have a bigger say in the running of the Community's affairs, and it is conceivable that during the next decade the balance of power will shift from the Council of Ministers and the Commission to an emergent European Cabinet, representing the Community as a whole. Critics of the Community will regard this development as an unwelcome additional threat to national sovereignties. Whatever view is taken, the evolution of the European Parliament on these lines will undoubtedly bring to the Community what it conspicuously lacks: responsible and accountable government.

Other international obligations

Before joining the European Community the United Kingdom became a member of the **United Nations Organization**: in fact, a founder member. The United Nations is an association of states which have pledged themselves, through signing the Charter, to maintain international peace and security and to cooperate in establishing political, economic, and social conditions under which this task can be achieved. There are 155 members and they cover states of all sizes, races, languages, and philosophies. Each contributes to the United Nations budget on a percentage scale which recognizes the national income of each member. In 1983, for example, the United States contributed 25 per cent of the annual budget, the USSR just over 11 per cent, Japan just under 10 per cent, and the United Kingdom 4.5 per cent.

In addition to the main institutions, such as the **General Assembly** and the **Security Council**, the United Nations acts as an umbrella organization for a number of other important international bodies all of which this country is a member. They include:

the **International Atomic Energy (IAEA)**, whose main function is to accelerate and encourage the peaceful uses of atomic energy; the **International Labour Organization (ILO)**, whose principal aim is to formulate international standards of labour relations in the form of International Labour Conventions and Recommendations; the **Food and Agriculture Organization (FAO)**, which gives international support to national programmes for increasing the efficiency of agriculture, forestry, and fisheries; the **World Health Organization (WHO)**, which assists countries throughout the world to improve their health services and to eradicate disease; the **International Monetary Fund (IMF)**, whose aims are to promote international monetary cooperation and, through it, encourage the expansion of international trade: the **International Bank for Reconstruction and Development** (popularly called the World Bank), whose purpose is to provide funds and technical assistance to help facilitate economic development in the poorer countries of the world; the **International Finance Corporation (IFC)** is an affiliate of the World Bank and its main activity is to help finance new ventures particularly where local venture capital is difficult to obtain; the **International Civil Aviation Organization (ICAO)**, which establishes technical standards for safety and efficiency of air navigation; the **Universal Postal Union (UPU)**, whose purpose is to assist in improving the organization of postal services throughout the world and to develop international collaboration; the **International Telecommunications Union (ITU)**, which allocates radio frequencies and promotes efficiency and safety in the field of telecommunications; the **World Meteorological Organization (WMO)**, which promotes international cooperation in weather forecasting and helps to establish meteorological stations and centres all over the world; the **Inter-Governmental Maritime Consultative Organization**, which is charged with increasing cooperation between nations in maritime matters and particularly in the interests of safety at sea; and the **General Agreement on Tariffs and Trade (GATT)**, which functions as a multilateral treaty that lays down a common code of conduct for international trade and as a forum for negotiation to overcome trade problems and reduce trade barriers.

As a European nation, the United Kingdom, in addition to her EEC membership, has other international commitments. The most important organizations of which we are members are: the **Organization for Economic Cooperation and Development (OECD)**, which is the successor to OEEC, which as we have seen, started life as the agency for distributing Marshall Aid funds (its particular interest now is to encourage the wealthier nations to assist the less developed; its membership includes the United States and Canada as well as the countries of Western Europe); the **North Atlantic Treaty Organization (NATO)**, to which we have already referred; the **Western European Union**, which acts as a European forum for discussing political questions; and the **Council of Europe**, whose aim is greater European political, social, and cultural cooperation, and whose membership includes most West European countries, including those who are not yet members of the EEC. Some people see the Council of Europe as the possible forerunner of a United States of Europe, and they are prepared to wait a long time for the realization of this ambition. The United Kingdom is a party to a number of mutual defence agreements in addition to the NATO commitments. The chief of these are: the **South-East Asia Collective Defence Treaty (SEATO)**, whose signatories are also Australia, France, New Zealand, Pakistan, the Philippines, Thailand, and the United States; and the **Central Treaty Organization (CENTO)**, whose other members are Turkey, Pakistan, and Iran. The United States, although not a full member, is closely associated with it.

119

The implications of Britain's overseas commitments

Britain has only been an island nation for a comparatively short period. For most of the time she has acted out her role on the world stage. We have traced in this chapter the history of the discarding of imperial possessions and of a transition from a first- to second-rank world power. Yet even with this new status the international obligations are enormous. Fortunately, years of Empire and Commonwealth have provided government institutions accustomed to thinking in international terms and the main departments of state have adapted remarkably well to this new European role. The most significant effects, and they will become more apparent as time goes by, have been the limitations that international obligations have placed on Britain's freedom to determine her own economic, social, and commercial policies.

It has always been accepted that a price has to be paid for any political and economic gains derived from membership of international groupings. In the case of United Nations membership and participation in mutual defence arrangements the price has been reasonable and expected. EEC membership has, however, clearly resulted in a gradual loss of control by the United Kingdom Parliament over legislation falling within the Community's spheres of influence. The main areas of impact so far have been in agriculture, international trade, company law, taxation, regional aid, insurance, professional qualifications, environmental matters, and consumer protection. Parliament can no longer legislate in isolation from the rest of Europe. Indeed there is an increasingly large area over which national power to legislate is disappearing or has disappeared.

Some senior civil servants are spending as much time in Brussels as in London and there is now a 'mini-Whitehall' permanently sited there. Parliament has found it necessary to establish two new select committees, one in each House, to scrutinize the increasing volume of delegated legislation which is flowing from the EEC.

The weakness in the present arrangements lies in Parliament's inability to develop a firm view on proposed EEC legislation. It has so far been unable to give clear advice to representatives on the Council of Ministers on the lines they should adopt in negotiations with their European opposite numbers. The absence of an authoritative European Parliament has, to many observers, been a crucial weakness in the European Community's organization. That is why the future development of the new directly elected assembly will be watched with great interest.

Assignments

EEC may plunder jobless funds

Farm reforms come too late to avert EEC budget crisis

British face rise beef and lamb prices

Majority in Britain favour leaving Common Market

Ministers in all-night battle to save summit

EEC on brink of Dublin milk deal

18. Critically evaluate the EEC Common Agricultural Policy. How would you reform it?

Sources: Any of the following: *The European Communities, a Keesing's Research Report*, 1975, pp. 68–92; D. Swann *The Economics of the Common Market*, Penguin, 1975, pp. 116–38; W. Farr (ed.) *Guide to the Common Market*, Collins, 1972, pp. 84–102; de la Mahotière *Towards one Europe*, Penguin, 1970, pp. 139–75; also Anthony Sampson, *The Changing Anatomy of Britain*, Chapter 21.

19. 'The political implications of European Community membership are more important than the economic.' Do you agree with this statement? Give a reasoned answer.

    This topic can also be used as a basis for a debate on the motion: 'This House believes that the political unity of Europe is more important than the economic.'

Sources: As for Assignment 18.

Part Three   People in public administration

12

The public service in Britain

The concept of a public service

In 1983 there were just over six hundred and fifty thousand non-industrial and industrial civil servants and between two and three million people working in local government. If we add to this list another third of a million in the armed forces, we have a formidable total of more than three million people, or more than 12 per cent of the working population, in some kind of public employment. If we include the quasi-government and nationalized bodies then the percentage is appreciably higher. It is not surprising that the public sector spends about 40 per cent of the Gross National Product.

When we consider this vast workforce we tend to think of people in discrete, watertight compartments. Thus we speak of the civil service, the local government service, the health service, and so on. Very rarely, if ever, do we use the expression the 'public service'. Is it possible—is it helpful—to speak of a public service?

It might be a useful concept if we were able to identify common features in the structure, organization, or methods of these separate groups of employees. Then we could analyse and judge them on the basis of common characteristics.

The first thought that probably springs to mind when the public service, or public servants, are mentioned is one of bureaucracy. 'Government from a desk' seems the most obvious characteristic of a civil servant or local government employee. However, when we try to define bureaucracy, as we shall do a little later, we are forced to the conclusion that it is by no means confined to the public sector. The majority of people work in bureaucracies. Professor Elliot Jaques, of Brunel University, estimates that 90 per cent of the working populations of the United States and the United Kingdom operate in some kind of bureaucratic organization.[1] Bureaucratic structure is not a very reliable characteristic to look for in search of common ground.

Are there other criteria we can use? At the start of this book we emphasized the point that public administrators are working, whether they are aware of it or not, within a political environment. Of necessity, this conditions their approach to their work. We should avoid over-emphasizing this point, however, as far as the great majority of public servants are concerned. In both the civil service and the local government service it is really only those people in senior positions, and who work reasonably close to the 'political coal face', who are constantly aware of the political obligations and constraints confronting them: the majority of employees are just 'doing a job'. A similar point can be made about the private sector. We often stress that private enterprise is conditioned by the profit motive, but it would be misleading to think that every worker in every firm, however lowly his position, had profitability at the forefront of his mind. Most of them, too, are just doing a job.

Nevertheless, the political context containing the public sector does create something which is peculiar to it: close political control and accountability. This brings an additional dimension to decision taking at most levels. In other words, before a decision is taken, it is not just a question of whether it is right technically or administratively, but also whether it will be politically acceptable and, as such, will it stand the test of political scrutiny? The political context must, then, be viewed as a reliable characteristic of the public service. Are there others?

There are, although there is nothing quite so clearcut and distinctive. Many large organizations in the private sector, and most of those in the quasi-governmental sector, display these characteristics, but only rarely in the developed form we find in central and local government. They may be summarized as: the absence of patronage and nepotism in selection and promotion procedures; the concept of anonymity whereby it is the temporary politician who is in the public eye while the permanent official is in the background; and the presence of a national structure and machinery for pay and working conditions. We should remember, however, that, at chief officer level in local government, the 'anonymity rule' does not apply so obviously.

Using these characteristics as our criteria, we are forced to the conclusion that only the civil service and the local government service completely qualify for inclusion in the 'public service'. Employees in *ad hoc* regional authorities lie on the fringe of such a service; people working in the nationalized industries may be in the public sector but we cannot regard them as part of the public service. Even defining the public service as narrowly as this produces problems. If we are to think of a common body of people forming a public service we should really see them as being in common employment with opportunities to move and progress within the total organization. In practice this happens only rarely; there is still little movement between the civil service and local government. Whether or not there should be more is one of the questions we will discuss in our final, evaluating chapter.

Before we look at the two parts of what we are calling the public service, let us consider a little more closely the concept of bureaucracy.

Bureaucracy

Bureaucracy is a word more often used as a term of abuse than as a description. To many people it signifies delay, 'red tape', coldness, impersonal attitudes and inefficiency. Whereas private enterprise suggests dynamism, relevance, and adaptability, bureaucracy—epitomizing 'public enterprise'—suggests sluggishness, remoteness, and rigidity. Both impressions, if used as generalizations, are travesties of the truth.

Only a minority of privately run organizations are, by international standards, highly efficient, and some of them display many of the characteristics for which the public sector is often criticized. Equally, the British public service, although now not perhaps the best in the world, has certainly served as a model for many others and is still copied today. How, then, has public administration become so closely associated with bureaucracy, and why has bureaucracy acquired such a bad name? Public administration is associated with bureaucracy because it is, in its structure and methods of working, essentially bureaucratic. Having said that, most organizations of size are bureaucratic, and this is not necessarily to be deplored: it is inevitable. Bureaucracy has a bad reputation largely because of the consequences of badly run bureaucracies. A highly bureaucratic organization which is ill-managed is likely to reveal more obvious defects than a non-bureaucratic one. To explain this, let us look at the essential characteristics of bureaucracy.

The first person to write, in sociological terms, about bureaucracy was the German, Max Weber (1864–1920). He saw bureaucracy as a very advanced and rational form of human organization, and although he was aware of its imperfections, believed that, on balance, the good features more than outweighed the bad.[2] The characteristics of a bureaucracy, developed from Weber's ideas, may be summarized as:

1. a hierarchical system of authority;
2. a systematic division of labour;
3. a clear specification of duties for everyone working in it;
4. clear and systematic disciplinary codes and procedures;
5. the control of operations through a consistent system of abstract rules;
6. a consistent application of general rules to specific cases;
7. the selection of employees on the basis of objectively determined qualifications; and
8. a system of promotion on the basis of seniority or merit, or both.

Both the civil service and the local government service in Britain display these characteristics to greater or lesser degrees. In theory, and to a considerable extent in practice, they imply that the whole organization is more important than any of its individual parts. They also imply that the organization, personified by a central or local government department, can carry on its work with little or no loss of continuity whatever changes take place in the personnel within it. These characteristics are both the strength and weakness of a bureaucracy.

The strengths and weaknesses of bureaucracy

A hierarchical system of authority means that the administration of policy is clear and unequivocal: what is decided at the top is passed down for implementation in a precise and direct manner. It also means that decision taking can take a long time if the discretion of the man at the bottom is limited and he has to refer constantly to the man above.

A systematic division of labour makes the fullest use of training and expertise but it can lead to excessive departmentalism. This, in turn, can inhibit good communications to the ultimate detriment of clients. All too often we have heard the phrase 'I don't know anything about that: it's not my job'. At the same time it is obviously advantageous that everyone in the organization should clearly know what his duties are. Ideally, each person should know what he is responsible for, whom he is responsible to, and what authority he has. A well-designed, well-managed bureaucratic system ensures that all these things are known and understood.

Clear and systematic disciplinary codes and procedures imply firmness but fairness of treatment, and the majority of people will respond well to this. There will, however, inevitably be exceptions to the general rule and the inability of a bureaucratic system to deal easily with the 'special cases' is one of its weaknesses.

The most recognizable characteristics of a bureaucracy are that operations are controlled through a system of abstract rules and then subsequently the general rules are applied to specific cases. It will be obvious that if a unit of a few hundred civil servants or local government servants is dealing with a clientele of several hundred

127

thousand it will be impossible to consider the case of every applicant for a benefit or a service on its individual merits. Public administrators inevitably deal in generalities and general treatment can often be unfair as far as an individual is concerned. Dealing in generalities is rather like dealing in averages. If you were to take the individual weights of a small group of people, aggregate them, and then calculate the arithmetic mean average, it is quite possible that no single member of the group had the exact weight of the average. Administration for the 'average case' can often mean that no single client is completely satisfied with the way he is treated.

Recruiting people on a basis of objectively determined criteria of age, qualifications, and experience seems, at first glance, the best method of selection, and in most cases it is. Again, however, this method tends to ignore the 'special case'. Bureaucracies are not happy resting places for eccentrics, even though eccentricity may be an expression of high talent. It is sad, but true, that most people entrusted with recruiting into the public service would prefer to appoint a 'second-best' who would be likely to conform than a 'genius' who would not.

The final characteristic of a bureaucracy which we have identified is a system of promotion on the basis of seniority or merit, or both. The best bureaucratic organizations would put merit clearly before seniority, without completely discarding the latter. All too often, however, seniority is the dominant criterion and this can mean that the ability to survive, without ruffling anyone's feathers, is the surest route to the top.

In this brief examination of bureaucracy we have looked at its strengths and how these strengths are its potential defects. What lessons can we learn from this?

First, the objectives of the organization must be clearly defined, and continually reviewed and redefined. Second, more attention should be paid to informal structures and informal relationships. In most large organizations, for example, in addition to the formal channels of communication, there is the informal system, usually known as 'the grapevine'. Trying to ignore the grapevine, or even suppress it, is seldom profitable: it is more sensible to appreciate it and even use it. A third piece of advice to be considered is that apparent operating costs should not be allowed to obscure 'real' costs. An example of this advice can be taken from a highly successful organization in the private sector, Marks and Spencer. Many years ago Marks and Spencer embarked on a study of the cost-effectiveness of their administrative procedures and came to the conclusion that the cost of operating many controls was greater than the losses they were supposed to prevent. Thus, over the years, they progressively made a number of procedures redundant and in their head offices, in London's Baker Street, they now have a 'museum' of discarded forms. It is no coincidence that the man brought in from business to set up a unit for the elimination of bureaucratic waste and improvements in efficiency, Lord Rayner, was seconded by Marks and Spencer. Because of the political context within which public administration operates it is obviously more difficult to streamline procedures which are intended to provide public accountability. Nevertheless, if the 'unacceptable face of bureaucracy' is to be avoided more experimentation with procedures must be attempted.

Origins of the modern civil service

The modern civil service can trace its origins from the middle of the nineteenth century when a demonstrably corrupt system, based on nepotism and patronage, was

128

gradually replaced by one based on competitive selection, objective promotion, and political neutrality. The event which prompted these reforms was the publication in 1854 of a report by Sir Stafford Northcote and Sir Charles Trevelyan.[3] Northcote and Trevelyan had been asked by the Treasury to consider the conditions which were common to all the public establishments and to report.

They criticized the existing system of recruitment, promotion, and organization and recommended sweeping changes. These included the establishment of a **Civil Service Commission**, to recruit on merit by open competition, and the introduction of promotion on the basis of merit and seniority. They also recommended the creation of general grades of civil servants which would provide a clear career for all entrants with opportunities for promotion not only within a particular department or ministry but from one department to another. They became known as the Treasury classes.

The changes following the Report did not occur overnight. The Civil Service Commission, consisting initially of three commissioners, was established in 1855 and a system of open competition was gradually introduced throughout the service. There was still considerable opposition to radical change and it was several years before major parts of the Report were implemented.

Treasury control

The Treasury had asked Northcote and Trevelyan to report and it was the Treasury which came to dominate the civil service in the years that followed. Initially it was mainly the case of 'the man who pays the piper calls the tune' but the Treasury's influence began to extend far beyond financial control. The whole system of grading of posts within the service was controlled by the Treasury, through the Civil Service Commission. The full pattern of the Treasury classes is shown in Table 12.1. The grades are set out in hierarchical order, the levels corresponding to approximately similar salary points. These were the 'general', as distinct from the specialist, posts in the service. The specialist included ambassadors in the Foreign Service, scientists, doctors, psychologists, information officers, architects, engineers, surveyors, and so on. The highest salaries, such as those of ambassadors, accorded with those at the top of the administrative class, the others were comparable to those in all the general classes.

Table 12.1 Treasury classes prior to the changes following the Fulton Report 1968

Administrative class	Executive class	Clerical and clerical assistant classes
Permanent Secretary		
Deputy Secretary		
Under-Secretary	Controlling posts	
Assistant Secretary	Principal Executive Officer	
Principal	Chief Executive Officer	
	Senior Executive Officer (SEO)	
	Higher Executive Officer (HEO)	
Assistant Principal	Executive Officer (EO)	Higher Clerical Officer (HCO)
		Clerical Officer (CO)
		Clerical Assistant (CA)

The philosophy behind the creation of Treasury classes was to recruit generalists to administer and execute policy and to provide the clerical support. The Treasury, following the thinking of Northcote and Trevelyan, believed that intellect, developed in whatever discipline, was the prime quality a top administrator needed. If expert knowledge was required he could turn to his specialist experts for advice. Thus, although it was possible to progress from the Executive Class into the Administrative Class and right up to the top of the service, the normal entry point for administrators was as Assistant Principal. This was primarily an administrative trainee grade, and, as such, attracted only a modest salary. However, after a few years' service, an Assistant Principal could expect to jump quite significantly in salary to Principal, and, from there, if he had the ability, to Assistant Secretary and above.

Treasury control grew in the nineteenth century and became all pervasive. It included the determination of departmental establishments, job gradings, selection and promotion procedures, training policies, working procedures, financial estimates, and, of course, departmental expenditure. There was little a department could do without prior Treasury approval. The most obvious consequence of Treasury control was that it created a unified service: it made it possible for someone entering the civil service to make his career in virtually any Department, irrespective of where he began. This is in stark contrast with local government where, as we have seen, professionalism has dominated and where the general administrator still has limited career opportunities.

The Fulton Report

The Treasury had its critics, however, and they grew more vociferous and influential in the post-1945 years. The main grounds for criticism were that the Treasury took a too negative approach to the control of expenditure, that its control of establishments and methods of work was too restrictive and encouraged the least desirable aspects of bureaucracy; that its responsibilities were too wide for it to undertake efficiently; that, because of its concern with departmental spending, it was less able to take a wider, positive view of economic policy; and that in building up its own empire it had inhibited the acceptance of responsibility by other Departments.

The criticisms were considerable but the Treasury was powerful. Not powerful enough, however, to silence its critics. Substantial changes were made in its internal organization in the early 1960s but these were not considered to be enough by some outsiders. In 1965 the Estimates Committee of the House of Commons published a report on *Recruitment to the Civil Service*[4] which hinted at certain deficiencies in the service. It recommended an inquiry into the structure, recruitment, and management of the civil service, and in 1966 a departmental committee under the chairmanship of Lord Fulton, Vice-Chancellor of the University of Sussex, was appointed. Its other members were Dr Norman Hunt, later Lord Crowther-Hunt, of the University of Oxford, four senior civil servants, two MPs, one Conservative and one Labour, and four other 'independent' members, drawn from business, the trade union movement, and the universities. The Committee published its report in 1968[5] and it has since been revealed that the greatest influence on it, and its main author, was Lord Crowther-Hunt.

The main points in the Report may be summarized as:

1. The civil service was still largely a product of the nineteenth century and its attitude was to support the 'gifted, generalist amateur'.
2. What was needed was to 'look at the job first' and to bring a more professional approach to working procedures.
3. A new Civil Service Department should be created to take over the establishment work of the Treasury and to oversee the Civil Service Commission.
4. The system of Treasury classes should be abolished and replaced by one unified grading structure.
5. A Civil Service College should be established.
6. Principles of 'accountable management' should be applied throughout the service.
7. Management service units should be set up in all major departments.
8. In most Departments there should be a senior policy adviser, in addition to the Permanent Secretary, to advise the minister.
9. Ministers should be allowed to employ temporary experts to advise them.
10. There should be more 'openness' so that the outside world could see more readily who was taking the decisions.

The Report was strongly influenced by the experience of successful business in the private sector and by civil service methods in other countries. The recommendations for accountable management and management service units were obviously intended to copy business practices. The proposals for a Civil Service College and the introduction of policy advisers drew from experience of the French civil service, whose recruitment and training policies for its top civil servants are world-renowned and where the use of 'ministerial cabinets', to which we have already referred, is widely quoted.

The post-Fulton civil service

The government accepted most of the recommendations of the Fulton Committee and most have been progressively implemented. The **Civil Service Department** was created in November 1968, taking over the personnel functions of the Treasury, and the **Civil Service College** opened soon afterwards at Sunningdale, Berkshire. A decision, in principle, to abolish Treasury classes and merge them with the professional and specialist grades was taken immediately, and over a period of years this has taken place. Genuine steps have been taken to create units to which could be applied what Fulton called 'accountable management' and this has included a deliberate process of 'hiving-off' which we have already discussed in an earlier chapter. The use of special advisers has grown, albeit slowly.

The Civil Service Department must be considered to have been a relative failure in view of the high hopes which its creation had generated. Although its chief became head of the entire service, it was not successful in matching, let alone eclipsing, the long-established dominance of the Treasury. In the end it was the man who paid the piper who called the tune. In announcing its abolition in November 1981, Prime Minister Thatcher said the government had arrived at its decision because the existence of the Department divorced central responsibility for the control of manpower from responsibility for the control of expenditure.

The new **Management and Personnel Office (MPO)**, established within the Cabinet Office, is essentially what would be called in management terms, a 'staff' department, supplying advice and assistance to the service as a whole. The Treasury is again the 'line management' department, with a clearly stated responsibility for the control of civil service manpower, pay, superannuation, and allowances: in fact the very things which the Fulton Committee thought could be better performed by a new, separate department.

The Civil Service Department could probably have worked successfully if it had been allowed to. The same might well be said of the other department to challenge the power of the Treasury, the Department of Economic Affairs. It too was, of course, eventually abolished. It would not be beyond the bounds of possibility if, at some point in the future, the Civil Service Department, or something like it, returned.

The Civil Service College, although generally approved as a necessary development, has not really lived up to its expectations. Some observers have compared it, unfavourably, with its French equivalent, *L'Ecole Nationale d'Administration*, in Paris, and have said that it does not provide a sufficiently relevant and rigorous training for the very top administrators in the civil service.

A comparison of Tables 12.1 and 12.2, which show the pre- and post-Fulton structures of the civil service, will give an indication of the extent to which most of the old Treasury classes have been linked together to form a main administration group and the specialist groups placed in equivalent positions beside it. It will be seen that the main route for 'generalists' is to Assistant Secretary level. Beyond that point is the élite group of top civil servants. A better idea of the hierarchical nature of the service is given in Table 12.3, which shows the numbers and percentage distributions of groups and grades.

It is now more than fifteen years since the Fulton Report was published: apart from the organizational changes, what effects has the Report had on the composition and character of the civil service? Little that is obvious. Promotion for the vast majority is still very slow, although there is a 'fast' route to the top for a few. A new grade of administration trainee was introduced in 1971 for graduates able to pass the rigorous selection tests. An opportunity for people already within the service to move upwards more quickly was provided by creating the post of Higher Executive Officer

Table 12.2 Civil service structure post-Fulton

Open structure	Administration group	Specialist groups
Permanent Secretary Deputy Secretary Under-Secretary		
	Assistant Secretary Senior Principal Principal Senior Executive Officer Higher Executive Officer Executive Officer	Social Security Professional and technology * Inland Revenue Tax grades Secretarial Science
	Clerical Officer Clerical Assistant	* These are at CO grade and upwards

(Administration) HEOA, later to be termed Higher Executive Officer (Development) HEOD. The results have not been dramatic, as Table 12.4 shows.

Oxbridge candidates still constitute the majority of people coming into the fast route via the Administration Trainee Competition, despite attempts to attract graduates from other universities and colleges. Indeed, the selection is so discriminating that in recent years it has not been found possible to fill all the vacancies available without some lowering of standards. In 1982, for example, 2174 external and 169 internal applications were received to fill 44 vacancies, yet only 24 appointments were eventually made.

The local government service today

Local government employs nearly four times as many people as central government. The total labour force of about 2.5 million is as big as most of Britain's manufacturing industries combined. The reason for this labour intensity is not hard to find: local authorities are essentially providers of services, many of them personal, and few of them can be automated or in other ways depersonalized.

Individual local authorities are usually very significant employers. In many county towns the county hall or shire hall provides work for more people than any other single undertaking. On average, and the extremes will differ greatly, a local authority will probably employ about 3000 people, with larger bodies, such as the Greater London Council, having 20 times that number on their payrolls.

Table 12.3   Distribution of civil service in main groups and grades 1983

Group or grade	Numbers	Percentage of whole service
Administration group	230 500	35.3
Social Security group (CO and EO grades in DHSS local offices)	48 100	7.4
Professional and technology group	35 100	5.4
Inland Revenue Tax grades	31 900	4.9
Secretarial group (Secretarial and typing staff)	26 000	4.0
Prison officers	16 700	2.5
Science group	14 600	2.2
Open structure (top civil servants)	852	0.1
Other non-industrial grades	116 500	17.9
Total non-industrial grades	520 252	79.7
Industrial grades	132 200	20.3
Total	652 452	100

Source: Civil Service Statistics, 1983, HMSO.

Table 12.4 Results of Higher Executive Officer (Administration) Competition 1973–80 and Higher Executive Officer (Development) Competition 1981–82

Year	Number of candidates nominated by departments (HEOA)	Number of candidates successful at Final Selection Board
1973	43	8
1974	47	4
1975	44	8
1976	36	1
1977	38	8
1978	31	2
1979	20	1
1980	25	1
	(HEOD)	
1981	41	10
1982	40	8

Source: *Report on Selection of Fast Stream Graduate Entrants*, MPO, February 1983.

It is misleading to talk about a 'local government service' as if it were an exact, or even near, equivalent of the civil service. It is not. Although there are national grades for salary purposes, individual occupations vary enormously.

Apart from the diversity of activities, the other main contrast with the civil service is in the backgrounds of local government officers. Whereas the non-industrial civil service, as Table 12.3 shows, consists mainly of 'generalists', the local government service is still dominated by professionals: teachers, engineers, architects, planners, accountants, and so on. Table 12.5 sets out the main occupational groups.

Although the structure is not nearly so clearly defined as in the civil service, local government employees fall into one or other of the following four main groups:

1. chief officers—0.2%;
2. administrative, professional, technical, and clerical staff—19.8%;
3. teachers , police, and firemen—30.0%; and
4. manual workers—50.0%.

If we are to speak of a local government service, as a civil service equivalent, then it is the 20 per cent group of chief officers and administrative, professional, technical, and clerical employees which really constitutes it.

Table 12.5 Local authority manpower as at September 1983 (full time or equivalent)

	Numbers employed (thousands)	% of total
Education: lecturers and teachers	610	24
others	400	16
Construction	191	7.5
Transport	82	3
Social services	300	12
Libraries and museums	39	1.5
Recreation and leisure	137	5.5
Environmental health	25	1
Cleansing	99	4
Housing	54	2
Town and country planning	17	0.5
Fire service	50	2
Police (including cadets, wardens, etc.)	177	7
Courts administration	2	14
Others	340	
Total	2523	100

Source: Monthly Digest of Statistics, HMSO.

Recruitment and training for the public service

The standard way of entering the civil service is still on the basis of open competition. The Civil Service Commission operates an elaborate system of written examinations and interviews which over the years has been improved and refined. For clerical posts GCE 'O' levels are normally required; for executive officer grades, 'A' levels or a degree; and for direct entry into administrative posts, through the administration trainee scheme, an honours degree. In all cases there are written examinations and interviews. The high levels of unemployment in the 1980s, and the consequential competition for jobs, have had their effect on the civil service so that it has become not uncommon to find 'A' level, and even degree, candidates for clerical officer vacancies, and the executive officer grade is becoming increasingly a graduate route.

Administration trainees undergo what was developed in the last war as the 'Method 2' selection process, which involves a series of written tests followed by extensive and intensive interviews by the Civil Service Selection Board. Method 1 which preceded, and then for a time operated alongside, Method 2 put its main emphasis on written examinations.

It is possible to criticize the composition of the present-day civil service but it is difficult to fault the thoroughness and objectivity of the Civil Service Commission's recruitment methods. They are generally more advanced and more rigorously designed than anything operating in local government or in many organizations in the private sector.

Recruitment to local government is not a national function and there is no equivalent of the Civil Service Commission. Each local authority recruits its own staff in its own way. In general it is by open competition, as in the civil service, but usually in a much less structured and developed form. In contrast with the civil service, selection for posts above a certain level involves both permanent officers and elected representatives. The normal pattern of recruitment consists of an open advertisement, written application, and face-to-face interview. Written tests are rarely given and the interview is usually much less elaborate and scientifically designed than its civil service counterpart.

Recruits, who may be school leavers and, increasingly, graduates, will expect to enter one of the professional departments and, if they do not possess an appropriate qualification already, will be required to train in the appropriate profession in order to obtain promotion. The highest levels are normally attained by moving jobs from one authority to another with the ultimate aim of becoming a chief officer of a department.

But the local government service is not run exclusively by the professions. There are general administrators although their role and career chances are relatively limited. They are normally responsible for running administrative and clerical services within departments. They are typically older and have served longer than those in the professional mainstream of a department who are at the same salary level, and the highest position they will normally achieve is that of office manager.

There is also a special kind of administrator in local government, the committee clerk, who normally works in the department of the chief secretary or administrator. His role of servicing the committee can be of key importance in that he will be responsible for assembling the agenda, taking the minutes of the meeting and ensuring that those responsible for taking the action are notified of the committee's decisions.

Training in the civil service is partly 'on the job' and partly external. Since the publication of the Fulton Report there has been an increased emphasis on management training and much of this has been done at the Civil Service College or by use of external agencies. On-the-job training has long been a feature of the service and has varied from, at its worst, 'sitting next to and learning from Nelly' to well-designed development programmes. There is evidence that internal training has improved considerably in recent years. The use of the Job Appraisal Review (JAR) system has helped to identify training needs and make training more systematic. The system involves an annual interview between a civil servant and an immediate superior in which the interviewee's job and the way he has performed it during the preceding twelve months or so are jointly evaluated. Most central departments operate the system for Executive Officer up to Principal grades. In some cases it has been used with lower grades.

Qualifications are an important factor in obtaining an appointment and for promotion in local government, and a concern that local authority staff should be properly trained for the job has been regularly expressed by the National Joint Council of the white collar trade unions and employers since its inception in 1943. However, despite this expressed concern and the fact that local government employs a large number of manual workers, much of the responsibility for training has been left to the professional associations and individual officers, and little emphasis has been placed on training for manual workers. It is also true that much of the training effort has been primarily concerned with the acquisition of professional and other qualifications by examination, perhaps to the extent that they are sometimes seen as ends in themselves rather than as means to the better running of a service. This contrasts with training in industry which was concerned until the 1960s, when management training grew rapidly, with craft apprenticeships aimed at improving work performance; training in industry has also traditionally been at the instigation and expense of the employer. It is surprising that since local authorities control further education, they do not make more use of its resources; a few undoubtedly do but in most cases it is the private sector which is the greatest user of further education.

Nevertheless, the **Local Government Training Board** set up in 1967 to ensure that training for local government was financed and carried out, has done something to advance training, especially in those areas not covered by the professional institutes, such as manual work, management development, personnel management, and general administration. It has also stimulated a concern for training within local authorities by encouraging the appointment of training officers and regular surveys by local authorities to check that manpower of the right kind and in the right numbers is available.

The image of the public servant

Public servants have rarely been popular. At best they are seen by the general public as a necessary item of expenditure. At worst they are considered to be an unnecessary extravagance. They are generally described as 'unproductive', with the implication that production is something which only occurs in factories and similar places. Few people stop to consider the *service* aspect of the civil service or the local government service. The emphasis tends always to be on cost rather than on output. This is something which people working in central and local government have lived with for a long time and most of them are resigned to it. How much of this public attitude is attributable to the behaviour and attitudes of civil servants and local government officers themselves? Some blame must surely be attached to them.

Anyone who has walked down the anonymous corridors of council offices or a government department inevitably has the impression of remoteness and impersonality. The worst features of bureaucracy seem to be reflected there. Why should not all local and central government offices to which ordinary members of the public have to go be bright and inviting, at least in the reception areas? Why should their hours of opening be geared to the needs of their employees rather than their clients and customers? Should there not be more positive attempts to let the public know of the services to which they are entitled and for which they are largely paying? Too often, however, 'public relations' is seen as a very low priority provision, particularly among elected representatives of local authorities.

It must, in honesty, be said that governments since 1979 have done little to improve this public image. Indeed, public service has been denigrated more frequently than it has been praised, resulting in an appreciable fall in morale in both the civil and local government services. This is an aspect we shall examine further in the next chapter.

References

1. Jaques, E. *A General Theory of Bureaucracy*, Heinemann, 1976.
2. Weber, M. *The Theory of Social and Economic Organization*, trans. Henderson and Parsons, Free Press of Glencoe, Illinois, 1964.
3. *Organization of the Permanent Civil Service*, Parliamentary Papers, 1854, vol. 27.
4. *Recruitment to the Civil Service*, HC 308, HMSO, 1965.
5. *Report of the Committee on the Civil Service*, 5 vols, HMSO, 1968.

Assignments

20. Discuss the pros and cons of seeking a career in the public service at the present time.
21. 'People who work in the public services are passengers we cannot afford.' Reply to this critical statement from the standpoint of either a civil servant or a local government employee.

    The statement could also be used as the motion for a debate.

Sources: Two articles in the quarterly journal *Public Administration* should be particularly useful: Sir Ian Bancroft *The Civil Service in the 1980s*, Summer 1981, vol. 59; and Sir Douglas Wass *The Public Service in Modern Society*, Spring 1983, vol. 61, no. 1.

13

Industrial relations in the public sector

The nature of industrial relations

By industrial relations we mean the relationships between the people employed and the people who employ them. In other words, the relationships between workers and management, because in the majority of cases 'employers' are institutions of one kind or another and are represented in their dealings with employees by paid, professional managers.

These relationships include four main aspects:

1. conditions of employment, including hours of work and remuneration;
2. the ways in which both sides, employers and employees, conduct their negotiations over conditions of employment;
3. the contractual obligations of each side to the other, and of both to the state; and
4. the degree to which the two parties consult each other about the way in which the organization for which they both work should be run.

At one time it was possible to speak of industrial relations in a strictly bilateral sense, with employers on the one side and employees on the other. Today there is a third party whose significance is growing year by year: the state. There has always been some government involvement in relations between employers and employees. In the post-war years, and particularly during the past decade, this involvement has grown immeasurably; not only has the state placed obligations on employers and employees towards itself, it has also placed obligations on them towards each other.

In this chapter we will be looking specifically at industrial relations in the public sector but, before we do so, let us identify the differences, if any, between such relationships and those in the private sector.

Public and private sectors compared

In its Report, published in 1968, the Donovan Royal Commission on Trade Unions and Employers' Associations said: 'Britain has two systems of industrial relations. The one is the formal system embodied in the official institutions. The other is the informal system created by the actual behaviour of trade unions and employers' associations, of manager, shop steward and workers.'[1]

The Report went on to say: 'The keystone of the formal structure is the industry-wide collective agreement. . . . The informal system rests on the wide autonomy of managers in individual companies and factories, and the power of industrial work groups.' These quotations from the Donovan Commission highlight one of the most significant differences between industrial relations in the public and private sectors: in the public sector national collective bargaining is the order of the day, whereas in the private sector, even though national or industry-wide agreements exist, they are liable to be overtaken by local plant or workplace bargaining.

The second major point of difference is that in the public sector the government is, directly or indirectly, the paymaster and therefore in a stronger position to impress its views on what should be acceptable conditions of employment than it is in the private sector.

These two differences are of supreme importance and have significant implications for employees in the public sector. In this chapter we will use a wide definition of the public sector and include not only the civil and local government services but also the *ad hoc* regional authorities and the public corporations and other bodies in the public field.

Collective bargaining in the public sector

Collective bargaining is a term used to describe an agreement concerning pay and conditions of work settled between trade unions on the one hand and an employer or association of employers on the other. It therefore covers any negotiations in which employees do not negotiate separately but collectively, through representatives.

The virtually universal instrument for collective bargaining in the public sector is the national joint council, which is usually reproduced at area and local levels. Each council consists of two groups, one representing the employers and the other the employees. In the civil service, local government, the health service, and some of the other *ad hoc* authorities, the joint bodies are referred to as Whitley Councils. In the nationalized industries they are usually called joint industrial councils. Whichever term is used the origins of the bodies are the same. In 1916 the government set up a committee, under the chairmanship of J.H. Whitley MP, to suggest improvements in industrial relations. The Committee produced five wide-ranging reports[2] which recommended, among other things, the formation of joint industrial councils as a means of bringing employers and employees together to discuss common interests and, in particular, conditions of employment.

Many people hoped that the **Whitley Council** idea would spread to all parts of industry and so create a straightforward method of anticipating and resolving disagreements between management and labour, and also develop joint consultation about ways of improving working methods as well as working conditions. The idea did not attract the widespread support that had been anticipated although in the two years immediately following the publication of the Whitley Committee's Reports 73 joint industrial councils were set up. This number had dropped to 45 in 1938 and, although support for the system revived in the post-war years, the maximum number has been around two hundred.

The Whitley Council concept is now found predominantly, but not wholly, in the public sector. The system was adopted for the civil service in 1919, and in the same year a National Joint Council for local authority manual workers was set up; similar arrangements for local authority administrative, and clerical staff followed soon afterwards, and eventually, over a longer period of time, it spread to all levels of local authority employees.

The nationalized industries which had local government origins, such as gas, electricity, and water, had had experience of national joint negotiating bodies. Those

140

which had previously been privately owned were mostly new to the idea. In each case the legislation setting up the public corporation which was to control the industry placed an obligation on the board to establish national joint councils for conciliation and consultation. In evidence given to the Donovan Royal Commission, the senior managements of the nationalized industries said, without hesitation, that had there not been a legal obligation to set up the machinery they would still have adopted it as the best method of bringing the two sides of industry together.

Whether called a Whitley Council or a joint industrial council, the membership, structure, and methods are broadly similar. A council consists of two corresponding groups, one representing employers, or the official side, and one representing employees, or the staff side. In the civil service the chairman is invariably a member of the official side. In other cases the council usually decides from which side the chairman should be drawn, or whether there should be a chairman for each side, or whether he should be an independent person from outside the organization. Questions discussed by Whitley Councils are not settled by vote: either the two sides reach a unanimous decision, probably on the basis of compromise, or there is deadlock and no decision at all; in the event of this happening recourse to arbitration is available.

An arbitration tribunal normally consists of an independent chairman presiding over two equal-sized groups: one nominated by employers and the other by employees. In theory, following a failure to agree in a Whitley or joint industrial council, either side can seek arbitration. In practice, usually the staff, or employees', side does so.

Public sector trade unionism

Negotiations in Whitley Councils or joint industrial councils are conducted, on the employees' side, by their union representatives. A civil servant is free to be a member of any association or trade union and, indeed, is normally encouraged to join, although the banning from union membership of staff employed in sensitive security areas, such as GCHQ at Cheltenham, has raised doubts about the willingness of all governments to encourage union representation. Membership of trade unions is open and generally encouraged in the local government service and other parts of the public sector.

Non-industrial civil servants are represented in negotiations by staff associations or by the Civil Service Union. A staff association is really a trade union, and any civil service association is free to register officially as such, and to affiliate to the TUC, if it chooses. There are eight associations nationally recognized for negotiation purposes within the Whitley Council machinery. The biggest are:

Civil and Public Services Association (CPSA): about 220 000 members, mainly performing clerical duties
Institution of Professional Civil Servants (IPCS): about 100 000 members, mainly in professional and technical posts
Society of Civil and Public Servants (SCPS): about 100 000 members performing administrative and executive work
Inland Revenue Staff Federation (RSF): about 65 000 members in the Inland Revenue
Civil Service Union (CSU): about 47 000 members who are mostly in manual, non-industrial posts.

141

Some civil service staff associations are quite small, such as the Association of First Division Civil Servants, which represents the more senior administrators.

In the Civil Service National Whitley Council the staff side consists of representatives from the various staff associations while the official side comprises, not ministers, but senior civil servants, including most permanent secretaries of the main central departments. The full composition is shown in Table 13.1.

Table 13.1   Normal composition of Civil Service National Whitley Council. (There are also departmental Whitley Councils)

Chairman:	Cabinet Secretary and Head of Home Civil Service		
Vice-Chairman:	Secretary General, Civil and Public Services Association		
Official side:	Treasury	6	
	Department of the Environment	1	
	Department of Employment	1	
	Department of Education and Science	1	
	Ministry of Defence	1	
	Cabinet Office/MPO	3	
	Scottish Office	1	
	Department of Health and Social Security	1	
	Ministry of Agriculture Fisheries and Food	1	
	Home Office	1	
	Board of Inland Revenue	1	
	Customs and Excise	1	
	Department of Trade and Industry	2	
	Department of Energy	1	
	Department of Transport	1	
	Law Officers' Department	1	
	Treasury Solicitors	1	
	Welsh Office	1	26
Staff side:	Civil and Public Services Association	9	
	Civil Service Union	3	
	Inland Revenue Staff Federation	2	
	Society of Civil and Public Servants	4	
	Association of Inspectors of Taxes	1	
	Prison Officers' Association	1	
	Institute of Professional Civil Servants	4	
	Association of First Division Civil Servants	1	
	Association of Government Supervisors and Radio Officers	1	
	Assistant Secretary	1	27

Industrial civil servants enjoy a slightly more complex form of Whitleyism. For them there is no single National Council but three Trade Joint Councils (for shipbuilding, engineering, and miscellaneous trades) and Departmental Councils. The main trade unions for industrial civil servants are the **Transport and General Workers' Union (TGWU)**, the **General and Municipal Workers' Union (GMWU)**, and the **Amalgamated Union of Engineering Workers (AUEW)**. The TGWU and GMWU are both general, as distinct from craft, unions and they represent, in negotiations with employers, a wide range of occupational groups. The AEUW has a more specific representation of industrial civil servants in engineering posts. All these unions perform a similar role, in the collective bargaining process, to the one they have in the private sector, except that they do so through established Whitley Council machinery.

In local government Whitleyism operates through Joint Negotiating Committees for senior officers, and National Joint Councils for Administrative, Professional, Technical and Clerical Services, and for manual workers. Employers are represented on these bodies by a range of local authority associations. Non-manual staff are represented by a number of trade unions, associations, and institutions, the biggest, and most significant, being the **National and Local Government Officers' Association (NALGO)**. Manual workers' main unions are the **National Union of Public Employees (NUPE)**, the GMWU and the TGWU. In addition to the National Councils, there are Provincial or District Councils. Specific councils have been set up to negotiate terms and conditions of service for the fire service and the police, and teachers have their own national joint committees for negotiating purposes. The Health Service has another set of Whitley Councils for its various constituent parts.

As we have already noted, joint collective machinery is well established in all the nationalized industries, most of it set up in accordance with the Act of Parliament which created each individual public corporation or authority. In each case the employers' side consists of representatives of the board of the public corporation or authority. There is a wide range of unions representing workers at all levels and in all kinds of occupations in the nationalized industries and other public bodies, each usually reflecting a specific kind or area of work. Some of the best known ones include the **National Union of Mineworkers (NUM)**, the **Union of Communication Workers (UCW)**, formerly the Post Office Workers' Union, the **Confederation of Health Service Employees (COHSE)**, the **National Union of Railwaymen (NUR)**, and the **Post Office Engineering Union (POEU)**. This is just a cross-section: there are many more.

Public sector pay and working conditions

It would be misleading to exaggerate the operational differences between the public and the private sectors. The methods and working conditions, particularly at operative level, are not very dissimilar. It is nearer the top, in the policy-making area, that public and private sectors tend to diverge.

In the nationalized industries, apart from the emphasis on national collective bargaining which we have already noted, methods of determining pay are also similar to those in the private sector. Plant productivity bargaining is as much in evidence in public enterprise as in private enterprise; this is demonstrated, for example, by the widely publicized productivity agreements in the coal mining industry. In some nationalized industries levels of pay are among the highest in the country, coal-face workers being a good example: in others they lag behind those in the private sector. Much depends on the strength of bargaining power the unions have and the profitability of the particular industry. In the civil service and in local government it is not possible to use profitability as a criterion for determining competitive rates of pay and other standards have to be taken into account.

The Priestley Royal Commission on the Civil Service,[3] which reported in 1955, argued that it was necessary to establish general principles governing civil service pay so as to ensure 'the maintenance of a civil service recognized as efficient and staffed by members whose remuneration and conditions of service are thought fair both by themselves and by the community they serve'. The Report went on to say that the primary principle determining pay should be 'fair comparison with the current remuneration of outside staffs employed on broadly comparable work, taking account of differences in other conditions of service', and that internal relativities should be used to supplement this primary principle. The Royal Commission's recommendations were considered by the National Whitley Council which announced in April 1956 its acceptance of 'fair comparison' as a valid and valuable principle in civil service pay negotiations, although not the only determinant. Both sides of the National Whitley Council agreed on the setting up of a fact-finding body to be called the Civil Service Pay Research Unit, under the general control and direction of the National Whitley Council, to do two things: first, to establish job comparability between the civil service and outside occupations; second, to discover the pay and conditions of service attached to jobs regarded as comparable.

Following a major dispute in 1981, the government appointed Sir John Megaw, a retired High Court judge, to chair an inquiry into civil service pay. The Report was published in July, 1982.[4] Its main conclusion was that fair comparison should continue to be used as the basis for pay evaluation but that other factors, such as 'recruitment and retention of staff', should also be taken into account. The Megaw Inquiry obviously tried to reach a compromise between the Priestley view and that of the government of the day which wanted to see a much stronger reflection of market forces.

This principle of 'fair comparison' therefore underlies all pay and conditions of service in the civil service and has gone some way towards ensuring that civil servants do not lag behind their opposite numbers, as the Civil Service Pay Research Unit identifies them, in the private sector. The principle is not always put into practice, however, and the series of strikes by civil servants in the early months of 1979 were mainly the result of the government's disinclination to pay awards on the basis of comparability because of their anticipated inflationary effects.

There is no exactly comparable principle or organization operating in local government. The thought of 'comparable pay for comparable work' undoubtedly lies beneath the surface and is often argued in negotiations between employing authorities and employees' representatives. One fairly common way in which the pay of local authority employees is determined objectively is by the use of *ad hoc* committees and review bodies. A good example of this practice is the Houghton Committee on Teachers' Pay[5] which made its recommendations in 1974. The disadvantage of adopting an *ad hoc* approach, as opposed to having a permanent review body, is that in a period of high inflation a pay award resulting from an objective *ad hoc* review can soon be overtaken by events and become out of phase with the pay of comparable workers whose conditions of service are more closely geared to market forces and inflationary trends.

To ascertain the appropriate rates of remuneration for the chairmen and board members of the nationalized industries, judges, senior civil servants, senior officers in the armed forces, Members of Parliament, and other 'top people' in the public sector, the government appointed, in May 1971, a Top Salaries Review Body. It reports directly to the Prime Minister. As soon as it was set up it was asked to undertake an immediate review of the salaries of these senior groups, and to carry out further reviews at two-yearly intervals. Its current chairman is Lord Plowden.

An incomes policy in the public sector

There is considerable debate about what is an incomes policy, let alone whether it is advisable to have one. A statutory incomes policy which clearly states norms and maxima for pay awards, with penalties for employers exceeding the maxima, is understandable even if its merits are debatable. A voluntary incomes policy whereby the government enunciates criteria for pay awards and urges employers to adhere to them 'in the national interest' is rather less understandable, in that it is difficult to see how it can be enforced if it is voluntary, and hence more debatable. One thing is certain, however, whether the government of the day professes to have a statutory incomes policy, a voluntary incomes policy, or no incomes policy at all, is that as a direct or indirect employer it can do a lot to influence pay and conditions of service in the public sector. Indeed, it will often feel obliged to set an example for pay awards in the public sector so as to influence awards in the private sector. Virtually all post-war governments, whether or not they have confessed to having one, have employed an incomes policy in the public sector, and most have used it as an overt or covert way of applying one to the economy in general.

It can be argued, with some justification, that the ability, and often the determination, of the government to influence, and sometimes even control, public sector pay, as an example to the private sector, is unfair discrimination. Yet, seen from the government's viewpoint, the temptation to intervene in such a significant sector of the national economy is virtually irresistible. The way to avoid similar 'discrimination' against public sector employees in the future would be to strengthen and extend the fair comparison principle used in the civil service and apply it generally throughout the public sector, or at least to that part of it which is well insulated from normal market forces.

The significance of good industrial relations in the public sector

Before we can assess the significance of good relations in the public sector we must try to define what we mean by *good*. Most people would probably interpret good industrial relations as meaning harmonious relationships between managements and workers, to use generalized terminology, particularly in the four aspects which we identified at the beginning of this chapter.

Harmonious relationships need not mean that managements are always getting things done in exactly the way they wish or, conversely, that workers are getting everything they demand in terms of working conditions, methods, and remuneration. There is such a thing as a 'style' of management, and some managers will achieve and maintain harmonious relationships on the basis of consultation, compromise, and agreement while others will succeed with a much firmer and more positive approach. The methods or styles are less important than the results achieved.

Good industrial relations are perhaps best identified by looking at recognizable indicators, such as a willingness to accept change and improvements; a willingness to use the available channels for airing grievances; and an absence of open disputes. In every work situation differences of opinion will arise over working methods, conditions, and rates of pay. If relationships are poor these differences will develop into confrontations, and they in turn may result in open disputes involving either

145

strike action or failure of workers and management to cooperate with each other. Apart from the loss of output which a dispute can cause, its effects on long-term cooperation can be considerable; thus any individual organization must suffer from the effects of bad industrial relations.

As we have frequently noted, the public sector constitutes, in economic terms, a significant part of the total national picture. If bad industrial relations exist there the repercussions will be great because of the sheer size of the sector. There are other reasons for their significance. First because of direct or indirect government involvement, the public sector is often seen as setting the national pattern of industrial behaviour: irresponsibility there can breed irresponsibility elsewhere. Second, much of the public sector is concerned with providing vital goods and services: often under monopolistic conditions. If we think for a moment of the kinds of things the public sector provides we will readily appreciate the implications: the maintenance of law and order; fire prevention and fighting; the provision of coal, gas, electricity, oil, and atomic energy; the supply of water, sewage disposal; medical and hospital services; the provision of a national communications system; traffic control; consumer protection, and so on. Some services we can manage without for short periods of time: some are indispensable; the loss of any would, in the long term, at the very least lower the standard of life.

Industrial relations in the nationalized industries have been, at best, patchy. Indeed, we have experienced major disputes in most of the major publicly owned industries. The failure of the nationalized industries significantly to improve their methods and machinery of industrial relations is disappointing, and perhaps surprising. There has been more successful innovation in the private sector than in the public; consultation procedures, conciliation methods, and productivity bargaining have more often than not been pioneered in the private sector. We can speculate on the reasons for this: greater freedom to innovate, perhaps; the enjoyment of more flexibility than a large bureaucratic organization allows; greater recognition, through the profit motive, of the need to be efficient and cost effective. Whatever the reasons, it must be said that public ownership has not so far achieved the improvements in industrial relations which most of its proponents want.

For most of the post-war period the situation in the civil and local government services has been good, even though, because of government economic and financial policies, relations have been subjected at times to some strain. In view of this generally good record, it is sad to comment that there has been a marked deterioration in the 1980s.

The, sometimes understandable, need of the government of the day to try to restrict public spending by putting restrictions on public pay settlements has been accompanied by an often publicly expressed view by ministers that the public sector is, at best, a necessary evil. It is conceded that some services cannot be provided other than by government but there has recently been a progressively active campaign to reduce the size of the public sector by a policy of 'privatization'. Its effect has been to make many public servants feel almost parasitic with a consequential lowering of their morale. If such a policy were embarked upon in the private sector it is certain that it would be deplored by everyone, in and out of government.

Perhaps some of the arguments set out in the Northcote-Trevelyan Report of 1854,[6] to which we have already referred, might usefully be remembered. The following quotation seems particularly apposite:

. . . as matters now stand, the Government of the country could not be carried on without the aid of an efficient body of permanent officers, occupying a position duly subordinate to that of the Ministers who are directly responsible to the Crown and to Parliament, yet possessing sufficient independence, character, ability, and experience to be able to advise, assist, and to some extent, influence those who are from time to time set over them.

It would be unfortunate, indeed dangerous, if in the future we were, as a nation, to be served by a body of people disenchanted about their role, uneasy about their future, and no longer proud to be of public service.

References

1. *Report of the Royal Commission on Trade Unions and Employers' Associations*, Cmd. 3623, HMSO, 1968.
2. *Reports of the Committee on Relations between Employers and Employed, 1916–18*, Cmd. 8606, Cmd. 9001, Cmd. 9099, Cmd. 9153, HMSO.
3. *Report of the Royal Commission on the Civil Service*, Cmd. 9613, HMSO, 1955.
4. *Inquiry into Civil Service Pay*, Cmnd. 8590, HMSO, 1982.
5. *Report of the Committee of Inquiry into the Pay of Non-University Teachers*, Cmnd. 5848, 1974.
6. *Organization of the Permanent Civil Service*, Parliamentary Papers, 1854, vol. 27.

Assignments

22. 'Whatever government is in power it always has an incomes policy for the public sector.' Do you agree with this statement? Give a reasoned answer.
23. Why, despite Whitley Council and other national consultative machinery, have industrial relations in the public sector been less than perfect in the past 20 years?

Part Four   The state and the economy

14

Policies: the end-product of government

Policies as the justification of government

Earlier in this book we concluded that politicians and their parties seek power so that they can use the machinery of government to make what they believe will be improvements in social and economic conditions. Although not everyone is likely to agree that what politicians want to do will in fact be improvements, we must accept that these are their intentions. The proposals put forward to effect these improvements we call policies. In a representative democracy all the apparatus of representation through election has, if we pause to think about it, only one end-product: policies.

A political party which does not gain power is ineffectual, a politician who does not win an election will lose credibility; an interest group which is unable to influence the government in areas of concern to its members will eventually forfeit their support. At the end of the day, to use a cliché favoured by politicians, it is action which counts and policies represent action, or, at least, proposals for action.

Sources of policy

A policy, then, is a proposal to do something. Where do policies come from? We can identify the main sources, in no intentional order of priority:

Party conferences
Study groups within political parties
Interest groups
Formal advisory bodies
Ministers
Civil servants
Policy reviews
Public opinion
Backbench MPs
International commitments

Political party conferences are obvious arenas for policy making. Indeed, the resolutions carried at the end of each conference debate are intended to form the basis of policies for the party when in power. The likelihood of a conference proposal ever becoming government policy depends on a number of factors, the chief of which is whether, in the eyes of the politicians who have to take the final decision as members of the government, it is a practical proposition. The practicability of a proposal will be influenced, and even in some cases determined, by the views of senior civil servants, as we shall see later.

Traditionally and philosophically, Labour governments have felt more obliged to implement conference decisions than the Conservatives, but even a Labour government, with a sincere belief in democratic decision taking, may find that practical politics prevent implementation. The views of conference are likely to have their strongest influence in the early stage of a new government when the 'policy slate' is clean. After some years in office conference decisions have to be more and more trimmed to the realities of life.

The major political parties have research departments which from time to time produce papers that may eventually provide the basis for policy proposals. **Research departments** and **study groups within parties** are likely to be most active when manifestos to be used during general election campaigns are being drawn up. Like conference decisions, proposals from internal party studies have eventually to pass the test of political practicability.

We have considered the characteristics and activities of **interest groups** in some detail earlier in this book. Their views can sometimes find themselves translated into firm policy, but it is more usual for interest groups to be influential in shaping the details of policy than in instigating completely new proposals.

Formal advisory bodies are a rich source of policy formulation. At the present time there are about 500 national advisory bodies which have been set up by government. Additionally, there are those operating at regional and local levels. National advisory bodies are of two main types: 'standing' bodies which have been established on a more or less permanent basis to give advice to a minister on a particular aspect of the work of his department, and *ad hoc* bodies which are set up to look at a specific problem and which are wound up after they have reported. Standing advisory bodies are used chiefly for monitoring the progress of policy and suggesting adjustments to it. Advice for major, long-term policy is generally sought from the *ad hoc* bodies.

There are two main forms of *ad hoc* advisory bodies: the **royal commission** and the **departmental committee**. The essential differences between them are not easy to determine. Indeed, an examination of them in recent years does not readily explain why sometimes a government will use a royal commission as its advisory vehicle and sometimes a departmental committee. Each usually consists of about twelve people under a chairman, selected and appointed by a minister and given precise terms of reference to inquire into a particular problem or aspect of life and to draw conclusions and make recommendations. Chairmen of royal commissions or departmental committees are usually people of some eminence and are more often than not experienced lawyers. Each commission or committee normally has a secretariat consisting of civil servants seconded to it for the duration of its existence. Members of a royal commission or departmental committee are generally drawn from the 'central list' or the list of the 'good and the great', as it is popularly called, to which we have referred in earlier chapters.

The royal commission, as its name implies, has greater status than a departmental committee. Its members are appointed under royal warrant, and once set up it has a life which can only be self-terminating. This means that if, for example, a Labour government appoints a royal commission to inquire into some particular matter it will continue to do its work, according to its terms of reference, even when the government which set it up has gone and has been replaced by a Conservative one. In most cases a departmental committee, once established, will also be given an opportunity to complete its work but it could be wound up by the minister who set it up or by his successor.

Having identified these differences between royal commissions and departmental committees it is still difficult to determine why sometimes one is used and sometimes the other. For example, the civil service has, during the present century, been the subject of investigations by both royal commissions and departmental committees and the fact that it was at one time a commission reporting and at another time a committee seems to have had little bearing on the importance of the inquiry or the standing of the subsequent report. It is surprising that the inquiry into higher education under Lord Robbins, between 1961 and 1963, was at departmental committee level, whereas university education in Dundee was investigated under Lord Tedder, between 1951 and 1952, by a royal commission. Some notable royal commissions and departmental committees in recent years have been the Kilbrandon Royal Commission on the Constitution (1973), the Fulton Departmental Committee on the Civil Service (1968), and the Donovan Royal Commission on Trade Unions and Employers' Associations (1968).

As a source of policy formulation royal commissions and departmental committees are undeniably important. A survey of the Acts of Parliament which have been passed during the present century confirms the extent to which they have been the result of royal commission or committee reports. The total is impressive.

Departmental ministers will occasionally propose policies which are clearly personal to them. Just as many people have a book within them waiting to be written, so a politician sometimes cherishes an idea which he hopes eventually to translate into something tangible. Often he is prevented from doing so because he is not given the department of his choice, or because resources are not available, or there is insufficient parliamentary time. Ministers, obviously, can have a considerable influence on policy. It would, however, be an exaggeration to say that they frequently formulate it themselves.

The influence of **senior civil servants** on policy is immeasurable. After all, it is they who have to live with policy implementation long after the temporary politicians who introduced it have moved on to other things. It is therefore understandable that they will be anxious to ensure that any proposed policy is implementable. As far as the initiation of the policy is concerned the role the civil servant plays is complex. If a minister clearly knows what he wants to do there is no doubt, as we have already agreed in our discussion of the minister–permanent secretary relationship, that the civil service will accept his views and implement his policies, only interrupting to advise him of any potential problems which may result. If, however, the minister has no clear policy proposals in some particular area it is equally certain that the civil service will not permit a gap to exist for very long and will fill it with views of its own.

We should also note that there are always long-term, 'internal' policies in most central departments which are retained by the permanent civil servants through successive changes of ministers. This permanent policy provides the continuity of action which political changes potentially can destroy. In some cases a policy becomes firmly embedded within a department and a minister will have to be extremely resolute and strong-willed if he is to change it.

Policies are subject to **continual review**, either at the instigation of a minister or of civil servants. In other words, the effects of policy decisions are monitored, and if

153

thought necessary changes are made. The outcome of such a review can be, in effect, more than a restatement of policy: it can be the formulation of a completely new one. Policy formulation should really be seen as a circular process which is self-feeding and self-regulating as Fig. 14.1 shows.

Occasionally **popular opinion** on a particular topic can become so intense that it breaks through any political barriers and forces itself on the government of the day. In recent years there has been a national outcry in this country each autumn against proposals to cull, or weed out, grey seals in the Orkney Islands so as to preserve fish stocks. The government's view, on the basis of expert advice, has been that the culling is necessary because of the vast quantities of fish the seals consume. Other expert opinion has been divided, but mass opinion has been overwhelmingly against the practice. Special interest groups, such as the RSPCA, have naturally been active in trying to persuade the Secretary of State for Scotland to reconsider his policy, but popular opinion, through the mass media, has in the long run had the greatest effect. This negative action, against policy, is more common than positive proposals stemming from popular opinion, mainly because it is rare that a mass view crystallizes into a coherent policy proposition.

Backbench MPs are often thought of as almost 'politically emasculated', obeying the party whips and voting as ordered. On major issues of party policy this may be so, but in other areas they can be very influential. In recent years two backbench Labour members immediately spring to mind: Leo Abse and Jack Ashley. Both have had notable successes in introducing policy proposals on controversial issues and having the satisfaction of seeing them translated into Acts of Parliament. Mr Abse was successful in securing radical amendments to divorce law, and Mr Ashley brought about major changes in social service policy and legislation. The obstacles in the way of an ordinary MP are considerable and the chances of his making a great impact on policy are not great. Nevertheless, as Leo Abse and Jack Ashley have shown, it can be done.

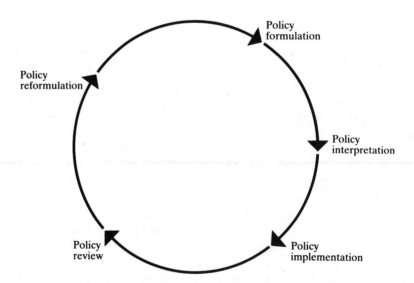

Fig. 14.1 The circle of policy formulation

The reports of the **House of Commons specialist committees**, which we shall look at in Chapter 19, can also be a source of policy.

Finally, policy can be strongly influenced, and sometimes determined, by decisions taken outside this country. As discussed in Chapter 11, membership of international bodies, such as the EEC, NATO, and the United Nations Organization, compels Britain to adopt policies, or modify existing policies, to comply with the obligations of membership. Some of the clearest examples of these can be found in the effects of the Common Agricultural Policy (CAP) of the EEC. Some aspects of this policy have been fiercely questioned and contested by British ministers and sometimes they have been successful in getting the policy changed. Nevertheless it is having an increasingly evident effect on the domestic economy and it is an inexorable process which will not stop until the agricultural policies of all EEC members are completely harmonized. This is just one example of how **international obligations** can force policy upon us. There are many more.

The policy-making process

Let us pause for a moment to consider the policy-making process. How does an idea translate itself into a firm policy for action? We have considered the main sources from which a policy can arise. The original source is, of course, an idea or group of ideas which, after discussion, is formulated and set out as a coherent proposal. Before a proposal can become an item of major policy it will need to secure Cabinet endorsement but before this happens a long process of consideration will take place.

Initially the idea will be turned over, usually within a department, by both ministers and civil servants. The advantages and disadvantages will be weighed one against the other, and the consequences that would be likely to follow its implementation are analysed. Throughout this process, which could last for weeks or months, the idea will gradually harden as ambiguities are resolved and consequences more clearly identified. Then at some stage the hardening process will be such that the original idea has become a firm basis for policy and from then onwards it will become more and more difficult for the proposal to be blocked. When this stage has been reached a policy proposition will be ripe for Cabinet consideration and, with the Prime Minister's full agreement, it will be put on the Cabinet agenda. Before it is considered by the full Cabinet it is likely that it will be given to an appropriate Cabinet committee for examination and then, in time, placed before a normal Cabinet meeting.

Once approved by the Cabinet the policy will usually be published for external consideration in the form of a White Paper. This is, in effect, a public notification of a major policy proposal and a White Paper is normally the basis of a Bill to be placed before Parliament.

We shall be discussing the extent to which ordinary members of the public should, and can, participate in the policy-making process in a later chapter, and we will see then that an intermediate stage is sometimes introduced before the publication of a White Paper, in the form of a discussion document, often called a Green Paper, the purpose of which is to stimulate popular discussion before firm policy is announced. Whether or not this intermediate stage is used, it is obvious that the policy-making process is often long and complicated. An interesting thought emerges from all this. It is that public decision making is, more often than not, taken not by individuals but by groups of people. What is perhaps even more interesting is that, during the process of discussion we have just looked at, a decision is just as likely to 'emerge' from the logic of the arguments presented, as from any one individual or group of individuals taking part in discussion.

Assignment

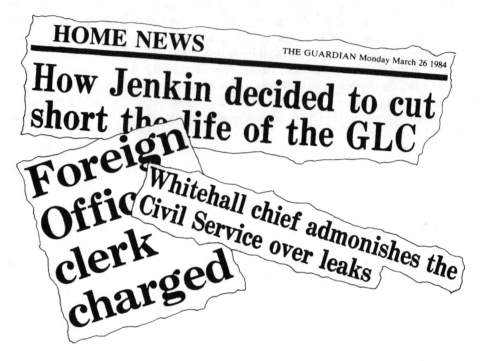

24. The development of the government's policy for abolishing the metropolitan counties was 'leaked' in *The Guardian* on 26 March 1984. Read *The Guardian*'s account and compare its conclusions with those reached by at least two other newspapers.

15
The government as a planner

The nature of planning

Planning is a word that has been in and out of favour with politicians over the years. The left-winger will embrace the concept of planning because it implies for him the control of communal resources to secure socialist aims. The right-winger will perhaps deplore it because for him it implies an unnecessary interference by the state in the affairs of private individuals and groups. Both kinds of politician, if pressed on the point, would acknowledge that their own personal lives involve a mixture of planned and unplanned activity. It would not be surprising to find that the right-wing politician plans his life more thoroughly than his left-wing counterpart. Nevertheless, in a political context, planning can be an emotive word. Stripping emotion from it, we can analyse it as a statement of possible activity. Planning involves three elements:

1. forecasting future events or situations which are not within immediate control;
2. preparing action to be taken to secure certain ends in the light of these forecasts; and
3. forecasting the likely effects of such actions.

All successful organizations plan. Without planning the future becomes a lottery and the present a series of pragmatic responses to unpredictable happenings. Some element of planning is part of all our lives: we keep diaries to regulate and record our activities; we use maps to prepare routes for journeys we intend to make; we have to budget our incomes for a week, or a month, or even longer. The concept of 'family planning' is no longer a novelty but a part of everyday life. There is, therefore, nothing particularly novel about planning itself: the novelty in the post-war years has been attempts by governments to plan the social and economic affairs of the whole nation.

In this chapter we will consider three areas, or kinds, of planning which governments have practised increasingly in the post-1945 years: manpower planning, physical planning, and indicative economic planning. In all three cases planning has been seen as necessary because resources are limited and consequently have to be husbanded and used to their greatest effect. If there was no economic problem, in other words, if resources were not scarce relative to the demands we wish to make on them, planning would be largely unnecessary. Even time, which is arguably the scarcest resource, needs to be planned. How many times have you secretly regretted that you 'missed the boat' through lack of planning?

People: the ultimate scarce resource

With over three million, or nearly 12 per cent, of the working population, unemployed, it may seem ironic to speak of people as a scarce resource. It is nevertheless true. Labour is and always will be a scarce resource, and as such it is the major part of the cost of many products, even agricultural products. An illustration of this can be found in circumstances when farmers decline to harvest an over-plentiful crop because they fear that if they did so they would depress market prices below the level of the labour costs incurred in harvesting.

Admittedly, the scarcity of labour is sometimes artificially created, even in times of significant unemployment. Particular crafts or professions will, by means of restrictive entry qualifications, try to limit the number of newcomers. Some trade unions still support outdated apprenticeship arrangements, not because they are convinced that lengthy training is necessary but because they are a means of containing the size of a skilled labour force. Even if all these artificial restrictions were removed it is virtually certain that people, as a factor of production, would be in short supply. Not perhaps as a total, unclassified factor, but as an aggregate of specific, identified skills.

At the present time, when unemployment in most people's opinion is at an unacceptably high level, there are still obvious shortages of skilled labour. The computer and data processing industry needs more programmers, systems analysts, and maintenance technicians. Accountants are at a premium in industry. Skilled and experienced secretarial workers are in great demand in most large cities, particularly in the Greater London area. People, then, when they have a developed, usable skill, are almost invariably in demand. Sometimes, of course, their specific skills become obsolete because they have been overtaken by some technological development. Sometimes, in an attempt to meet some anticipated demand, too many people are trained in a particular skill and the market is saturated. When, therefore, we consider people as a scarce resource we must remember that we are looking at them in a dynamic, rather than static, situation. The situation is dynamic because demands are changing, technology is changing, and social and economic aspirations are changing.

It might seem from all this that a successful business, or a successful country, will be the one which is able to anticipate these changes and prepare for them by ensuring that the right kind of labour is available at the right time. In general terms we call this process of anticipation manpower planning.

Manpower planning

Manpower planning has been described as 'a strategy for the acquisition, improvement and preservation of an enterprise's human resources'.[1] In practice it consists of three stages of action:

1. taking an inventory of existing labour resources;
2. forecasting future labour requirements if the organization's objectives are to be achieved; and
3. ensuring that the necessary labour resources are available at the appropriate time.

Although, at first glance, it seems an obvious and straightforward operation, only a comparatively small number of organizations have embarked on manpower planning as a serious, practical exercise. Many have professed to do so but only paid lip-service to it; others have not even considered it. The main reason for this dearth of effective manpower planning is that, as a realistic operation, it is not as simple as it may seem. Nor is it, on evidence, particularly reliable, and it is understandable that 'hard-nosed' businessmen will view with scepticism an exercise which consumes a large amount of time for few tangible results.

The difficulty about manpower planning is that of forecasting labour requirements with precision in a rapidly changing situation. A company may define its objectives over, say, the next five years only to find that, because of a change in government policy, or improvements in technology, or changes in consumer tastes, or the effects of competition from rival companies, these objectives have to be changed.

Part of the manpower planning process consists of training or retraining people to perform certain jobs and often the training period is such that by the time it is over circumstances have radically changed. It is perhaps understandable, therefore, that firms, faced with these seemingly unpredictable prospects, discard manpower planning in any rigorous sense and follow the practice of buying-in appropriately skilled labour as and when an immediate need arises. This might seem a sensible thing to do provided that at the time a particular skill is needed it is available on the labour market, but if individual employers give up the challenge of anticipating training needs and adopting appropriate training policies, who ensures that the right sort of labour is available at the right time? The government?

This would seem a task wholly appropriate to government. After all, it controls, or strongly influences, the educational system, and it is through this system that the first stages, and in some cases all stages, of training occur. The number of scientists produced will be determined to a significant extent by the number of science teachers in schools. The quality of the end product will be influenced by the number and quality of teachers.

Applying the three stages of manpower planning, which we have already identified, in a national context, the government would obviously first like to know how much and what kinds of labour are available: in particular, it would wish to know the stock of skilled labour. Secondly, it would like to have as accurate a forecast as possible of the nation's future requirements of labour, particularly skilled labour. Thirdly, it would wish to ensure that the education and training systems were geared to meet these future demands. How have governments in this country tried to do these things?

National manpower planning in Britain

The first tentative attempts at manpower training on a national basis were made after the Second World War. They were not very successful partly because they were undertaken on a fragmentary, *ad hoc* basis, and partly because the available statistics were far from adequate. What came out of these early inquiries resembled intelligent guesses more than reliable forecasts. The best attempt, in a specific manpower sector, was made by the Barlow Committee which looked at the demand for scientific labour in 1946.[2]

By the 1960s politicians on both sides of the House of Commons were coming to some sort of consensus about the need to expand and improve industrial training. It was felt that the examples set by the most enlightened employers should be followed by the rest. How to achieve this became the centre of a major debate. Eventually, towards the end of 1962, the Conservative government announced its intentions in a White Paper.[3] They included proposals to set up training boards in each major industry, with powers to impose a training levy on employers and to repay some or all of the levy in the form of grants to enable them to provide approved training for their

159

employees. During the debate on the Bill which followed the White Paper arguments were advanced for setting up machinery for forecasting manpower requirements and the Industrial Training Act of 1964, in addition to establishing **Industrial Training Boards**, included provision for a **Manpower Research Unit** in the Ministry of Labour. The Act also set up a **Central Training Council** to act as general adviser to the Minister on the exercise of his functions in the field of industrial training.

The first Industrial Training Board was created soon after the Act came into effect and by 1969 there were 26 established under the Act and two voluntary organizations, the Local Government Training Board and the Insurance Industry Training Council. The new Boards undoubtedly did much to stimulate and assist training. At the same time they attracted considerable criticism. The main grounds for criticism were that they were, in most cases, unnecessarily bureaucratic; that at times they encouraged irrelevant training for the sake of training and stimulated 'empire building'; and that they did little to help the small firm. Enoch Powell, who was probably the most outspoken opponent of the system established under the Act, endorsed the description which was being popularly canvassed of 'the Great Training Robbery'.

The 1970 general election brought the Conservatives back to power and they initiated a review of the Act which they had put on the statute book six years earlier. By early 1972 the government felt able to reveal its hand and indicated in a Consultative Document,[4] that it wanted to replace the levy-grant system with an alternative form of financing, and also to provide 'global' as well as industry-based training. After a lengthy period of public discussion a White Paper[5] was published in March 1973, which was eventually translated into the Employment and Training Act 1973. The Act created the Manpower Services Commission (MSC) which replaced the Central Training Council in a much more comprehensive and autonomous form. It was to be a statutory body responsible to the Secretary of State for Employment for the coordination and management of both employment and training services. We have discussed the work of the Commission in some detail in an earlier chapter.

The levy-grant system was retained but now gave a firm the opportunity of claiming exemption from the levy if it could show that it was making adequate provision for its training needs itself.

In addition to its responsibilities in the fields of current employment and training needs, the MSC is concerned with the future needs of the nation: in other words, with national manpower planning. In pursuance of this policy it published, in December 1977, a consultative document *Training for Skills*,[6] in which it invited employers to identify future industrial and commercial training needs. This exercise was intended to be as realistic an assessment as possible, undertaken in the real world of business and not in some academic ivory tower. In September 1979 the MSC published a report, *Hard to Fill Vacancies*,[7] which contained calculations of what are technically called 'v/u ratios', in other words the figures for vacancies divided by the figures for unemployed. The deficiency of such calculations arises from the difficulty of defining a 'skill'. The report made little immediate impact.

Meanwhile, the Commission had embarked upon a variety of training initiatives, some more successful than others. The **Training Opportunities Scheme (TOPS)** attracted many recruits but too few of them ended up in real jobs. The **Special Temporary Employment Programme (STEP)** was criticized as a palliative for youth unemployment rather than a serious contribution to training. In 1978 the MSC launched the **Youth Opportunities Programme (YOP)** and this too was attacked on the grounds of inadequate training and a poor success rate in job placements.

The Commission's consultative document *A New Training Initiative*,[8] of May 1981, was followed by a White Paper *A New Training Initiative: A Programme for Action*,[9] announcing the replacement of YOP by YTS, the **Youth Training Scheme**, intended to be a permanent programme of integrated training and work experience for all 16-year-olds and some 18-year-olds. The YTS programme was given a budget of £950 million for 1983–4, rising to £1.1 billion in the following year. It was launched with the support of the TUC, CBI, and education authorities but, nevertheless, soon ran into opposition, mainly from sections of the further education teaching profession.

If national manpower planning is to succeed then not only must the identification of future education and training needs be reliable but the satisfying of those needs must be effective. There are now two central government departments with an interest in both sides of the national manpower planning equation, the Department of Employment, overseeing the work of the MSC, and the Department of Education and Science, overseeing the work of the public education sector. For a long time it has seemed as if a genuine dialogue between the two was not taking place but early in 1984 there were indications of cooperation, albeit on a somewhat unbalanced basis.

In February 1984 another White Paper on training was published, but this time jointly by the Department of Employment and the Department of Education and Science. It was called *Training for Jobs*.[10] Its main proposal was that the MSC should, progressively over a period of three years, become responsible for a quarter of non-advanced further education. Although the Department of Education and Science was involved, there was little evidence of prior discussions with either local education authorities or further education colleges, whose work would, obviously, be affected. It was, perhaps, understandable that the White Paper met with considerable initial opposition, particularly as one reason it gave for the transfer of work from local education authorities to the MSC was that colleges were not sufficiently in touch with employer needs. It was this self-same criticism that was often levelled at the Commission.

This rather sorry history of events inevitably poses a final question. Is effective national manpower planning achievable in a country such as the United Kingdom when there is, apparently, so little understanding, let alone cooperation, between the disparate groups and organizations which, ideally, ought to be agreed on a common purpose?

Manpower planning in the public sector

Public administration is essentially labour intensive. For this reason alone there is a strong case for at least attempting to operate a manpower planning policy in the public sector. To have too many people with the wrong skills half-employed is probably worse than a shortage of skilled persons with those who are available being overstretched and overworked. It must be every manager's dream in the public or private sector to have an infinitely adaptable and malleable workforce which he can retrain and redeploy at a moment's notice as and when circumstances change.

The civil service has done much to pioneer objective techniques for analysing the content of jobs, the values to be attached to them, and the qualities needed in the people required to fill them. As we have already seen, the recruitment methods of the

161

Civil Service Commission, are highly sophisticated and generally well regarded. Local authorities vary in their approach and in the degree of success they achieve in the techniques associated with manpower planning. There is evidence, however, that some authorities have developed approaches comparable to the best in the civil service and the private sector.

It is in the area of prediction of needs that the weaknesses of manpower planning are most evident. The over-provision of training places for prospective teachers is a recent, striking example of this defect. The identification some years ago of a growing demand for town and country planning staff and a subsequent over-reaction in their production is another. Most skills obviously take time to acquire. The higher or more sophisticated the skill the longer the acquisition time. Thus, at the very minimum, a full professional qualification will take at least four years to obtain. During that time circumstances can have changed dramatically and an acute need can have become an embarrassment. This, unfortunately, is the cross which manpower planners must carry.

Physical or environmental planning

The Town and Country Planning Act of 1947 established a national system of controlling the development of land in England and Wales using local authorities as the local planning authorities and central government as the central supervisor. The local planning authorities were required to produce five-year development plans for their areas and submit them to the Minister for approval. The details of these plans were centrally recorded and there was a provision for people to object to a development proposal or appeal against a refusal of a planning authority to allow development to take place.

In 1964, after the original Act had been in operation for more than fifteen years, a group mainly composed of civil servants and local government officers was asked to review the system, and their report,[11] published in 1965, eventually resulted in a new piece of legislation, the Town and Country Planning Act of 1968. The Act attempted to distinguish between strategic policy decisions about environmental planning and tactical decisions. In other words, it required central government to concern itself with the broad physical structure of an area and local authorities with the allocation of sites and the details of implementation. The Act also sought to give the public greater opportunities to participate in planning decisions.

Before the 1968 Act was passed the government had set up the Skeffington Committee to advise on the best method of securing the participation of the public at the formative stages of making development plans, and the Committee in its report *People and Planning*,[12] made a number of specific recommendations for publicizing local plans and giving the public more opportunities to comment on them and suggest amendments before adoption.

We will look at the degree of success which has been achieved in this area of public participation in policy making in a later chapter. For the moment we can remind ourselves of the problems which environmental planners face. There never will be an 'ideal' planning proposal. Almost invariably a plan to build a hypermarket outside a town, or a shopping centre within a town, or a motorway near a village, will upset someone. The traditionalist will resist change at almost any cost; the entrepreneur will object to what he regards as 'bureaucratic interference' in his aspirations to develop his enterprise. The planner should, however, take comfort from the lessons of the past. The permanent scars which the industrial revolution left on areas of the Midlands and the North and the untidy ribbon development of the 1930s are reminders of what has happened and what could happen again if uncontrolled development were permitted to return.

Indicative economic planning

In a 'collectivist' state, where decisions about kinds and amounts of all forms of production are taken by government or governmental agencies, it might seem sensible to speak of a 'national plan'. In a democratic state, where substantial parts of productive enterprises are privately owned, the idea of economic planning seems less appropriate and practical. Yet in Western democratic countries it has been done, or at least, attempted.

The kind of planning possible in this sort of environment can best be described as 'indicative'. In other words, the government gives a reasonably firm indication of how it would like the economy to develop and encourages individual enterprises to draw up their separate plans in the hope that the aggregate will approximate to the optimum model which the government has in mind. Thus the government might plan for an annual rate of increase in production of 3 per cent and set this as a target over the next five years for individual undertakings in the public and private sectors. It is, of course, a comparatively easy thing to indicate a target such as that, but it is a much more difficult proposition to achieve. The ill-fated *National Plan*[13] which George Brown, as Secretary of State for Economic Affairs, produced in 1965 is a case in point. The plan itself looked impressive. Equally impressive was the Secretary of State's achievement in getting the leaders of both sides of industry to sign a 'declaration of intent' to implement the plan. In the event, everyone concerned said that the targets in the Plan were sensible and worth achieving, but they were not achieved. The Plan was an indication and became no more than that.

Nothing quite as ambitious as George Brown's National Plan has been attempted since, but, whatever their political hue, and whether or not they espouse the concept of economic planning, all governments feel obliged to try to direct the way in which the national economy is developing or not developing. This is such a crucial area of government concern that we devote the whole of our next chapter to it.

References

1. *Company Manpower Planning, Department of Employment and Productivity*, HMSO, 1968, p. 2.
2. *Scientific Manpower*, Report of a Committee appointed by the Lord President of the Council (Barlow Report), Cmnd. 6824, HMSO, 1962.
3. *Industrial Training: Government Proposals*, Cmnd. 1892, HMSO, 1962.
4. *Training for the Future—a plan for discussion*, Department of Employment, HMSO, 1972.
5. *Employment and Training: Government Proposals*, Cmnd. 5250, 1973.
6. *Training for Skills*, Manpower Services Commission, HMSO, 1977.
7. *Hard to Fill Vacancies*, Manpower Services Commission, HMSO, 1979.
8. *A New Training Initiative*, Manpower Services Commission, HMSO, 1981.

9. *A New Training Initiative: A Programme for Action*, Cmnd. 8455. HMSO, 1981.
10. *Training for Jobs*, Cmnd. 9135, HMSO, 1984.
11. *The Future of Development Plans*, HMSO, 1965.
12. *People and Planning*, Report of the Committee on Public Participation in Planning, HMSO, 1969.
13. *National Plan*, Cmnd. 2764, HMSO, 1965.

Assignment

25. 'The so-called National Plan of 1965 was more a pipe-dream than a plan.' Do you agree with this statement? Give a reasoned answer.

Sources: Back issues of *The Economist* and any contemporary economics textbook. R.H.S. Crossman, *Socialism and Planning*, Fabian Tract 375.

16

Economic management

The concept of economic management

Expressed in simple terms, economic management means controlling and influencing the economy so that it develops in ways which the government of the day believes to be beneficial.

In an unmanaged economy, subject only to market forces, the government would be just another element in the production-consumption cycle and an observer, rather than a manipulator, of economic change. But even if it had no wish to practise economic management, the sheer size of the public sector would have a significant impact on prices and other indicators of economic activity. By public sector we mean that part of the economy which is wholly or partly owned by the state, centrally, locally, and regionally, and which, consequently, makes demands on public funds. It now accounts for more than 40 per cent of the nation's total spending.

Nineteenth-century Chancellors of the Exchequer, such as Gladstone, believed that their sole task was to 'balance the nation's accounts', as if they were conducting a huge housekeeping operation. If they turned to the academic economists of their generation this is the advice they would almost invariably receive. Thus an annual budget would consist of collecting enough revenue, and no more, to pay for the limited activities of government. The idea of budgeting for a surplus or a deficit was made academically respectable by later economists thereby changing the whole rationale of public accounting. Before, Chancellors would be almost entirely concerned about *how* they acquired their revenue and whether this tax or that tax would be politically acceptable. Their successors would be just as much concerned about the effects of their decisions on the economy as a whole. Should they stimulate demand and perhaps raise prices, or stimulate production, or, perhaps, put a damper on economic activity?

Even today a Chancellor will talk about producing a 'neutral budget', meaning that it is not intended to generate or dampen demand. But no Chancellor today, whatever his political hue, would deny that public sector revenue raising, whether by taxation or by borrowing, has a significant effect on total economic activity.

The aims of economic management

Although each of the main political parties in this country has its own particular view of what is or is not 'good' for the nation, there has been, for the past forty years or so, a reasonable consistency in certain basic aims. The differences between the parties have been chiefly about priorities. This consistency has, to some extent, been inevitable because these aims are interdependent, in that the achievement of one makes that of the others automatic or necessary. These aims may be summarized as follows:

1. the maintenance of a reasonably stable price level;
2. the maintenance of a high and stable level of employment;
3. the maintenance of a favourable balance of payments; and
4. the achievement of sustained economic growth.

If a government makes economic growth its primary target and achieves success, it is highly likely that unemployment will fall and the balance of payments will, as an indicator of international indebtedness, be favourable. These three aims might be achieved, initially at any rate, at the expense of rising prices, but, in the long run, if growth is sustained, prices would be expected to fall and stabilize.

Making the reduction of unemployment the main target would not, in itself, ensure economic growth or a favourable balance of payments, and might certainly, in the short term, result in rising prices, but, again, the attainment of this aim would be likely, in the longer term, to ensure that of the other three.

Clearly, sustained economic growth is the most attractive aim in political terms, and the one which makes best economic and social sense. In practice, however, it is the most difficult to achieve. The evidence of its benefits is irrefutable: the West German 'economic miracle' of the 1950s and 1960s; the resurgence of France in the 1960s; the commercial and industrial dominance of Japan from the 1970s onwards; and the revival of the United States economy in recent years.

The main obstacle in the path of achieving sustained growth is that it requires a consistency of policies over a longer period than the life of a single government in this country, or even one that enjoys a second term of office. The swing of the political pendulum, which we discussed in an earlier chapter, has precluded consistent economic management. The Attlee government, of 1945 to 1951, which, in retrospect, pursued a modest and responsible programme of socialist reform, was replaced by the government of Churchill which reversed certain policies and tolerated, rather than consolidated, others. And so the process has continued, with successive governments, although in broad agreement, as we have suggested, about the four major aims, deeply divided at times about priorities, and even more sharply disagreeing about the methods.

Economic and social priorities

These disagreements about priorities are starkly evident at the present time. In its election manifestos of 1979 and 1983 the Conservative Party made the control of inflation its prime target. It argued that the other major aims would inevitably be achieved once inflation was brought under control. The opposition parties argued that, for social as much as for economic reasons, the reduction of unemployment should be the major aim and said that the achievement of this would eventually secure the other aims. Indeed, they argued that economic growth and the full employment of the nation's resources were inextricably interwoven.

Since 1970 the level of unemployment in this country has risen from about one million, or 5 per cent of the working population, to over three millions, or more than 12 per cent. There have been appreciable increases in unemployment levels in many other countries during the same period, with one or two notable exceptions. It has been possible, therefore, for the Conservative government to argue that the increase in unemployment in the United Kingdom has been the inevitable result of a world recession coupled with rapid technological change. Its opponents have said that during most of this period of Conservative rule North Sea oil has been on full stream, with all the consequential financial and economic benefits, so that the country's economic performance, in contrast with those which have not enjoyed this advantage, has been comparatively poor. Above all, they have complained, the nation's resources, human and material, have been grossly underutilized at a time of great economic opportunity.

The critics of Mrs Thatcher have argued that, had she pursued alternative priorities, the current state of the economy would be profoundly different. She has, naturally, rejected this charge. Unfortunately, 'ifs' cannot be evaluated so the debate is inevitably sterile. The only point which can be made with reasonable certainty and objectivity is that if, over a longer period than the life of two, let alone one, parliament, a social and economic policy consensus had existed, the prospects of achieving all the four main aims of economic management would have been much greater.

The methods of economic management

In recent years governments of all parties have sought the advice of academic economists for guidance on how they should manage the economy. Before the present century not only did governments not consider economic management their responsibility, but economists argued that it was not necessary, or even possible. Adam Smith, for example, in his famous book *An Inquiry into the Nature and Causes of the Wealth of Nations*,[1] produced a convincing case for the believers in market forces, arguing that if every individual were allowed to pursue his own economic advantage that of the whole community would automatically result. On such theoretical bases the philosophy of *laissez-faire* was built.

The idea that Chancellors of the Exchequer needed merely to keep the nation's accounts in balance persisted through to the present century, despite rising unemployment in the 1930s. It needed a bloody and unnecessary war to reverse the trend. In Germany hyper-inflation and a crumbling economy allowed Nazism to grow and flourish and the 'New Deal' policy of Franklin Roosevelt owed more to an enlightened social conscience than economic teaching.

Yet during this period a new school of economic thought was developing. A young Cambridge economist, John Maynard Keynes, had already pointed out the dangers of extorting too much retribution from Germany after the Great War,[2] and then went on to develop a theory about the operation of the economy which argued that governments could, by influencing consumption and investment, raise the level of economic activity and so create employment opportunities.[3] Out of this grew the concept of 'full employment' expressed by Sir William Beveridge, later Lord Beveridge, in his personal report *Full Employment in a Free Society*,[4] which was immediately endorsed by all the main political parties, and became the cornerstone of post-war economic policy.

As expressed in the Beveridge Report, full employment implied the absence of avoidable unemployment and postulated an acceptable level of unemployment, caused by natural friction restricting the full mobility of labour and other resources.

167

A national maximum figure of 3 per cent of the working population was seen as acceptable, although the precise percentage was not that important. For about thirty years unemployment remained below, and sometimes appreciably below, this level. A combination of events and factors produced it, including the stimulation of economic activity by two major wars involving the United States, in Korea and Vietnam, and a growth of state activity as the so-called welfare state was expanded and consolidated.

The initial sharp rise in unemployment in the 1970s occurred for various reasons, the most significant being the increase in world energy prices and the faltering United States economy. Economic activity in the United States is so significant that any major change inevitably affects the rest of the Western world. If the European Community had cohered into a tighter economic and social unit it might have resisted both major changes in economic circumstances, particularly as the United Kingdom was progressively becoming more self-sufficient in energy, but such cohesion was not achieved.

The Labour government of James Callaghan had begun to tackle unemployment by essentially Keynesian policies but the problem facing it was exacerbated by the effects of rapid technological change.

The Conservative Party under Margaret Thatcher fought and won the 1979 general election on a pledge to reduce inflation, and, thereby, unemployment. At the general election in 1983 the Conservatives could justifiably claim significant success in bringing down the rate of inflation but, their opponents claimed, at the cost of enormous numbers out of work. Furthermore, during this period from 1979 to 1983 industrial output had failed to rise, in stark contrast to such countries as Japan and the United States.

In making the control of inflation its prime target, the Thatcher government had eschewed Keynesian economic policies and embraced a particular view of how economies should be managed which, in shorthand terms, may be called monetarism.

Monetarism offers a superficially simple, and hence attractive, solution to rising inflation. It resurrects and reaffirms theories which 'classical economists' propounded long before the 'Keynesian revolution'. In simple terms, it argues that there is a direct relationship between the money supply and the price level. Control the money supply and you control inflation. As 'public money' accounts for nearly half of that in circulation, a Chancellor of the Exchequer could, understandably, see a straightforward way of tackling inflation by controlling public spending.

The chief seminal influences on Margaret Thatcher and her supporters in the Conservative Party seem to have been the Austrian philosopher Friedrich Hayek, who wrote *The Road to Serfdom*[5] in the 1920s, and the American Milton Friedman who wrote, among other things, *Capitalism and Freedom,*[6] in the 1960s.

It should be said that the policy of setting cash limits on public spending was not something peculiar to the government of Mrs Thatcher. It is a policy which has been attempted by earlier Conservative administrations and by Denis Healey when he was Labour Chancellor. No previous government, however, had put such reliance on the limitation of public spending, and had so obviously turned its back on an expansionist, Keynesian approach.

Two controlling methods of economic management had emerged, based mainly on economic priorities, but also on differing philosophical standpoints: a Keynesian approach of using public sector resources for stimulating economic activity, particularly through investment in the infrastructure; and a monetarist approach of neutralizing, as far as possible, the economic effects of public spending so that market forces could operate more freely. The ultimate targets of both approaches were the same.

Both the Conservative Party, following a monetarist line, and the Labour Party, more boldly Keynesian, dismissed the use of an overt incomes policy as something that had been tried and found wanting. Only the Liberals and Social Democrats, advocating a middle route between the two major parties, openly acknowledged that the success of their policies would be dependent on an incomes policy, voluntary if possible, but statutory if necessary.

The tools of economic management

Until 1961 central government spending in this country was planned on a year-to-year basis. A departmental committee under the chairmanship of Lord Plowden recommended in its report of 1961[7] that five-year spending plans should be introduced. This recommendation was adopted and until 1976 five-year public expenditure plans were published, expressed in volume, rather than financial, terms. In 1976 the use of volume plans, such as numbers of public employees or number of miles of roads to be built, was discontinued and forward expenditure was expressed in cash terms. Spending departments were given cash limits to which they were expected to adhere. If they were in danger of overspending they could either try to persuade the Treasury to raise the cash limit or cut back their expenditure. It was recognized that the imposition of cash limits could not control all public spending. Indeed, as much as 60 per cent of the total was determined by circumstances outside the departments' control and could only be altered by taking major political decisions. For example, expenditure on social security benefits rises as the number of people eligible to receive them increases. If savings are to be made in such areas then the government has to face the odium of public disapproval.

From 1980 onwards, with a more obvious swing towards monetarist policies, the government's control of public sector spending became enshrined in what is called the **medium-term financial strategy**. The medium-term strategy has three main aims:

1. a progressive reduction in the growth of the money supply so as to reduce inflation;
2. a progressive reduction of taxes and of the size of the public sector; and
3. a progressive reduction in the size of the **public sector borrowing requirement (PSBR)**.

The PSBR is simply the excess of government spending over its income: in other words, what it needs to borrow to finance central government, local government, and other public bodies.

The theory behind the medium-term strategy is that increased public sector borrowing raises interest rates, which increase costs and fuel inflation, and an increase in the supply of money has similar effects. Reduce the money supply and the size of the public sector, and hence its need to borrow, and inflation will come down, industrial costs will fall, economic growth will be generated, and the economy will flourish.

The theory does not enjoy unqualified support and several economists have pointed out that in a sophisticated economy, using every available means of exchange from

169

cash to credit, it is becoming increasingly difficult to *define* the money supply with any accuracy, let alone control it.

The medium-term financial strategy is the form of economic management developed by the Conservative government under Mrs Thatcher. Since the Treasury has responsibility for it, it obviously contains some elements of earlier policies. What makes it distinctive is its reliance on monetary targets and its belief in the progressive limitation of state activity. Another government could have adopted a more expansionist policy, placing more reliance on increased economic activity reducing inflation, and even extending, rather than contracting, the boundaries of the state.

With unemployment standing at over 12 per cent of the working population, the amount of public money needed for social security payments is considerable and only reducible as unemployment reduces. The 'long haul' solution to unemployment is, therefore, costly. A shorter term approach, on Keynesian lines, would run the risk of generating inflation and might only be successful if accompanied by an effective incomes policy, operating on the demand side.

The National Economic Development Council machinery

The government can exercise direct control over the public sector but it must rely on influence and persuasion as far as the private sector is concerned.

In our earlier discussions about the role and activities of interest groups we concluded that there was some evidence to suggest that we are now a pluralist society, with governments operating on the basis of working agreements with groups representing particular interests. This is apparent in the field of social and economic policy and, indeed, successive governments have over the years encouraged the development of this pluralist approach.

In 1961 the Conservative government of Harold Macmillan set up the **National Economic Development Council (NEDC)** as a means of bringing together, for regular exchanges of views, under the chairmanship of the Chancellor of the Exchequer, or sometimes the Prime Minister, representatives of organized business, organized labour, the nationalized industries, and the government. Its membership, in 1983, is set out in Table 16.1. The actual membership can change frequently but the basic balance has remained.

In setting up NEDC in 1961, Harold Macmillan, impressed by the success of consultative economic planning in France, had used the French *Commissariat au Plan* as his model. This kind of planning by general consent reached its peak in this country in 1965 with George Brown's National Plan,[8] which did not survive the economic crisis of 1966. After 1966, during the governments of Wilson, Heath, Wilson again, and Callaghan, NEDC was seen as a useful and significant forum for discussion and, although it never achieved the power and influence of some of its European counterparts, was generally appreciated by both sides of industry. Its 'little Neddy' sector working parties produced useful reports on aspects of specific parts of the economy and the **National Economic Development Office (NEDO)** was well regarded.

The Thatcher government seemed distrustful of NEDC, perhaps because of its earlier associations with attempts to achieve 'planning by consent'. At the time of writing it is in a state of balance. It offers the only formal opportunity for government, employers, and the trade union movement to sit down together to discuss common problems in a non-adversarial setting and if it were to disappear

Table 16.1   NEDC membership 1983

Government representation
Prime Minister (occasionally chairing)
Chancellor of the Exchequer (normally chairman)
Secretaries of State for   Employment
                                          Trade and Industry
                                          Energy
                                          Environment
                                          Education and Science   6/7

Employers' representation
President and Director-General of the Confederation of British Industry
Industrial companies
Currently: Dunlop
                 British Aluminium
                 Eldridge Pope   5

Nationalized industries' representation
Currently: British Rail
                 Bank of England
                 British Telecom   3

Trade union representation
Currently: Trades Union Congress
                 General and Municipal Workers' Union
                 Electrical, Electronic, Telecommunications, and Plumbing Union
                 National and Local Government Officers' Association
                 Amalgamated Union of Engineering Workers
                 Transport and General Workers' Union   6

Other members
Representative of the Consumers' Association
Chairman of the Manpower Services Commission
Director-General of the NEDO   3

'confrontation politics' would be even more obvious. There is evidence that employers and unions still find it valuable but without clear support from the government it would have a questionable role to play.

Economic management in perspective

Despite the Conservative government's determination to reduce the size of the public sector, the United Kingdom is clearly a mixed economy and always will be. This means that the government will always be able to exert considerable influence over economic affairs through its control of the public sector. Whether it chooses to do this in a positive or negative way is, obviously, a political choice.

The history of economic management by all governments, whatever their political complexions, is not good, largely because of the lack of consistency and continuity in policies over a reasonable period of time. Some sort of consensus, social and economic, is arguably desirable, but the prospects of its being achieved are not bright.

References

1. Smith, A. *An Inquiry into the Nature and Causes of the Wealth of Nations*, Dent, 1977.
2. Keynes, J.M. *The Economic Consequences of the Peace*, Macmillan, 1971.
3. Keynes, J.M. *General Theory of Employment, Interest and Money*, Cambridge University Press, 1936.
4. Beveridge, W.H. *Full Employment in a Free Society*, Allen and Unwin, 1945.
5. Hayek, F. *The Road to Serfdom*, Routledge, 1976.
6. Friedman, M. *Capitalism and Freedom*, University of Chicago Press, 1967.
7. Report on the Control of Public Expenditure, Cmnd. 1432, HMSO, 1961.
8. *National Plan*, Cmnd. 2764, HMSO, 1965.

Assignment

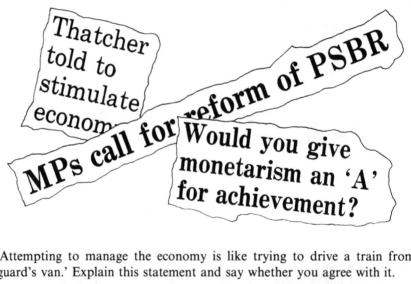

26. 'Attempting to manage the economy is like trying to drive a train from the guard's van.' Explain this statement and say whether you agree with it.

Sources: Anthony Sampson's *The Changing Anatomy of Britain*, particularly Chapters 12 and 19.

17

Government and business

The concept of a mixed economy

There are some states where it is impossible for individuals or groups of individuals outside the government to own property or to engage in any entrepreneurial activity on behalf of themselves. They are, however, a minority. There is no state in the world where government is not involved in some way with entrepreneurial activity, by regulating it, supporting it, or participating in it. In other words, although we can visualize, at one end of the scale, a completely free, unfettered market economy and, at the other end, a completely government-controlled socialist economy, in practice most states operate at a point between the two extremes: with a 'mixed economy'.

The difference between one mixed economy and another is reflected in the proportion of economic activity generated in the public sector compared with that in the private sector. The main difficulty in measuring, or even estimating, these proportions stems from the problem of defining the public sector. We can include in this central and local government, the fringe, as we have identified it in an earlier chapter, and the nationalized industries, but should we go further and include those industrial and commercial activities in which the state has a partial rather than a complete involvement? In the end, defining the public sector is an arbitrary exercise but the precision with which its boundaries are delineated is not of crucial significance to our discussion of the concept of a mixed economy or, for that matter, to our examination of the relationship between government and business.

By a mixed economy we simply mean a situation where there is a mixture of private and public ownership of property; a mixture of private and public enterprise; and a partial, but not total, control by government of all economic activity.

The growth of state intervention in industry and commerce

It is, of course, inevitable that the government of any country will have some involvement in industry and commerce. At the very least it will have established the basic political, social, legal, and economic framework within which industry and commerce operate. After all, that is the major role of government: if it did not provide this framework it would be superfluous.

In Britain the government's interventionist role has increased progressively during the nineteenth and twentieth centuries. The need to regulate so as to ensure minimum safety requirements and other working conditions was not immediately apparent during the early years of the industrial revolution, but particular individuals and interest groups brought pressure to bear so that by the second half of the nineteenth century working conditions in factories, mines, and on the railways were controlled by Acts of Parliament and regulations made under them.

Possibly the first significant example of the government's involvement in entrepreneurial activity was the purchase, in 1875 by Benjamin Disraeli, of shares in the newly formed Suez Canal Company. In 1914 the government obtained a controlling interest in British Petroleum Limited, and between the two world wars public boards or corporations were set up in specific sectors of the economy as the government of the day saw the need for involvement arising. In the period 1945–51 a planned legislative programme was undertaken to create a series of public corporations to own and operate basic industries including coal mining, gas and electricity supply, transport, atomic energy, and the manufacture of iron and steel.

We thus see the state performing a variety of roles: as a shareholder, as a business promoter, and as an external regulator.

The state as a shareholder

The earliest examples of state involvement in business were on an *ad hoc* basis and various organizational forms were used. The British Broadcasting Corporation, for example, started life as the British Broadcasting Company and other undertakings were given titles such as boards or authorities.

From 1946 the standard device used for taking previously privately run enterprises into public ownership was the **public corporation**, and the politician who most strongly favoured this form of ownership was Herbert Morrison, or Lord Morrison of Lambeth as he later became.

The Morrison concept of the public corporation was that of combining, in a legally constituted body, an acceptable degree of public accountability with a large measure of commercial freedom. Thus the chairman and other members of the board of a corporation are appointed by a minister to whom they are ultimately responsible. The Act of Parliament, or royal charter, which establishes a public corporation sets out its obligations, as an arm of state enterprise, and indicates the functions it must perform, the services it must provide, or the profits it must produce which, if purely commercial criteria were applied, might not be performed, provided, or produced. Thus the National Coal Board is required, under its nationalization Act, to ensure that adequate supplies of coal at reasonable prices are available, and the British Railways Board is charged with providing an adequate public transport system. Comparable obligations are placed on the other nationalized industries.

The degree of commercial freedom enjoyed by public corporations has been developed over the years on a largely pragmatic basis in an endeavour to provide some measure of ultimate control by the responsible minister, some measure of responsibility to Parliament, and as little interference as possible in the running of the corporations' day-to-day business. It would be misleading to say that this three-part balance has been achieved with complete success, and there have been times when relations between chairmen and their respective ministers have been distinctly cool.

The choice of chairman has usually been crucial to the success of a public corporation. Two former Labour ministers, Lord Robens and Lord Marsh, as they now are, were appointed chairmen of the National Coal Board and British Railways, respectively, by Conservative governments. Sir Peter Parker and Sir Michael Edwardes accepted substantial salary cuts to move from the private sector to head British Rail and British Leyland, and Ian McGregor was 'head hunted' by Sir Keith Joseph and persuaded to move from a lucrative post in New York to become chairman of British Steel. Until the administration of Mrs Thatcher chairmen had been chosen irrespective of political background or outlook. Appointments since 1979 have tended to be of people more obviously in sympathy with current Conservative policy. 'Is he one of us?' seems to have been an important question to ask.

Whatever government has been in power, nationalized industries' chairmen have often felt themselves to be shuttlecocks in the game of adversarial politics, finding it difficult to formulate and adhere to long-term plans with any confidence. When he was chairman of the National Coal Board, Lord Robens started a monthly 'luncheon club' for his fellow chairmen and this developed into the **Nationalized Industries Chairmen's Group (NICG)**, with a current membership of 21. The Group has its own small staff to undertake studies of common problems and arranges annual lectures on industrial matters. The Group started as a largely social exercise but now has become a powerful buffer against the inconsistencies of government policies.

The public corporation model was the instrument for the programme of planned nationalization which was largely concluded with the re-nationalization of the iron and steel industry.

Another method of controlling industry without using the device of the public corporation is that of involvement with the classic instrument of private enterprise in this country, the **joint stock limited liability company**. We have already noted that as long ago as 1875 a British government thought it wise policy to buy shares in a joint stock company, the Suez Canal Company, and that it took a similar view of British Petroleum in 1914. This approach has been revived significantly in recent years.

In 1966 the **Industrial Reorganization Corporation (IRC)** was established by statute:

(a) to promote or assist the reorganization or the development of any industry; and
(b) if requested by the Secretary of State, to establish or develop any industrial enterprise.

It was given £150 million of public money to spend on loans and it had power to buy shares in joint stock companies on the open market, but it had no powers compulsorily to acquire them.

On its own initiative, the IRC intervened in certain areas to encourage, or even promote, mergers. The mergers of GEC with AEI and then GEC with English Electric are cases in point. At the request of the government it bought shares in Rolls-Royce and Cammel Laird Limited, and when it was known that the American Chrysler Company was proposing to take over the Rootes Group entirely, IRC was asked to ensure that the British government had shares in the company.

Most people would agree, in retrospect, that the IRC enjoyed only a limited success: by its own admission, it concentrated too much on encouraging mergers and not enough on selective investment. Its successor, the **National Enterprise Board (NEB)**, was to learn that lesson.

NEB was originally seen as an instrument for extending nationalization into the profitable areas of British industry, so as to assist the government in controlling prices, stimulating investment, encouraging exports, creating employment, and generally planning the economy. Its strongest supporter, in its original form, was Tony Benn. When firm proposals for its establishment appeared in the White Paper, *The Regeneration of British Industry*,[1] its powers of 'nationalization by the back door', as the critics put it, had been emasculated and it was only to be allowed to

175

acquire shares 'by agreement'. These proposals were eventually embodied in the Industry Act 1975.

The NEB was to become one of the largest holding companies in the world, with either a total, majority or minority holding in a wide range of formerly privately owned companies. They include such well-known undertakings as British Leyland, Rolls-Royce, Chrysler UK, British Petroleum, ICL, the computer manufacturers, Cable and Wireless, Ferranti, Harland and Wolff, Short Bros and Harland, Beagle Aircraft, Alfred Herbert, the machine tool manufacturers, and Upper Clyde Shipbuilders.

After winning the general election of 1979 the Conservatives began to emasculate NEB, removing Rolls-Royce, and later British Leyland, from its control. Eventually what was left of it was merged with the **National Research Development Corporation (NRDC)**, which had originally been set up by Harold Wilson during his first administration. The new merged group was given the title **British Technology Group (BTG)**, with the objective of linking university research with industry.

One of the leading members of Mrs Thatcher's Cabinet, Nigel Lawson, is reported as having said: 'The government of business is not the business of government.' This view encapsulates the outlook of the Thatcher administration towards business. Its answer to nationalization has been privatization, that ungainly but expressive word. But even a government believing so strongly in the virtues of private enterprise has to accept that a substantial public sector is part of our mixed economy and will not go away entirely.

The state as a business promoter

One way in which the state can intervene in industrial activities without becoming totally involved is by lending financial support to promising new, or ailing old, businesses.

Tax allowances are an obvious method of providing financial help and one used by governments throughout the world. The Industrial Development Act 1966 introduced **investment grants** as an alternative to tax allowances but the Industry Act 1972 converted them to **development grants** for particular regions whose economic problems were particularly acute. We will look more closely at regional policy later in this chapter.

During the late 1970s and 1980s the importance of the small business was belatedly recognized and both Labour and Conservative governments set up units within the Whitehall departments to identify and provide for the needs of the small firm.

There has, however, been little evidence of consistency of policy or purpose in much of this promotional activity and it is small wonder that businesses, large and small, have viewed much of the attention which governments have sporadically paid to them with apprehension rather than appreciation.

The state as an external regulator

All governments, however committed to a free enterprise economy, are obliged to provide a social, economic, and legal framework in which businesses can flourish. English law has placed emphasis on the protection of property, rather than protection of the person, and this has encouraged businessmen to invest with confidence.

176

During the nineteenth century and the first half of the twentieth state regulation has developed mainly on safety and humanitarian grounds. This has been evident in, for example, factory and mines legislation. In other respects a *laissez-faire* tradition has persisted, even to the extent of granting legal immunities to trade unions beyond those available to other organizations.

In the United States, often regarded as the home of free enterprise, the state had become concerned about the abuse of monopoly power by big corporations and about the possible exploitation of the consumer as early as the 1920s and 1930s: many years before a similar interest was shown in this country. The **Monopolies and Mergers Commission** was first set up by the Attlee Labour government in 1948. It proved to be, in many ways, a pale shadow of its counterparts in America and Europe. It has no powers to initiate an investigation and must wait for the government to request it to do so, and its reports are not binding. Conservative governments have tended to be non-interventionist about mergers, but even Labour governments have been more tolerant than the United States federal government, for example.

The Conservative Party's concern for the consumer has usually been prompted by the wish to encourage free competition. It was Edward Heath who guided the Resale Price Maintenance Bill through the final months of the Macmillan–Douglas Home administration. The commercial repercussions of abandoning the fixed price system were unprecedented, leading to an explosive growth of supermarkets, hypermarkets, and discount shops. It was the Heath government which set up the **Office of Fair Trading** in 1973, with the task of overseeing the consumer's interests, assisted by the local trading standards service, investigating restrictive trade practices, and reporting potential monopolies to the Monopolies Commission.

The Labour Party has shown a more active interest in the rights of the consumer *per se*, and, following the fall of the Heath government, in 1974, established a new central **Department of Prices and Consumer Protection**, assisted by a **Price Commission** and a publicly-funded **National Consumer Council**.

This structure proved to be too socialist and interventionist for the government of Mrs Thatcher, which, when it came to power in 1979, abolished the Department of Prices and Consumer Protection and demoted the consumer minister to the rank of minister of state within the Department of Trade.

Regional policy

Governments have attempted to influence the location of industry in the United Kingdom since the 1930s. The stimulus has invariably been the uneven distribution of employment opportunities.

Unemployment in South Wales and the North East of England in the 1920s and 1930s persuaded the government to establish new industrial and trading areas to which the unemployed could move, accounting, for example, for substantial Welsh communities in southern industrial towns such as Slough. In the decade or so after the last war governments were generally passive about regional policy but in the late 1950s concern about localized unemployment was rekindled. By 1979 about 40 per cent of the population of the United Kingdom lived in areas eligible for some kind of regional aid. A summary of regional policy since 1934 is given in Table 17.1.

This summary provides yet another example of how governments of all parties have tended to react to problems in the world of industry and business as they have

177

Table 17.1   UK regional policy 1934–84

1934	Special Areas (Development and Improvement) Act (Coalition)	Four Special Areas designated, leading to establishment of new industrial estates
1945	Distribution of Industry Act (Labour)	Special Areas extended and redesignated Development Areas
1947	Town and Country Planning Act (Labour)	Industrial Development Certificate (IDC) introduced, controlling new industrial development
1950	Distribution of Industry Act (Labour)	Increased grant and loan powers for Development Areas
1958	Distribution of Industry (Industry Finance) Act (Conservative)	Development Areas extended; development in other areas restricted through use of IDCs
1960	Local Employment Act (Conservative)	Distribution of Industry Act repealed; Development Areas replaced by Development Districts
1965	Control of Office and Industrial Development Act (Labour)	More stringent restrictions on development outside Development Districts
1965	Highlands and Islands Development Act (Labour)	Established a Highlands and Islands Development Board to assist Scottish development
1966	Industrial Development Act (Labour)	Development Districts replaced by broader Development Areas; powers to make grants and loans extended
1967	Regional Employment Premium (Labour)	Subsidies introduced to induce employers to retain labour in the Development Areas
1967	Special Development Areas (Labour)	Additional assistance provided for areas of greatest need

occurred, rather than to initiate activity as a result of anticipated developments. It also confirms the failure to achieve consistency and continuity in policy making.

In summary, regional policy, at the time of writing, is based on grants and loans to assisted areas, classified as Special Development Areas, Development Areas, and Intermediate Areas; Enterprise Zones; Development Agencies for Scotland and Wales; Development Boards for the Highlands and Islands of Scotland and Rural Wales; and specific assistance for Northern Ireland. Additionally, the New Towns, started in the pre- and post-war years have been expanded. Figures 17.1 and 17.2 show the locations of assisted areas, new towns, and enterprise zones in the United Kingdom. There is also a Council for Small Industries in Rural Areas (CoSIRA). If, as we discuss towards the end of this chapter, there were a coherent, long-term industrial policy, as exists in several European countries, a more rational and less proliferative arrangement of regional aid institutions might exist. It should also be noted that EEC aid is available for investment projects likely to create or safeguard employment in assisted areas of the United Kingdom. In 1982 about £200 million was received from this source.

178

Table 17.1 (*continued*)

1970	Intermediate Areas (Labour)	A new class of assisted area introduced, qualifying for a lower rate of support than Development Areas
1972	Industry Act (Conservative)	Regional development grants replaced by depreciation allowances; restrictions on industrial development relaxed; regional selective assistance introduced
1974	Regional Employment Premium (Labour)	Rate of premium doubled; IDC control tightened
1975	Development Agencies (Labour)	Scottish and Welsh Development Agencies established, with powers to build factories and engage in other forms of industrial development
1974	Policy revision (Labour)	Relaxation of IDC limits
1977	Regional Employment Premium (Labour)	Abolished for Great Britain, but retained for Northern Ireland
1980	Enterprise Zones (Conservative)	Areas experiencing unusually high unemployment could be designated Enterprise Zones, enjoying certain tax and rates exemptions, investment allowances, and customs-free warehousing
1984	Policy revisions (Conservative)	Greater emphasis on job creation, including more selectivity in aid and less discrimination against service, as compared with manufacturing industries

Source: J. Marquand *Measuring the Effects and Costs of Regional Incentives*, Department of Industry.

North Sea oil policy[2]

In little more than a decade North Sea oil has become the United Kingdom's biggest industry. Its effect on the nation's balance of payments has been considerable, allowing the welfare state to be maintained despite falling manufacturing output and the highest levels of unemployment yet experienced.

When we imported all our oil the government was chiefly concerned with safeguarding overseas supplies and protecting the interests of largely British-owned companies, such as Shell and British Petroleum. The prospect of moving from a position of being a total importer to that of a major net exporter required a drastic review of policies.

Prospecting for oil in the North Sea began in earnest in the 1960s. At unprecedented speed, the Conservative government of Alec Douglas-Home passed the Continental Shelf Act of 1964 and immediately invited applications for licences to explore 960 designated blocks, each comprising about 100 square miles. By September 1964 nearly half the blocks had been applied for and licences issued.

Harold Wilson's Labour government, which came into power in October 1964, was concerned about the large American stake in North Sea oil exploration and wanted a

179

Fig. 17.1 UK new towns and enterprise zones 1982
Source: 'Invest in Britain' (Department of Industry). Reproduced with the permission of the Controller of Her (Britannic) Majesty's Stationery Office.

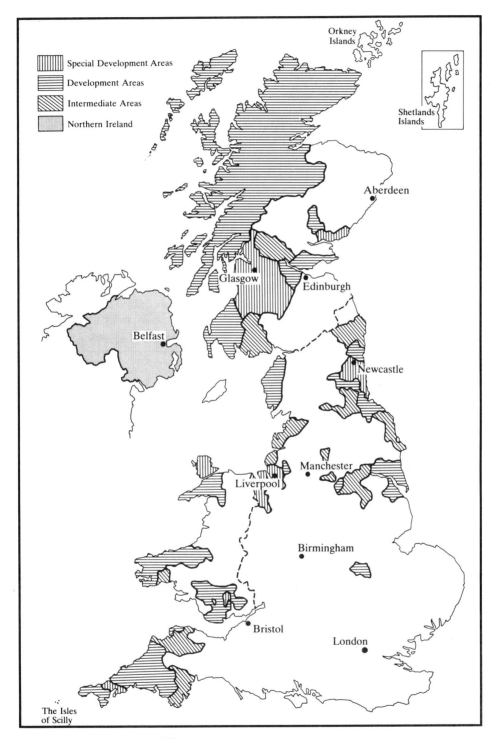

Fig. 17.2 UK assisted areas 1982
Source: London Enterprise Agency (LENTA).

181

greater British involvement. It continued the previous government's policy, however, in broad terms and in the following year invited applications for a further 1102 blocks. Meanwhile, there was a growing lobby within the Labour Party for the establishment of a National Hydrocarbons Corporation, to take over the established offshore investments of the National Coal Board and the Gas Council. The government responded by announcing a modest increase in public sector investment and issued invitations for a third, but smaller, round of 157 blocks before it lost power to the Conservative government of Edward Heath in 1970.

By the time of the fourth round of licences, in 1972, British progress in North Sea oil development compared favourably with other European countries, and the United Kingdom was well on the road to net self-sufficiency in 1981. There were critics, however, the most notable being the House of Commons Public Accounts Committee, who felt that the licensing arrangements had been too generous to the oil companies. The Heath government embarked on a major policy review but before it was completed it went out of office. It had, however, given sufficient recognition to the importance of North Sea oil by creating a separate Department of Energy.

Harold Wilson's second administration, from 1974, continued the Heath policies but again came under pressure from its own backbenchers for greater public sector involvement. It responded by introducing a new tax, the **Petroleum Revenue Tax (PRT)**, to supplement corporation tax which the oil companies paid, and set up the **British National Oil Corporation (BNOC)** to oversee public participation. BNOC was formally established on 1 January 1976 and soon demonstrated its effectiveness. By 1981 it was showing pre-tax profits of £500 million.

The return of the Conservatives under Mrs Thatcher, in 1979, resulted in a new chairman for BNOC and a new Energy Secretary. The first chairman, Lord Kearton, had had wide industrial experience while his successor, Philip Shelbourne, was a City man. The new Energy Secretary, Nigel Lawson, announced that he proposed to split BNOC into a publicly-owned trading organization, and a part-private/part-public production and exploration company, Britoil. The announcement caused considerable comment largely because of its timing. The sale of Britoil shares realized less than might have been anticipated because of falling world oil prices.

The need for a coherent industrial policy

Industrialists, managers, and trade unionists have been sharply critical of government industrial policies, whichever party has happened to be in power. Indeed, the fiercest critics have questioned whether any government has ever had an industrial policy at all.

Certainly, such policies as have been outlined in this chapter have suffered from a lack of continuity, as they have fluctuated with the swing of the political pendulum, and have lacked a clear coherence, in that no long-term objectives have been discernible. In particular, they can be contrasted unfavourably with the industrial policies of some of our major competitors, notably West Germany, France, and Japan. Each of these countries, while following policies developed from different economic and cultural bases, has demonstrated an obvious long-term 'plan', in which national and international priorities have been firmly identified.

The main weaknesses in the United Kingdom's approach to industry and business may, perhaps, be summarized as:

1. an absence of a clear indication of aims;
2. an inability, or unwillingness, to demonstrate to industry that there is a long-term view of the kind of economy the government wishes to develop;
3. a lack of continuity, as evidenced by attitudes to state intervention and the perennial 'nationalization versus privatization' argument; and
4. an overall lack of coherence, demonstrated by numerous instances of the policy of one central department being at odds with that of another.

The solutions to these deficiencies are more political than economic. There are already instruments and institutions in being which, if differently used, might lead the nation into a coherent industrial policy. The NEDC and NEDO have more often than not had lip service paid to them rather than allowed to become a genuine industrial forum and planning centre. A reformed House of Lords, based on regional and group representation, could make the plurality of our society real and practical. Above all, British governments could usefully follow the example of some of their colleagues in the EEC. The Community itself might, with British support, develop an industrial strategy which might help to fulfil the original ideals of its founders.

Pricing policies in the public sector

As we have already noted, the nationalized industries in this country have social, economic, and financial obligations which are different from and additional to those accepted by organizations in the private sector. A privately owned company has obligations to its shareholders, whereas a public corporation has obligations to the state and ultimately to the public in general. In view of these obligations what prices ought they to charge for their products or services? If they apply purely commercial criteria while being obliged to take on non-commercial commitments they will be at a serious disadvantage. Should they be allowed to use their monopoly positions and let their prices cover the full costs of activities which would not normally be commercially viable, or should they 'subsidize' the public by making a loss on them? If they do incur losses, who should cover them? These are questions which lie at the heart of pricing policies in the public sector.

The boards of the nationalized industries have not been helped by the vague and inconsistent advice they have received from the government about their financial obligations. Since most of the corporations operate in conditions where there are no direct competitors, charging 'what the market will stand' is not an acceptable criterion. The advice governments in the past have given is to relate prices to long-term marginal costs. As a broad guideline this advice has considerable merit. If what the economist calls 'normal profit' is included in total costs, then over a long enough period of time corporations should break even. Most of the nationalized industries, however, employ very large amounts of fixed capital: the permanent way in the railway system, the coal mines, the electricity generating plants, and so on. This capital needs to be maintained and replenished. Again, over a long enough period of time capital costs can be included in marginal costs, but in times of inflation 'full life cycle costing' is difficult to achieve without a substantial amount put aside for capital replacement. The gas and electricity industries have generally managed to finance investment out of income. The railways, coal mining industry, and, to a lesser extent, the nationalized airlines, have been less successful; all, at some time or another, have had capital losses written off by the government.

Another feature which is peculiar to some of the nationalized industries is the need to have 'surplus' capital for use only at times of peak demand. The electricity supply industry and the railways are confronted with this problem. An obvious way of dealing with it is to apply differential pricing: in other words to charge more for the product or service at the times of peak demand: thus electricity boards make a fixed charge plus one which varies with consumption; British Rail encourages passengers to spread their travelling over the week and over the working day by selling off-peak, reduced price tickets. The Post Office imposes a rental charge for a telephone and then a variable charge according to the number of calls made. It also charges more for its connections during weekday mornings.

There is evidence that the accounting systems of the nationalized industries have improved immeasurably during the past ten years or so and that they are now in a better position than they were to identify cost centres and profit centres. Governments in recent years have also shown a better awareness of the long-term financial needs of the public corporations and the difficulties they encounter in trying to reconcile social with financial obligations. The organizations which are able to use essentially commercial criteria for their pricing policies, such as British Airways and British Leyland, have shown clear evidence that a publicly-owned venture can compete fairly and successfully with private sector companies.

Entrepreneurial activities in local government

We may not readily associate local government with the cut and thrust of the market place and the drive for commercial profit, but its involvement in the provision of services for which a full charge is made to the user is one of the more traditional activities of local authorities. We would not include here services such as the letting of council houses which, although a rent is payable by the occupier, is a highly subsidized activity. The kind of services which are entrepreneurial in character and which have been traditionally called 'trading services' are the provision of open markets, cemeteries, entertainment centres, public transport, and, until they were hived off to national and regional bodies, gas, electricity, and water supplies. The powers to undertake such enterprises have been conferred on local authorities by various statutes, sometimes in response to emergencies, as in the case of the municipally-run British Restaurants set up to serve blitzed areas during the Second World War. The variety of enterprises is wide: Birmingham has its own municipal bank; Hull operates the only public telephone service outside the monopoly of British Telecom; Doncaster runs a racecourse, and a number of authorities operate airports.

The reasons for local government becoming involved in commercial activities vary widely according to the activity and the date the power was acquired. The power to provide markets, for instance, often stems from the grant of royal charters in earlier centuries. However, the main reasons put forward are that the whole community benefits from profits made by municipal enterprises and that local authorities, not having shareholders' dividends to put at risk, will be more innovative and experimental in marginal enterprises such as the provision of entertainment. Counter-arguments are that by spreading their activities local authorities will threaten the efficiency of their main services and that their management structures are not suitable for the quick decisions and risks which go with a business enterprise.

Whatever the arguments may be, there has been a steady trend in post-war years for authorities to become more involved in commercial activities. The two main characteristics of this trend are that the enterprises have generally involved the acquisition of land and buildings, and they have often taken the form of partnerships with private enterprise. The first characteristic arises from the growth in importance of town and country planning and, in the case of a number of towns and cities, the need to rebuild war-damaged areas. This early momentum was continued in the 1960s by the need to renew many worn out and outmoded city centres and in the 1970s by the drive to revitalize the inner city areas around the centres. The second characteristic results from a realistic assessment by the public and the private sectors of the real benefits each can bring to an enterprise.

Many of the post-war town centre schemes have involved the provision of new shopping facilities in which the local council has sought a revitalized town centre and the developer and shopping interests have wanted more up-to-date, attractive, and therefore profitable, retailing facilities. The average scheme, although providing a commercial rate of return, is not so spectacularly profitable that a local authority can afford to finance it on its own, so a partnership with a private finance organization becomes necessary in order to avoid undue risk. The large sums of money involved in industrial or commercial development make this course of action a worthwhile and practical exercise for a firm wishing to expand its activities. The main features of such a partnership are usually that the local authority acquires the land and keeps the freehold. As landlord it can control design and will have a constant share of an increasing revenue after the centre has started trading. The private developer is helped in getting together the necessary land, which may originally be in many different ownerships. The local authority can overcome this problem through its powers of compulsory purchase. He also gets planning permission and usually a long lease, which is an asset he can sell at any time. In return, he supplies finance at rates much cheaper than on the open market, provides management, and takes the commercial risk. In addition to the financial benefits and an up-to-date town centre, the local authority may also obtain other planning gains, such as a free library or community centre. Not all town centre schemes are successful, of course, and, like any other commercial activity, they are vulnerable to economic changes. The failures are, however, the exceptions rather than the rule.

One of the most significant instances of local government taking on the role of entrepreneur, often with the help of central government, as well as in partnership with the private sector, is in the field of fostering industrial growth. We have already seen how the government provides funds for the so-called 'assisted areas' in a number of ways, including investment grants, tax concessions, employment premiums, and so forth, and special help is afforded to inner cities under the Inner Urban Areas Act and, less directly, through Rate Support Grant settlements. However, it appears that local government is coming to be regarded as the most suitable agency for actively assisting in industrial regeneration at the local level. It is a way of contributing to the industrial strategy. As with town centre schemes, the most usual arrangement is for the local authority to invest in land or new buildings, which are then leased as factories and warehouses to the private sector. Typical of this new enterprise is the construction of 11 moderately-sized warehouse/factory units at Sandgate Street in the London Borough of Southwark. The units, financed jointly by the local authority and a pension fund, are leased to private manufacturers. The main advantages to this

London Borough are the reduction of unemployment and the gradual regeneration of the area's prosperity.

Some imaginative and energetic local authorities have been successful in regenerating what were at one time 'one industry towns' by attracting new industries to them. The former steel town of Corby and the railway town of Swindon are two outstanding examples of this kind of enterprise.

The policy of establishing enterprise zones has given local authorities additional opportunities for assisting and developing industry in their localities. The results have not always been entirely as had been hoped, however, and the establishment of some zones seems to have resulted more in a redistribution of unemployment rather than a reduction.

The opportunity to establish **freeports** in approved locations was announced in the 1983 Budget. They are policed areas into which goods can be imported, stored, processed, manufactured, and exported free of customs duty. Duty becomes payable only when goods are moved from the freeport to somewhere else in the country. Freeports would normally be established at major communications centres, such as ports or large airports, and would require customs officers on site, absolute security, and efficient stock control. They provide another opportunity of improving local employment prospects and already applications for their establishment have been made by a number of local authorities.

References

1. *The Regeneration of British Industry*, Cmnd. 5710, HMSO, 1974.
2. For a fuller account see *Without Precedent: The Development of North Sea Oil Policy* by John B. Liverman *Public Administration*, vol. 60, no. 4.

Assignments

27. Discuss the advantages and disadvantages of privatizing British Airways.
    This topic can also be used as the basis of a debate on the motion: 'This House believes that British Airways would be more successful if privately owned.'
28. Identify any functions of your local district and county councils which, in your view, could be usefully privatized. Give reasons for supporting your conclusions.

18
Paying the piper: central and local public finance

The central taxation system

The *Concise Oxford English Dictionary* defines a tax as a 'contribution levied on persons, property or business for support of government'. It is a means of raising money. It is unlikely to be the only source of finance, although often it is the major one. The other main means of obtaining revenue are borrowing and levying a charge on services provided.

At first glance the purpose of taxation would seem clearly to be that of financing government spending, but this is only part, and not necessarily the most important part, of the story. The prime purposes of taxation are economic and social. An economic justification is that of diverting demands on the country's productive capacity from the private sector to the public; a social justification is that of redistributing wealth from the affluent to the less affluent.

We can consider other economic and social arguments when we look at the *kind* of tax imposed. A tax can encourage idleness and discourage industry. It can encourage thrift or it can encourage profligacy. Sometimes the intentions behind a tax are distorted by the way in which it is levied or collected. To the taxpayer the 'psychology' of a tax is important. A tax which in terms of the total amount of revenue it is intended to collect is quite modest, can be seen as swingeing by an individual taxpayer.

A distinction is often made between direct and indirect taxation. A **direct tax** is paid direct by the taxpayer to the taxing authority, whereas an **indirect tax** is included in the price of a commodity or a service the consumer purchases, and the tax itself is paid indirectly to the tax authority through the retailer or wholesaler who acts as the collecting agency. Economists are usually not very concerned about the distinction between direct and indirect taxation. They prefer to distinguish between taxes on income, wealth, or property, which are the main forms of direct taxation, and taxes on consumption which is the category into which most indirect taxes fall.

It is useful, for other reasons, to distinguish between direct and indirect taxation. An individual has little chance of escaping a direct tax; it is a personal obligation imposed on him. He can, however, choose not to pay an indirect tax simply by not purchasing the article or the service which is taxed. He can, of course, ensure that he pays as little direct taxation as possible by making the fullest use of the allowances which are available but tax evasion, in contrast to tax avoidance, is illegal.

It is also useful to make a distinction between what an economist calls a **progressive** tax and a **regressive** tax. A tax is said to be progressive when it takes account of a person's ability to pay it; a regressive tax, on the other hand, mostly ignores the ability to pay. If we consider for a moment the main kinds of direct and indirect taxation in this country we will soon see how significant this concept of progressive and regressive taxation is.

The main direct tax levied by central government is **income tax**, a charge which varies according to a person's income. The more you earn the more tax you are likely to have to pay; if your income is below a certain level you will be completely exempt from payment. Not only is income tax related to the size of a person's income, but as income increases so the rate of tax increases. It is, from an economist's viewpoint, a highly progressive tax, because it clearly takes account of a person's ability to pay.

Income tax does, however, suffer from certain disadvantages. From the government's point of view the main disadvantage is that it is very obvious, in that it is a direct charge on the taxpayer. Since a large number of voters whose support the government seeks have to pay income tax whether or not they want to, it is a politically unpopular tax. Income tax also has an economic disadvantage: because it is inherently progressive it tends to be a disincentive to greater effort and productivity. Overtime earnings are particularly susceptible to the inroads of income tax.

Another form of direct taxation is that on **capital gains**. This is a tax on income resulting from the sale of a fixed asset which has increased in value since the date of its original acquisition. Thus, if you buy some property for investment purposes and later sell it at a higher price you may be liable for capital gains tax on the 'profit' you have made from the sale. Although not so overtly progressive as income tax, there is a strong implication in capital gains tax that an ability to make capital gains indicates an ability to pay tax.

Then there are the direct taxes which might be called 'hyper-progressive' in that the intention behind them is to redistribute wealth from the more affluent sections of the community into the public sector and, ultimately, into the pockets of the less affluent; collectively we can call them **property taxes**. The most obvious one in this country is **capital transfer tax**, which has replaced estate duty as a means of taxing property left to dependants on death.

During the present century successive Chancellors of the Exchequer have experimented with a wide variety of indirect taxes. The one thing they have had in common is that they have all been taxes on consumption or expenditure. Until the introduction of **value added tax (VAT)** in 1973, **purchase tax**, which was applied as a percentage addition to the price of identified goods, was the main form of expenditure tax in the United Kingdom. VAT has proved to be a more flexible, and hence more useful device. Because it covers such a wide range of goods and services, it can produce a large amount of revenue for a relatively small change in its rate. Using the device of zero-rating, essential goods, such as basic foods, can be made completely exempt. It is no wonder that VAT, in a number of guises, has grown in popularity on the continent of Europe. Even had Britain not entered into membership of the EEC, it would probably have eventually adopted VAT.

VAT is a general expenditure tax: most others in this country are specific. They include petrol tax, car tax, and excise or customs duties on particular commodities such as tobacco, beers, wines, and spirits.

All expenditure taxes are basically regressive, even when they attempt to discriminate between basic needs and so-called luxuries. Indeed, it is virtually impossible to make an objective distinction of this kind; one man's basic needs may be another man's luxuries, and, of course, the converse is true. The tax on an expensive watch is clearly more than that on a cheap one, but it is rash to assume that all wealthy people buy expensive watches and the less wealthy buy cheaper ones. A millionaire has the choice of buying an inexpensive item and, in consequence, paying relatively little VAT. The regressive nature of expenditure taxes is built into them.

Before 1966 companies in this country were required to pay income tax and profits tax on their earnings. The Finance Act of 1965 replaced these liabilities with a new **corporation tax**. Its effect was to increase the rate of profits tax and exempt undistributed profits, which were ploughed back into the business, from income tax liability. Apart from tidying up the tax system as far as companies are concerned, corporation tax is intended to act as a stimulant to investment. Tax theoreticians are by no means all convinced that it does this effectively. Some argue that, because companies use their own resources to finance investment and do not have to go to the open market for funds, they are unlikely to be sufficiently discriminating in their investment policies. It is also possible to argue that profits are an indicator of successful enterprise and, as such, should not be taxed, because this tends to penalize the efficient company and favour the inefficient which makes a smaller profit or no profit at all.

The main components of central government tax revenue are set out in Table 18.1.

Table 18.1   UK central government revenue 1982

		Amount (£m)	% of total
Taxes on income:	Income tax and surtax	30 275	29.7
	Petroleum tax and duty	5 039	4.9
	Corporation tax	4 986	4.9
Taxes on expenditure:	VAT	14 255	14.0
	Hydrocarbon oils	5 102	5.0
	Tobacco	3 540	3.5
	Beers, wines, and spirits	3 346	3.3
	Customs duties	1 077	1.0
	Car tax	600	0.6
	Betting and gaming	578	0.6
	EC agricultural levies	278	0.3
	Motor Vehicle duties	1 712	1.7
	National insurance surcharge	2 811	2.7
	Gas levy	476	0.5
	Stamp duties	833	0.8
	Other expenditure taxes	376	0.4
National insurance contributions		18 069	17.7
Royalties and licence fees on oil and gas production		1 600	1.5
Dividends and interest from local authorities		1 742	1.7
Dividends and interest from public corporations		2 637	2.6
Other net income		2 671	2.6
	Total	102 003	100.0

Source: National Income and expenditure, HMSO, 1983.

The finance of local government

It is not sensible to speak of the local taxation system as if it were the exact equivalent of the central one. There is one simple tax which is levied locally, the **rate**, but this accounts for less than half of the money local authorities need to finance their activities. The other sources of finance are shown in Table 18.2.

In a two-tier system of local government the upper tier authorities do not levy and collect rates themselves. They make their financial requirements known to the district councils in the form of a *precept* and the districts then add this to their own requirements to arrive at the total rate.

Rates are, as we have said, a tax on property: they are charged on the basis of the rateable value of property which is equal, in principle at least, to the yearly rent which a landlord would charge and a tenant pay, on the understanding that the former insured the property and kept it in good external repair, and the latter paid the rates. Since 1949 the task of assessing the rateable value has been the responsibility of the valuation department of the Inland Revenue. This brings greater objectivity and fairness into the system.

The actual amount payable by a ratepayer is determined partly by the rateable value of the property he occupies and partly by the rate in the pound charged by the local authority. The method of calculating the rate poundage can best be shown by a simple example:

Total rateable value for the area (say) £10 000 000
(summation of all separate rateable values)

Product of a penny rate $\dfrac{£10\,000\,000}{100}$ £100 000

Total revenue required (say) £4 000 000

Rate needed is therefore $\dfrac{4\,000\,000}{100\,000}$ 40p in the £

The simplicity of rates is their greatest strength: indeed, some people would argue, their only strength. They contain a number of significant disadvantages; they tend to be regressive, not intentionally, but rather because they are based on a number of assumptions which are not always valid. The chief assumption is that the value of the property occupied is a good indicator of the ability of the occupier to pay; this is sometimes not the case. If a person decides to spend more on his house than on a car, or clothes, or food, or holidays, he pays more rates than he would have done if he had chosen a more modest residence. There is also, perhaps, an implied assumption that the more expensive the property the more demands the occupiers make on the local authority's services. There is, of course, no justification for this: a man in a small terraced house may put out two dustbins a week for refuse collection and the man in the five-bedroom detached house only one. If you have a big garden of your own you do not need to use the public park.

There are two other significant drawbacks to rates. First, they are not a very buoyant form of income for a local authority. Expenditure taxes, such as VAT, because they are levied on a percentage basis, rise with inflation. A personal tax, such as income tax, also grows with increases in the taxpayer's incomes. The second

191

Table 18.2   UK local authority revenue 1972 and 1982

	1972 Amount (£m)	1972 % of total	1982 Amount (£m)	1982 % of total
To finance current expenditure				
Grants from central government	3233	47.0	16 000	47.5
Rates	2379	34.6	12 098	35.8
Rents, dividends, and interest	863	12.5	4 014	11.9
Trading surpluses	134	2.0	242	0.7
Other income	269	3.9	1 390	4.1
Totals	6878	100.0	33 744	100.0
To finance capital expenditure				
Surplus from current account	689	77.2	3608	89.4
Capital grants from central government	203	22.8	382	9.5
Miscellaneous receipts	—	—	44	1.2
Totals	892	100.0	4 034	100.0

Source: National Income and Expenditure, HMSO, 1983.

disadvantage is that their impact is very obvious to the persons paying them. It is possible to argue that, if a tax has to be paid, it is better to bring it out into the open where it can be clearly seen. Unfortunately, this tends to make the tax unpopular. Psychologically, most people are more willing to pay a 'hidden' tax than an obvious one. An indirect tax, such as VAT, clearly adds to the cost of living, but it does so in a relatively unobtrusive way.

Despite the fairly widespread unpopularity of rates, and despite numerous suggestions that they should be replaced by a more buoyant local tax, none has yet been introduced. In 1974 the government appointed a committee, under the chairmanship of Frank Layfield, to examine all aspects of local government finance. In its report published in 1976[1] the Layfield Committee recommended a reform of the rating system, including the rating of agricultural land, which has been exempt. It also suggested a local income tax which would go a long way towards removing the present anomaly whereby local government is financed, through direct taxes, by less than 50 per cent of the local electorate: 16 million pay rates and 19 million do not. The Layfield Committee Report was effectively shelved, the Labour government of James Callaghan, rejecting most of the radical proposals in a Green Paper published in 1977.[2] The Conservative government of Mrs Thatcher, despite expressed intentions to tackle the problem of rates, has failed to do so and so this regressive, disliked tax remains for want of an acceptable alternative.

Financial relations between central and local government

As Table 18.2 shows, local authorities are now dependent on central government for at least half their income. This, inevitably, places them in an inferior position in their relations with Westminster and Whitehall. If central government was willing to respect the autonomy of elected local councils, despite their financial dependence, these relationships could still work harmoniously. When, however, central government becomes obsessive about the need to reduce public spending generally, then it is understandable that it should, with local authorities accounting for about a third of all public sector spending, 'lean heavily' on councils showing signs of exceeding Treasury targets.

Central government grants to assist local authorities were first introduced in 1835 for the specific purpose of contributing to the cost of transporting prisoners. Subsequently, a number of other specific grants were introduced, for education, policing, and so on. Under the Local Government Act of 1929 non-specific, or **block grants**, were introduced, and from 1948 the block grant was paid only to those local authorities whose revenue from rates was below the national average. This grant was called the **exchequer equalization grant**. In 1958 the government decided to replace most of the specific grants with one block grant called the **general grant**. The exchequer equalization grant continued for those local authorities which could show a real need. Another major reform occurred in 1966 when the general grant, the exchequer equalization grant, and any remaining specific grants were combined into a single **rate support grant (RSG)**. It comprises three elements. The needs element, which is by far the largest of the three, is designed to increase the amount of money payable to those authorities with greater than average calls on their services; for instance, an authority with a large number of school children who would make heavy demands on the education service would be given additional money. The second element, the resources element, is aimed at balancing out the effects of the different rateable values per head of population between authorities. Finally, there is the domestic element which is a direct subsidy for private householders paying rates.

The announcement of the size of the RSG for 1984–5 caused disappointment for most local authorities. The grant assumed an average rise in local government expenditure of 3 per cent, whereas the government estimated that the cost of living would rise by at least 5 per cent. The new grant therefore represented a cut in real terms. In announcing the grant, the government indicated financial penalties to be imposed on councils which spent above the Treasury's target figures.

As the Thatcher government's main intention was to restrict public spending from whatever source, it did not consider it sufficient to put a ceiling on grants to local authorities because they could, if they chose, increase their revenue by raising rates, however unpopular this might be locally. In December 1983, therefore, a Rates Bill was introduced which would give the government power to limit rate increases for certain local authorities regarded by the government as traditional 'high spenders', with reserve powers to extend this 'capping' of the rates to other authorities, if it was thought necessary. Since the identified 'high spenders' are mostly metropolitan counties, such as the GLC, Sheffield, and Newcastle, all Labour controlled, it is perhaps understandable that this part of the Bill would be supported by Conservative backbenchers. The wider, 'reserve', powers have, however, been bitterly opposed by some Conservatives.

The government's justification for this pre-emptory behaviour has been that it was necessary in order to maintain the medium-term financial strategy and control the PSBR, and also that many people who are obliged to pay rates, for example businesses, do not have the voting rights of private ratepayers. Whatever the outcome of the Rates Bill, this strict control of local authority finance by central government has done much to sour relations, not only with Labour-controlled councils, but also with many that have Conservative majorities.

Central government also exercises tight control over local authority borrowing, which has to be authorized by a **loan sanction**. The loan sanction procedure gives central government very detailed control over local schemes for such things as the construction of libraries or recreation facilities. Certain items of capital expenditure fall into what is called the **key sector**: schools, colleges, and housing, for example. Key sector projects are closely scrutinized by officials in the appropriate central departments.

This financial dependence of local authorities on central government was examined at length by the Layfield Committee, to which we have already referred. The Layfield Committee's recommendation of a local income tax, to replace rates as a more buoyant form of revenue, seems even more relevant and necessary today. But even if local authorities became more financially independent of central government, could they still expect to escape from the strict financial curbs which any government might choose to impose because of its belief in the need to control public sector spending generally?

The central budgetary system

The prime object of operating a budget would seem to produce a desired relationship between income and expenditure. Most personal budgets start with an income and what is spent is then related to it. If income over a given period exceeds expenditure, then we have managed to save something. If expenditure exceeds income, then we must borrow or dip into our savings.

Budgeting in the public sector operates within similar constraints but there are important differences. The first is that the government, central or local, can look at future expenditure first and then decide how much income it needs to meet that expenditure. Of course, in practice it is not as simple as that. Both sides of the equation, income and expenditure, have to be looked at more or less simultaneously. In other words, the effects of obtaining more income, through taxes, rates, or borrowing, have to be considered and then, perhaps, proposed expenditure has to be trimmed in the light of these considerations.

The second difference between budgeting in the public and the private sector is one which applies more to central government than local. It is that the budget, representing this relationship between income and expenditure, is no longer merely a financial device: it has become an economic weapon.

In the nineteenth century, when Gladstone was Chancellor, it seemed essential to secure as exact a balance as possible between the income the government obtained through taxes and the money it proposed to spend. Today chancellors can budget for a surplus or a deficit, and often do. If they wish to reduce the amount of purchasing power in the economy, then they will aim at collecting more revenue than they wish to spend. If they wish to boost the economy by putting more money into peoples' pockets, they will do the reverse. In the case of local government, which we will consider shortly, these economic aspects of budgeting are less apparent.

Let us first look at the mechanics of central government budgeting and at the devices and procedures which have been developed to bring more accuracy into forecasting revenue needs and into the control of expenditure.

Most central government spending starts in the departments. In the autumn they prepare their spending estimates. At about the same time the Treasury will inform the Principal Finance Officer in each spending department of its view on how the economy is progressing. The departments are expected to take this into account in the preparation of their five-year spending forecasts which have to be sent to the Treasury. By February the annual estimates will have been submitted, together with statements justifying them in the light of the overall analysis of the state of the economy. The Treasury considers all the estimates and discusses them with the spending departments concerned and then, once they are agreed, they are presented to Parliament. The **Civil Estimates** are traditionally introduced in the House of Commons by the Financial Secretary to the Treasury and the **Defence Estimates** by the Secretary of State for Defence. Meanwhile the Chancellor, with his Treasury officials, has been considering how he will produce the revenue necessary to meet the expenditure proposed in the estimates: in other words, he has prepared his budget. Traditionally, on the day before he presents his budget in the House, sitting as the Committee of Ways and Means, he will have revealed his taxation and other proposals to a special meeting of the Cabinet.

The ways in which the House of Commons attempts to control public expenditure are considered in the next chapter. We look now at two particular aspects of what we might call central financial management: the role of the Treasury and the system of Public Expenditure Surveys.

The Treasury as a financial manager

The Treasury, although one of the smallest Whitehall Departments, has always been the most powerful. Its power rests partly on its political prestige, in that the Prime Minister is formally First Lord of the Treasury, and the Chancellor, arguably, the next most senior member of the Cabinet; partly on its prestige within the civil service; and partly on the fact that it ultimately controls the nation's purse strings.

Although respected, the Treasury has never been loved. A former Chancellor, Denis Healey, once described himself as Dr No, with his second in command, the Chief Secretary to the Treasury, as Oddjob. It is the Chief Secretary who has the unenviable task of leading the team that does the hard bargaining with departments over their spending plans.

Because it has been unloved, and even feared, the Treasury has always had rivals and, as we have already seen, several attempts have been made to wrest power from it. In 1964 Harold Wilson appointed James Callaghan, not the strongest member of the Cabinet at that time, as Chancellor, and then created the Department of Economic Affairs, with his deputy, the ebullient George Brown, as its head. After four years George Brown had gone, replaced by the less effective Peter Shore, and by 1969 the Treasury's rival had disappeared. A second rival, the Civil Service Department, was dissolved in 1981, and the Central Policy Review Staff (CPRS), which could have challenged the Treasury in the field of medium- and long-term economic planning, met a similar fate.

The only remaining potential rival was the Cabinet Office, whose Secretary is now officially head of the civil service, but the Cabinet Office is not a spending department and has no real aspirations to financial management.

And so the Treasury has retained its predominance. As Harold Wilson is reported to have said: 'Whatever party is in office, the Treasury is in power.'

Between 1945 and the present day a central system of public expenditure management and control has evolved, with the Treasury always at the centre or hub of the system. The two main objectives have been, first, to plan public spending according to the government's formulated objectives, and, second, to control it so that it stays within the limits set by the plan. The Treasury's role in this involves seven main activities:

1. maintaining a dialogue with the spending departments about their expenditure programmes;
2. coordinating these spending programmes and advising the Chancellor and other ministers on how they fit into the overall economic strategy;
3. developing techniques for measuring and analysing public spending;
4. producing an annual White Paper setting out five-year expenditure plans for the Chancellor to present to Parliament;
5. liaising with the Cabinet Office on the effective management of the spending departments;
6. liaising with the House of Commons Public Accounts Committee; and
7. operating the Public Expenditure Survey Committee (PESC) process and the departmental financial management systems.

The PESC process

The initials PESC stand for **Public Expenditure Survey Committee** which is an interdepartmental committee of senior civil servants chaired by a Deputy Secretary of the Treasury. It started life in the early 1960s as a Treasury Committee, with representatives from the spending departments on it, but it has now become the centre of the main machinery for internally coordinating and controlling the government's total spending policies. PESC is, however, more than just a committee: it is a complete system operating on a continuous basis throughout the year.

We have already seen that the departments produce their annual estimates by late winter, having borne in mind the Treasury's view on the state of the economy. While the annual estimates and the Budget are being considered by Parliament the Treasury continues its work of looking at the on-going spending predictions of the departments well into the summer. This work culminates in a meeting of the PESC whose main job is to produce a report suggesting the principal issues ministers should consider in the autumn when they look forward to the next financial year. The PESC report is presented to the Cabinet by the Chancellor of the Exchequer and discussions then take place at Cabinet level so that by December, or thereabouts, an annual White Paper is produced which sets out the government's economic and financial policy intentions over the next five years.

The PESC process is, therefore, continuous, with estimates and predictions being continually up-dated. The White Paper, which represents the public exposition of the process, is probably unique. There is no record of any other government in the world producing a state document setting out in such detail the total economic and financial strategy of the government and the plans of each spending department.

The Heath government, soon after it was elected in 1970, embarked upon an ambitious programme of central government reform, aimed at making policy making and its implementation more rational and effective. Many of the innovations of this period, such as the reorganization of central departments and the establishment of the CPRS, have already been discussed, another should be noted, although it, like the CPRS, has now passed into temporary or permanent oblivion. It was a system of expenditure control called **Programme Analysis and Review (PAR)**.

The purpose of PAR was to ensure that individual spending departments followed policies in accordance with the total strategy of the government. Each department was required to submit annual PAR returns which set out in detail those policies which incurred expenditure. Senior officials of the Treasury, with those of the spending departments, the CPRS, and the Civil Service Department, considered the PAR returns in relation to overall government policy and the results of these considerations were eventually conveyed to the Cabinet.

There were high hopes for PAR in its early days and it had the personal backing of Edward Heath. As the government became more and more involved in immediate policy issues, such as industrial relations and the attempt to make an incomes policy work, so the political support for PAR waned and, without that support from the senior politicians, the system lost its initial momentum. It gradually faded into the background and was officially disbanded in 1979.

Nothing has really replaced it and since 1979 the government has paid less attention to long-term issues, being more concerned about 'value for money' in day-to-day expenditure. Thus, instead of a remodelled PAR, we find the cost-effective Rayner scrutinies, and private sector type of management information systems and resource control. We will discuss these and other innovations in our final chapter.

The local budgetary system

Local government is responsible for spending large amounts of money. In the financial year 1977–8 it spent more than £150 billion, representing 27 per cent of total public expenditure and 12 per cent of the total value of all goods and services produced in the country. It follows that the expenditure of individual local authorities is large and must be carefully planned and controlled. An average county council would, for example, spend about £150 million. An authority's expenditure is set down in some detail in its budget document. This document is prepared annually through a process which is usually lengthy and complex and which culminates in the authority fixing the rate to be levied for the forthcoming financial year. It is done annually primarily because the rate must be fixed every year by law and because the government makes most of its grant to local government on an annual basis. However, most local budgets attempt to forecast requirements for some three to five years ahead, mainly to show the implications for future years of continuing to run existing services and to indicate the committed costs of major building schemes which will take more than one year to complete.

One job of a budget is, as we have seen, to relate income to expenditure. In the case of local authorities this is its principal purpose. Most of a local authority's budget will be concerned with a relatively detailed itemization of its expenditure. The budget will also distinguish between two fundamental types of expenditure, revenue and capital. Basically, any money to be spent on items that recur frequently, and at least annually, such as salaries, or the purchase of goods and materials, will be termed revenue expenditure and will be met from the annual revenue budget. Capital expenditure is that which is a once-and-for-all expense on something new and permanent, such as a new school or a new road, or possibly new vehicles. The distinction between the two is important mainly because of the way they are initially financed. Expenditure on capital schemes is paid for by borrowing money from a statutory body called the *Public Works Loans Board* or from the private money markets. The idea behind borrowing is to smooth out the effects of undertaking major new schemes which if they had to be paid for out of one year's income, would cause dramatic fluctuations in the rates. The principle is similar to buying a house with the aid of a mortgage; there is also an element of equity involved. Future generations will benefit from the construction of a new building or facility, therefore it is right that they should contribute to its cost through the rates they will pay, so authorities will borrow money and pay it back, with interest, over periods of up to sixty years. The repayments will be made a little at a time each year so that eventually all local authority expenditure is met through its annual budget.

The elements that make up the budget are put together each year through a process which involves the authority in estimating its spending for the coming year and matching this with its estimated income. Its income is arrived at by ascertaining the likely level of grant from central government, assessing its probable income from charges for services, and calculating what it needs to raise in rates to make up the remainder. The financial year begins in April, and in most authorities the budgetary process will begin in the summer or early autumn when the committees responsible for the main services will estimate what they think they will need to spend; at the same time they will put forward their proposals for capital spending. The overall level that each committee wants to spend will often be governed by guidelines laid down in advance by the council or one of its central committees such as the policy or finance committee. The council will have a broad indication of the degree of change that central government expects to see in each major service, from the public expenditure White Paper which we have already discussed. The separate committee estimates are brought together at about the end of the calendar year, and there usually follows a period of brisk activity for a month or two while estimates are trimmed so as to bring them nearer to the guidelines. In the course of these discussions the rate for the coming year is agreed. This stage usually involves intense debate as committees and the chief officers bid for larger slices of the money cake, while the finance or policy committee tries to strike an acceptable balance between maintaining essential services and avoiding a substantial rate increase. The process ends with the formal publication of the next year's budget and the fixing of the rate in February or March.

The nature of the budget and its production are strongly influenced by the national annual cycle of public accounting, and the need for an effective means of control; indeed many requirements are laid down by statute. However, it is arguable whether it provides the best means of ensuring that local government spending is both efficient and effective. The shortcomings of the budget procedure as an adequate method of local authority planning and management have been recognized by many councils and various attempts have been made to develop alternative or complementary systems which try to provide a broader context for estimating service provision and expenditure. One of the most developed of these is the Planning, Programming, Budgeting Systems (PPBS) approach. The critics of the conventional annual budget argue that it is primarily aimed at controlling expenditure to pre-set levels within a large number of detailed heads, and that because it takes this form, it encourages authorities to concentrate on what they are doing, rather than why they are doing it, or whether they are doing it well, or whether it could be done in a different way. For example, if a council has a highways department to provide highways, and a transport department to provide a bus service, these can too easily become ends in themselves rather than the provision of an integrated transport system.

PPBS is essentially an approach to management which is designed to concentrate thinking on identifying the objectives of providing a service, evaluating the effectiveness of that service, and examining whether there are better alternatives to meet the needs which the service is designed to satisfy. In so doing it encourages authorities to think about how activities relate to one another so that several apparently unrelated activities can be identified as trying to achieve the same objective, and can therefore be coordinated appropriately. For instance, the provision of school sports facilities and the provision of municipal sports pitches and swimming baths are all aimed at meeting the leisure needs of the local community; so a leisure programme might combine the activities of the parks and education departments in the provision of a community leisure centre based on a local school.

There is still a widespread reluctance to change conventional budgeting procedures but there are signs that more local authorities, however cautiously, will introduce the new systems over the coming years. This will result in a better balance between effective planning and objective evaluation of local spending and the traditional procedures of expenditure control. It can be seen, therefore, that, in separate but similar ways, the approach to expenditure planning and control in both central and local government is becoming broader based and more realistic.

References

1. *Report of the Committee on Local Government Finance*, Cmnd. 6453, HMSO, 1976.
2. *Local Government Finance*, Cmnd. 6813, HMSO, 1977.

Assignments

29. 'An annual budget statement is now an anachronism and could usefully be abandoned.' Do you agree? Give a reasoned answer.
30. In the past five years or so there has been a steady movement from direct to indirect taxation. Discuss the advantages and disadvantages of this movement.

Part Five The public interest and the private interest

19

Public accountability

The concept of accountability

We have argued earlier that the United Kingdom has maintained and developed its democratic traditions through a system of representative and responsible government. We can take the argument a stage further and say that for a government to be responsible it must also be accountable. In other words, there must be some means whereby public administrators, centrally and locally, are obliged to account for the decisions they take and the actions which follow. The questions we should now ask are, how and to whom should they be accountable?

When we looked at the structure and operation of the central government institutions we examined the concept of ministerial responsibility. We can now widen that concept into one of political responsibility and include in it the political–permanent relationships which operate not only in central government but also in local government and some of the *ad hoc* quasi-governmental bodies. What we are saying is that any decision in the public sector which is political should be subject to public accountability. Action taken by permanent public servants to implement a political decision is not normally publicly accountable although the fine line between policy and administration is not always easy to draw.

'Internal' decisions and actions, if we may call them that, are accountable to the politicians responsible for the department or unit in which the decisions have been taken. Politicians must, however, be prepared to justify and defend those decisions and actions which we can call 'external' and which have an impact on people outside the administration. Thus there is accountability in two stages. The first makes the public servant accountable to the politician; the second makes the politician accountable for all decisions of his department or unit, whether or not the decisions have been taken personally by him, or even whether he is aware that they have been taken. This accountability is ultimately, through the representative system, to the public at large. It seems a fair burden for a politician to bear: after all he is usually quick to capitalize on any successful operation he has been associated with so why should he not accept blame for the unsuccessful?

The need for public accountability has always been there. Because of growing government involvement in almost every facet of life, the need has been accentuated. According to the theory of representative government it contains its own, in-built accountability. The electors vote their representatives into office for a given term: if, at the end of that term, their record is thought to be unsatisfactory they are voted out of office. Furthermore, during their term of office the elected representatives are, according to the theory, continually challenged by their rivals who will be doing their utmost to reveal their faults and weaknesses so as to discredit them and, if possible, replace them. In very general terms the theory is still valid today but the traditional institutions for ensuring accountability have either become overloaded or their methods of operating have become outdated. We will now look at how these traditional institutions are managing and at attempts to improve them, replace them, or complement them with newer, more relevant bodies to plug the accountability gaps which have been found to exist.

In this chapter we will concentrate mainly on the institutional forms of public accountability. In the next chapter we will examine another aspect: the relations between the ordinary individual and the state. This is another facet of accountability but sufficiently important to merit separate consideration.

Judicial control and review

In a constitution based on the rule of law the judicial system obviously must play a big part in ensuring that the executive is accountable for the actions it takes. The basis of this judicial control is found in the concept of *ultra vires*. We have already mentioned this doctrine in earlier chapters but, because it is so central to the concept of public accountability, we must now look at it more closely.

The surest way of challenging an administrative action is to ask whether it is within the legal competence of the person or body taking it; in other words to ask the question: are you authorized in law to do what you are doing? If the answer to your question is not an unequivocal yes, then your objection will almost certainly be upheld.

To act in an *ultra vires* fashion is to act beyond your powers. It is something of which any person or body in the public sector can be found guilty although it is more likely to arise in local government or other bodies whose powers are derived almost entirely from Parliament. A minister, or civil servant acting on his behalf, can act *ultra vires*, of course, but be in a better position to make the action *intra vires* than someone in, say, local government. If the law prevents the government from implementing a certain policy it can use its parliamentary majority to alter the law, providing it is ready to face the political consequences of doing so.

The three main bases of complaints that a public body has acted *ultra vires* are, first, that it has simply done something that it was not authorized to do; second, that it has failed to do something which in law it is charged to do; and third, that it has done something which it is empowered to do but in doing it has acted in an improper way, usually by failing to follow a set procedure. In all three cases the courts can do something. There is a series of orders of the High Court which can be applied for by the person or body making the complaint. A **prohibition** may be granted which orders the minister or public body to refrain from some specified act. A **declaration** may be issued which formally sets out the rights of the person making the complaint. An order of **mandamus** may be issued which commands a public body to perform its duties. In some cases an executive action has been challenged in a lower court and the action upheld. In this case a complainant may take the matter to the High Court and, if his complaint is successful, an order of **certiorari** may be made which has the effect of quashing the decision reached in the lower court.

Local authorities are also subject to audit by the Audit Commission. The Commission is entrusted with the job of examining the financial accounts of a local authority to ensure that any expenditure has been properly authorized and is within its legal powers. The country is divided into audit districts with an auditor responsible for each. He has wide powers of interpretation and, applies in a financial context, the doctrine of *ultra vires*. If he believes some expenditure has been illegally authorized, and he can interpret this in the sense of its being 'unreasonable', he has power to surcharge the council members responsible for incurring or authorizing it. This means that they can be compelled, personally, to repay the illegal expenditure. If an officer of a local authority knowingly incurs or authorizes unlawful expenditure, even if instructed to do so by an elected member, he too may be surcharged.

Unfortunately, judicial control and review through the doctrine of *ultra vires* only really caters for those cases where a public body is clearly breaking the law. It is now possible for Ministers, or civil servants acting on their behalf, to exercise enormous powers which seem strictly within the law yet which can be interpreted so widely that it is difficult for someone without legal training or experience to judge whether they are abusing the spirit of the law or even straying beyond its bounds. The areas where ministerial powers have grown and where ministerial discretion is increasingly exercised are in the field of delegated legislation; in the use of administrative tribunals; and in the right of ministers to act as the final point of appeal against decisions by local authorities or even by their own civil servants.

Accountability for delegated legislation

The present century has seen a phenomenal growth in the amount of delegated legislation authorized in this country. Two world wars and the creation of the so-called welfare state have been the main reasons for this. As the government has involved itself more and more in day-to-day social, economic, and industrial affairs, so specialized legislation has been passed, and almost invariably the parent Act has had numerous offspring in the shape of regulations and other statutory instruments spelling out in detail the application of the general principles in the Act.

The job of producing this delegated legislation is given to civil servants working on behalf of ministers. Thus a Road Traffic Act will set out a series of general propositions and then regulations made under the Act will detail exactly how law enforcement officers and the courts interpret and apply these propositions. In effect, ministers have been given authority to make laws without going through the full legislative process.

To try to ensure that Parliament was not completely bypassed by ministerial fiat, the House of Commons, in 1944, set up a **Select Committee on Statutory Instruments**, as delegated legislation is officially called, to scrutinize it. It soon acquired the popular name of the **Scrutiny Committee**. It has 11 members, drawn from both sides of the House and chosen by the Selection Committee, and its chairman is always a member of the Opposition. It can draw the House of Commons' attention to delegated legislation on one or more of the following grounds:

1. that it imposes a charge;
2. that it makes unusual use of powers;
3. that it is retrospective, without specific permission of the enabling Act which authorized it;
4. that there has been an unjustifiable delay in its publication; or
5. for any other reason the Committee sees fit.

Once the attention of the House has been drawn to the offending legislation it is up to it to decide the next step. Although the government in power obviously has the

205

legislative whip hand, the Scrutiny Committee has a good record of success as a 'parliamentary policeman'. It is certain that its very presence ensures that a lot of doubtful or badly drafted subordinate legislation never sees the light of day. A similar body operates in the House of Lords.

In our examination of the European Community we saw that the great bulk of community law is in the form of delegated legislation issued on the authority of the Council of Ministers. Most, if not all, of this European legislation has, or will have, an effect on this country, so, alive to the possible dangers in this, the House of Commons has set up another Select Committee, on the lines of the Scrutiny Committee, specifically to look at this new, growing stream of delegated legislation.

Tribunals and inquiries

The government's increased involvement in social, economic, and industrial matters has led it into the area of judicial, or quasi-judicial, activity.

Civil servants, acting on behalf of ministers, are required at times to give a decision which is essentially based on their views of the rights and wrongs of arguments presented to them. As such, it contains all the hallmarks of a judicial decision. If such a decision were made in a court of law the rules of 'natural justice' would apply. These represent a fundamental approach to law which has been developed by the judiciary over the years and which is now generally regarded as being the best guarantee of fairness and objectivity in disputes dealt with by the judicial process. Natural justice involves four elements:

1. that no one should be a judge in his own case;
2. that, before a decision is taken, each side in a dispute should have an opportunity of presenting its case;
3. that both sides should be entitled to know the reasoning behind the decision given; and
4. that the decision should be based on the evidence presented and not on other factors.

When a minister, or a civil servant, takes a decision of a quasi-judicial nature, such as ruling whether or not someone is entitled to a grant, or should be allowed to develop his property, it is certain that not all of the rules of natural justice will prevail. Clearly, the minister is an interested party, and therefore virtually a judge in his own case.

Another way in which ministers, vicariously, play a judicial role is by setting up an administrative tribunal to deal with claims which would otherwise come to them. Tribunals of this nature are prominent in the social services. Someone claims that he is entitled to a pension, for example, and the ministry refuses the application. The applicant is advised to take his case to a pensions tribunal where his arguments are listened to and a decision given. Although the proceedings at an administrative tribunal are less formal, and less obviously judicial, than those in a court of law, and even though the tribunal includes lay as well as legally qualified members, a hearing there contains most of the essentials of the judicial process and, because of this, the rules of natural justice, it would seem, ought to apply.

A third way in which ministers and civil servants adopt a judicial role is when a public inquiry is held following an appeal to the minister about a decision by some other body, usually a local authority. Such inquiries are common in the field of environmental planning: someone wishes to develop an area of land for housing or industrial use and the local authority turns down his planning application; the would-be developer appeals against the decision and a public inquiry is held in the locality. The inquiry is conducted by a civil servant acting on behalf of the minister. He listens to the arguments presented to him by the applicants for planning permission, and by the local authority and other objectors and then advises the minister, either accepting the appeal or rejecting it. The minister is not bound to accept the inspector's advice, but at least the arguments for and against have been listened to and evaluated. There could, conversely, be an appeal against a local authority's decision to allow development. In some cases a minister has a proposal himself, possibly a new motorway or trunk road, and people living in the area decide to object. The method of resolving the dispute is, again, the public inquiry.

All three processes involve judicial or quasi-judicial activity. At first glance it might seem that the proper place for the disputes to be heard is an ordinary court of law. There are, however, several disadvantages in this. First, the law courts are already overloaded. If their jurisdiction were extended in this way the judicial system would probably break down. Second, although judges are trained to take judicial decisions, they are very much 'creatures of precedent'. They are experienced in interpreting common and statute law, and they have shown great flexibility and versatility in doing this, but they will always take the legal view and rely on non-legal experts for technical advice. Most of the cases which come before administrative tribunals or public inquiries are technical in nature and that is why members of them often have technical backgrounds. A purely legal approach would in many cases produce incongruous, even unjust, decisions. Finally, a tribunal or inquiry can adopt much more informal methods than would be acceptable in a court of law. This makes them more appropriate for the kinds of cases they are required to look into, and also speeds up the work of the hearings. The possibility of diverting the work of tribunals and inquiries into the ordinary law courts is therefore not really practicable. We should turn our attention towards ensuring that the people who appear before them get the fairest and most appropriate hearings possible.

The accountability of ministers

The first strong public stirrings of unease about the dangers inherent in the government's use of discretionary powers occurred in the late 1920s. The (then) Lord Chief Justice, Lord Hewart, took the remarkable step of writing a book criticizing the excessive use of delegated legislation and the exercise of powers by ministers in a quasi-judicial manner.[1] His complaints and those of others undoubtedly contributed to the government's decision to set up a departmental committee in 1929, under the chairmanship of Lord Donoughmore, to look into the use and abuse of ministers' powers in the areas of delegated legislation and administrative adjudication. The Committee had an ill-starred life. Because of illness, the chairman was replaced by Sir Leslie Scott, and its report, published in 1932, had a cool reception.[2] Despite the Donoughmore–Scott Committee's useful analysis of the problems involved, only one of its recommendations was acted on, and that 12 years after the Committee had reported. It was the setting up of the Scrutiny Committee on delegated legislation.

In the post-1945 period, as the nation returned to a peacetime existence, the feeling that ministers and officials exercised too much unchecked power returned. One particular episode seemed to crystallize this disquiet: the so-called Crichel Down Affair.

Crichel Down is an area in Dorset where, before the outbreak of war in 1939, the government had compulsorily requisitioned land for air force use. It was land farmed by the Marten family. When the war ended it was no longer needed for defence purposes and a decision was taken to return it to private ownership. Instead of giving the Marten family a first option on its purchase, civil servants in the Ministry of Agriculture decided to restock the land and sell it to a suitable purchaser as a viable farming unit. This was in accordance with a policy established by the Labour government of Clement Attlee. Officials in the Ministry, through their contacts, identified a prospective buyer and went a long way towards giving him a guarantee that the land was his if he wanted it. Meanwhile a member of the family who had originally owned it, Lieutenant-Commander Marten, made inquiries about possible purchase. Although there is no evidence of bribery, it is clear that the civil servants involved had committed the Ministry almost irrevocably to the sale of the land to someone outside the Marten family so that this new approach caused them considerable embarrassment. They therefore embarked on a policy of trying to dissuade Lieutenant-Commander Marten from pursuing his offer and, in the course of this, deliberately misled him with fictitious and incorrect information. He persisted with his claim, refusing to be deterred, and was eventually successful in obtaining an interview with the Minister, Sir Thomas Dugdale. For the first time, the Minister sensed that something was wrong and had the courage to order an immediate inquiry into the whole affair. The report of the inquiry, in 1954, took the view that the civil servants concerned had been guilty of maladministration. The fact that the Minister had not known of this was not seen as a satisfactory excuse. Sir Thomas Dugdale offered his resignation to the Prime Minister and it was accepted.

Crichel Down was seen by many people as a classic example of a minister over-reaching his powers. In fact it was nothing of the kind: it was a simple case of maladministration by civil servants. The two most significant aspects of the episode were, first, that it provided strong support for the doctrine of ministerial responsibility, and, second, that it revealed that there was, at that time, no immediate and adequate machinery for dealing with complaints of maladministration of this kind. Another interesting feature about Crichel Down is that the civil servants in the Ministry of Agriculture were still implementing Labour Party policy with a Conservative government in power. The policy introduced in the 1945–50 administration had become departmental policy, and the new minister had not initiated a change.

The Franks Committee

However wrongly it was interpreted at the time, the Crichel Down Affair provoked the government into setting up another inquiry whose effects were to prove widespread and long-lasting. In 1955 a departmental committee, under the chairmanship of Sir Oliver Franks as he then was, was asked to look at the constitution and working of administrative tribunals, and the operation of administrative procedures such as the holding of public inquiries. It is ironic that the question of maladministration, which was essentially what Crichel Down was about, was not included in the Committee's terms of reference. More time was to elapse, as we shall see, before that particular nettle was grasped. Nevertheless, the report of the Franks Committee in 1957 was timely, well-argued, and, as it proved, extremely influential.[3]

The Committee used as its guide for assessing the workings of administrative tribunals and public inquiries the three concepts of 'openness, fairness, and impartiality'. Using these criteria, it made a number of firm recommendations, most of which were accepted by the government and eventually implemented in the Tribunals and Inquiries Act of 1958. The most significant result was the establishment of a permanent Council on Tribunals, charged with the task of overseeing and monitoring the constitution and working of administrative tribunals. The Council closely watches tribunals and its members sit in on different hearings from time to time. It produces an annual report and specific reports if it sees the need to do so. It can be said without hesitation that the working of tribunals has improved immeasurably since the Council was established.

The Franks Committee also recommended specific reforms to increase the openness, fairness, and impartiality of administrative procedures such as public inquiries, and again there have been significant improvements in this area. The whole process is more open and reasons for decisions arrived at are now given.

Some lawyers and political observers argue that the British approach towards making ministers and public servants more accountable for their actions is still far from satisfactory and advocate the adoption of a complete and separate system of administrative law similar to that operating in France. To do this we would need a new set of administrative courts, operating alongside the ordinary courts, and a separate body of administrative law. Whether this could be successfully integrated into the existing system of common and statute law is a matter of judgement. In any event, it is very unlikely to happen. What is more likely is that, in a pragmatic fashion, present methods will be modified and improved as part of an evolutionary process.

Accountability through political control

The theory behind representative government is that the executive, meaning ministers and civil servants centrally, and chief officers of local authorities, is responsible and accountable to the members of the representative institutions, in other words Parliament and the local councils. However, we know that in practice the government in power, because of its majority in the House of Commons, is more in control of itself than controlled. It is also evident that because of councillors' lack of time and knowledge local chief officers are able to exercise much more discretion and take many more decisions than the theory of representative government admits. Are ministers and chief officers absolved then, from political accountability? Let us look at central government first.

There are four main ways in which Parliament exercises some control over the central administration and tries to make it accountable to it. The first and obvious way is by Members asking questions of ministers in the House of Commons. The first hour of the parliamentary day from Mondays to Thursdays is devoted to Question Time, and this has been broadcast live to the nation. MPs can ask for an oral or a written answer: if their prime purpose is to get information then a written answer is more likely to produce it; if, on the other hand, the question is designed to embarrass or assist the government an oral answer is more appropriate. Most questions for oral

209

answer are asked purely as part of party tactics. Thus the question normally addressed to the minister is often no more than a peg to hang a supplementary question on and the drift of the subsequent questioning may bear little relationship to its start. As an instrument of control and accountability there is little evidence that parliamentary questions are effective. The most they achieve is to keep civil servants on their toes in providing ministers with ammunition for dealing with possible supplementary questions. Ministers are not obliged to answer parliamentary questions and sometimes they refuse to do so. For example, successive Speakers have ruled that questions about the day-to-day operation of the nationalized industries are not admissible. In the 1971–2 parliamentary session a Select Committee on Parliamentary Questions was set up in the House of Commons and, as a result of its inquiries, a list was published of 95 items about which ministers have persistently refused to answer questions. MPs believe that if that list were to be brought up-to-date it would be even longer today.

The practice of using Question Time for 'planted' questions has also developed. In February 1984, for example, Labour backbenchers obtained copies of a list of questions given to Conservative MPs by government whips with the suggestion that they might usefully be asked during the Prime Minister's question session. The tactic was intended to occupy time with helpful questions which would provoke bland, self-congratulatory answers, and so squeeze out more searching, and potentially embarrassing, questions. The practice of planting questions is not confined to any one government: all have used the device in recent years. What made the 1984 episode distinctive was the fact that it had become so blatantly obvious.

It is not surprising that Question Time has become perhaps the least useful means of calling ministers to account. It has also become increasingly costly. In the 1980–1 parliamentary session, for example, 30 863 questions were asked in the House of Commons, the cost of which was £1 230 000, or an average of just under £40 per question. A minister has discretionary power to refuse to answer a question if the cost of preparing a reply would be likely to be more than £200.

An alternative way in which a Member of Parliament can require a minister to be accountable for his actions is by writing to him. Recent studies have shown that the practice of MPs corresponding with ministers on behalf of their constituents is likely to be much more effective than parliamentary questioning.

A third, obvious, way of requiring the executive to account for its actions is through formal debates. The parliamentary sessional timetable affords numerous opportunities for debating government policies and decisions. However, most of the debates arranged 'through the usual channels' are little more than set pieces, with government and opposition speakers taking turns to score points off each other. Furthermore, such debates tend to be too general to be effective as a means of ensuring accountability. The most effective debates are probably those at the second reading stage of a Bill, when the principles of proposed legislation are presented and discussed, and the emergency debates, under the House of Commons Standing Order 9, when the Speaker allows discussion of a matter of national importance and of extreme urgency. Such debates are quite rare because it means the suspension of the planned business of the House while the debate takes place. It is understandable that the Speaker accedes to a request for an emergency debate with considerable reluctance. When he does so, however, it is usually very effective.

210　　The fourth, and, in overall terms, clearly the most effective way in which

Parliament requires the government to be accountable is through the use of select committees.

Accountability to select committees

A select committee is so called because its membership is drawn from both sides of the House, by the Selection Committee, with the intention of making it as representative of and as much in sympathy with as many backbenchers as possible.

The Public Accounts Committee (PAC) was established by Gladstone in 1861 as the first parliamentary committee and it has survived to the present day. Until 1979 there were three other significant House of Commons select committees: the **Expenditure Committee**, concerned, as is the PAC, with finance; the **Nationalized Industries Committee**; and the **Statutory Instruments Committee**, to which we have already referred. In July 1978 the **Select Committee on Procedure** recommended the establishment of 12 specialist committees to shadow the work of the main central departments and the recommendation was accepted and implemented in 1979 by the, then, Leader of the House, Norman St John Stevas. The PAC and the Statutory Instruments Committee were to remain, but the Expenditure and Nationalized Industries Committees disappeared.

The Westminster system of select committees has been compared, usually unfavourably, with the congressional committees in the United States. The Senate and House of Representatives' committees have an enviable reputation as powerful bodies which can bring the federal government to account at the very highest level. The Watergate inquiries are a dramatic example of their power. It is perhaps not sensible to suggest that they could, or should, be duplicated in this country. The two systems of government are fundamentally different. In the United States there is a fixed-term executive which does not have daily access to the legislature, as in this country. It is mainly because of this gap between the Presidency and Congress that the committee system has been found necessary and has grown. Nevertheless, the importance of the select committee system in the United Kingdom should not be underrated.

The most prestigious and powerful is the PAC. It has 14 members and is chaired by a backbench member of the Opposition. It examines the annual financial accounts of the central departments and the reports on them made by the Comptroller and Auditor-General and his staff. The Comptroller and Auditor-General is an officer of the House of Commons and heads the Exchequer and Audit Department. He enjoys an independence and security similar to that of a High Court judge. His job is to audit all the central government accounts, to certify them, and then submit them to Parliament. In addition to ensuring that the accounts are technically correct and that there have been no illegal transactions, the Comptroller and Auditor-General also advises the House of Commons on whether, in his view, expenditure has been soundly and efficiently undertaken.

The PAC has acquired considerable standing and influence, and its reports carry great authority. Civil servants undoubtedly show it genuine respect and would always wish to avoid crossing swords with it. Its greatest disadvantage is that its work is, inevitably, *post facto*. It is bound to be nearly always 'closing the stable door after the horse has bolted'. Nevertheless, its very presence has reduced the number of occasions on which the horse has seen fit to bolt.

The 12 new committees set up in 1979 have now successfully established themselves and have demonstrated that they are not afraid to show a healthy disrespect for the government of the day. The **Foreign Affairs Committee**, for example, caused the government considerable embarrassment during the 1983 general election campaign by publishing a draft report arguing that the 'Fortress Falklands' policy was untenable in the long term. The **Defence Committee** has examined defence spending in some detail, questioning the government's policies over its contribution to NATO. The **Energy Committee** has queried decisions to increase energy prices, particularly those for electricity, without sufficient economic justification. The **Employment Committee** and the **Environment Committee** have, with Energy, looked at the politically-sensitive subject of safety in nuclear establishments, causing the government some discomfort.

The **Transport Committee** has probed the public financing of road, rail, air, and sea ferry services, including subsidy policies, and the **Social Services Committee** has investigated housing benefits, as well as the management of the National Health Service.

The **Treasury and Civil Service Committee** has proved to be a particularly powerful voice in Westminster, even though its recommendations have sometimes been ignored. The other four committees, **Agriculture**, **Education, Science, and the Arts**, **Home Affairs**, and **Trade and Industry** have been similarly active in their inquisitorial roles, and the **Scottish Affairs** and **Welsh Affairs** committees have diligently safeguarded the interests of the two countries.

Chairmanships of these committees are important and in the 1979–83 Parliament they were shared between Conservatives and Labour in the ratio of seven to five. Following the reduced Labour majority in the House of Commons in 1983, this ratio was changed to eight to four, in favour of the Conservatives. It should be noted, however, that Conservative backbench chairmen can be just as critical of their government as their Opposition counterparts. The Liberal–SDP Alliance has felt itself 'disenfranchised' in that, although it has select committee representation, it does not fairly reflect its political strength in the country.

Any objective evaluation of the new Westminster select committee system must judge it to be a success in terms of the committees' ability to cross-examine ministers and their civil servants vigorously and searchingly. In the final analysis, of course, Whitehall has many more resources at its disposal in this 'question-and-answer game', and whether or not the government decides to heed a committee's criticism is a matter of political choice. The committees are, nevertheless, a welcome and encouraging development.

Accountability in local government

As individuals, councillors have no direct power over officials except the right of access to documents which are necessary for them to do their duty. This power enables them to make some penetration into the administrative machine on behalf of electors, and the Robinson Committee on the Remuneration of Local Authority Members[4] noted that, on average, local representatives spend 13 hours per month dealing with elector's problems in addition to 54 hours on general council business. The evidence is, however, that members of the public are more likely to take complaints directly to an official in the local council offices, who is more readily identifiable than a committee chairman, and who can be expected to be able to take direct action.

Control by councillors as a corporate body is more effective but, as we have already seen, the links between the party group on the council and the permanent officials are likely to be weak. The party group has a large number of tasks to perform and has to take a view about a wide variety of technical matters which are often complex. Only a minority of its members, sitting on the relevant committee, will be reasonably familiar with the nature of a service under discussion; the rest will have to rely on the lay opinions of that minority since officers are rarely invited to be present at the group's discussions. The party group meetings are, therefore, likely to be hurried and ill-informed and the quality of their discussions must, in consequence, be questionable.

External local political control and accountability is limited by the comparative infrequency of elections: every three or four years. Within the council the crucial links between the party group and the officials are weakened by the secrecy surrounding the group's activities. The health of local democracy must depend upon the relationships between the electorate, politicians, and officials being strengthened and this would be greatly helped if this cloak of secrecy which seems to surround so much of party political activity were removed.

By law all local authorities are subject to external audit. Until 1983 this was done through a system of **district audit**, whereby the country was divided into districts, for each of which the Secretary of State for the Environment appointed a district auditor specializing in the work of local authorities. Although the district auditor was strictly speaking a civil servant, he did enjoy a large measure of independence from the Secretary of State.

The function of the district auditor was to inspect local authority accounts to detect any financial irregularities, to promote sound financial procedures, and to reveal any unlawful payments. He had power to disallow what he regarded as unlawful expenditure and to order repayment by councillors or officials who had authorized the expenditure. Over the years district auditors had increasingly concerned themselves with wasteful expenditure and had devised 'performance indicators' for comparing the provision of different services in different authorities.

In 1983 the district audit service was replaced by the **Audit Commission**, which is a body of people appointed by the Secretary of State but ostensibly enjoying even greater independence than the district auditors. The Commission is based on a system that has been operating successfully in Scotland for many years.

References

1. Lord Hewart, *The New Despotism*, Ernest Benn, 1929.
2. *Report of the Committee on Ministers' Powers*, Cmnd. 4060, HMSO, 1932.
3. *Report of the Committee on Tribunals and Enquiries*, Cmnd. 218, HMSO, 1957.
4. *Report of the Committee of Inquiry into the System of Remuneration of Members of Local Authorities*, HMSO, 1977.

Assignments

31. Who, in your view, was primarily responsible for the leak of radioactive material from the Sellafield nuclear power station? Who should accept responsibility for it?

Sources: The Economist, The Times, The Guardian, The Daily Telegraph, The Sunday Times, The Observer, or *The Financial Times.*

32. Which of the House of Commons specialist select committees has, in your view, been most successful.

214   *Sources:* As for Assignment 31.

20
The state and the citizen

The public versus the private interest

Democracy is, by definition, government by the people, of the people, and for the people—but what is meant by the people? Sometimes a law which is passed in the interests of the majority can be seen as positively harmful by a single individual. The construction of an urban motorway to take traffic away from central London may seem to be a desirable, and long overdue, development, particularly for people who have to travel regularly from one side of the city to another. But what about the people who live in the area where the motorway is to be built? It is unlikely that they would see it as in any way desirable.

Inevitably, there will be conflicts between the majority view, which we may call the public interest, and the minority view, which we may call the private interest. How to avoid or resolve these conflicts poses one of the most important problems confronting public administration today. If the public interest always prevailed a great many individuals would be, at the very least, disadvantaged and inconvenienced. If, on the other hand, the private interest was able to block every scheme or proposal which was put forward by the government or some other public body many worthwhile environmental improvements and other forms of social progress would be frustrated.

In the previous chapter we examined the ways in which public bodies are made accountable to the community for their actions. In this chapter we will take this examination a stage further by looking more specifically at the ways in which ordinary people, singly or in groups, can bring public bodies to account and challenge them when authority seems in danger of overriding individual rights and freedoms.

The redress of grievances

The Franks Committee on Tribunals and Enquiries had this to say: 'Over most of the fields of public administration no formal procedure for objecting or deciding on objections is provided . . . . It may be thought that in these cases the individual is less protected against unfair or wrong decisions.' That was written in 1957. Since that time a number of developments have taken place, some of them as a result of the report of the Franks Committee, to afford better protection to the ordinary person against abuse or unfair treatment by the state and its agencies. Despite these improvements, there are still grounds for disquiet. Some of the institutions and procedures which have been set up are working imperfectly. There are still gaps in provision or protection which have not been filled.

We shall now try to answer a number of questions which are vital as far as the individual is concerned. What kinds of grievances does the average citizen have against authority? What channels and opportunities are open to him to air these grievances? On the evidence of experience, how successful is he likely to be in pursuing his complaints? How might the existing institutions and procedures be improved? What gaps in 'grievance satisfaction' still remain?

To try to distinguish between one kind of grievance and another may seem, from the individual's point of view, largely irrelevant. If you park your car outside the public library and while you are inside a wall collapses, depositing a ton of bricks on it, your immediate concern is certainly not going to be whether the wall 'legitimately' crumbled or whether it was due to an act of maladministration. When Lieutenant-Commander Marten was fobbed off with misleading information in response to inquiries about the purchase of his family's former property at Crichel Down he saw it as a matter of personal grievance and probably did not consider whether the civil servants concerned had acted illegally or just unfairly. Yet, as it turned out, the distinction was important. If their actions had been illegal he would have had access to the courts. If they had failed to follow some set administrative procedures he could have appealed to the minister or to a tribunal. Because they had not acted illegally but had been guilty of maladministration no defined route to secure redress of his grievance lay open to him. The substance of a grievance is, therefore, important.

We have already discussed the machinery of tribunals and public inquiries. These are, of course, available to any individual who has a grievance in an area within the competence of a tribunal or an inspector. There are also the political channels through which a grievance can be taken up with an MP or councillor. In the case of an illegal action by a public body there is access to the courts. Before we try to evaluate the likelihood of the ordinary citizen obtaining effective redress of his grievance through these established institutions and procedures we must look at a problem area which has only comparatively recently come into prominence: the area of maladministration.

Maladministration and the individual

The events of Crichel Down were adjudged to be a clear case of maladministration on the part of the civil servants concerned and, although the Franks Committee was set up soon after the facts had been revealed, its chairman was at pains to point out that his committee's terms of reference excluded any examination of the question of maladministration. Three years later, in 1960, an unofficial body of lawyers, **Justice**, decided to institute its own inquiry and the committee it set up for this purpose reported in 1961.

Justice is the British Section of the International Commission of Jurists. It is an all-party association of lawyers pledged to uphold and strengthen the Rule of Law. The committee it set up was under the chairmanship of Sir John Whyatt, a former Chief Justice of Singapore, and the report, *The Citizen and the Administration*, is often referred to as the Whyatt Report. Having noted the inability of the Franks Committee to consider the problems of maladministration, the Whyatt Report identified two major areas of concern which it felt demanded urgent attention. They were:

1. the use, and possible abuse, of ministerial discretion; and
2. complaints that an administrative authority has failed to discharge its duties in accordance with proper standards of administrative conduct.

The Report observed that there was no machinery for appealing against a decision of a minister exercising his discretion under statutory or prerogative powers and suggested that the system of tribunals should be extended so as to provide the individual with an opportunity of challenging discretionary decisions. To deal with allegations of maladministration, the Whyatt Report cited the successful use of investigatory officials, on the lines of the Scandinavian 'ombudsmen', and suggested that a similar device might be introduced in this country.

The word 'ombudsman' is Scandinavian: the best English translation is probably 'complaints commissioner'. The office has its origins in the dissatisfaction of the Swedish Parliament, in the eighteenth century, with the Chancellor of Justice who had been entrusted by the monarch with the task of supervising the administration of justice by judges and other law officers. The Swedish Parliament was unhappy about the way in which the King controlled the judiciary and tried to break the connection between him and the Chancellor. Their attempts being unsuccessful, they created a new official, free from the executive and elected by Parliament. He was given the title 'ombudsman' and had power to investigate complaints by citizens about the administration of the law and then, as his powers were extended, about the activities of all kinds of officials. He was later given powers to initiate his own investigations.

The Swedish example became a model for the rest of the world. It was copied in other Scandinavian countries and in 1961 an ombudsman was appointed in New Zealand. Even before the Whyatt Report had been published there was some knowledge of and interest in ombudsmen in this country, mainly as a result of a visit to Britain by the Danish Ombudsman in 1958.

The sort of ombudsman proposed in the Whyatt Report was a very modest official compared with the Swedish model. The Committee was very concerned lest it recommended something which would conflict with the doctrine of ministerial responsibility and the relations between the executive and Parliament. It suggested, therefore, that he should have the title of Parliamentary Commissioner for Administration and that the general public should not have direct access to him, but only through their MPs. The question of direct access should be reviewed, the Whyatt Report suggested, after some years' experience with the new office. He would have power to ask for correspondence in files of the central departments, but not for internal minutes, and he would not be allowed to identify civil servants by name.

Despite the mild form in which the Committee's recommendations were couched, the Prime Minister, Harold Macmillan, told the House of Commons in November 1962 that he had serious reservations about the idea because it would, in his view, conflict with the principle of ministerial responsibility. The Labour Opposition, however, probably sensing that there was some political advantage in it, included in its 1964 general election manifesto a proposal to appoint a parliamentary commissioner and after being elected produced a White Paper[2] setting out its proposals, which finally became law in March 1967.

The other major recommendation of the Whyatt Committee, that there should be a right of appeal against the decisions of ministers and civil servants to an administrative tribunal, was rejected both by the Conservative government of Harold Macmillan and by the Wilson government which succeeded it. The Report was, after all, unofficial and there was no compelling reason why it should be accepted.

The British decision to introduce its own brand of ombudsman has given the concept greater acceptability and similar officials are now to be found, at national or local level or both, in Australia, Canada, Fiji, France, West Germany, Guyana, Hong

Kong, India, Israel, Italy, Mauritius, New Zealand, Papua-New Guinea, Switzerland, Tanzania, the United States, and Zambia, as well as the Scandinavian countries of Denmark, Finland, Norway, and Sweden.

The Parliamentary Commissioner for Administration

The 1965 White Paper which announced the government's intention to appoint an ombudsman, with the title of Parliamentary Commissioner for Administration, explained the prupose and status of the appointment in this way:

> In Britain, Parliament is the place for ventilating the grievances of the citizen—by history, tradition and past and present practice. It is one of the functions of the elected Member of Parliament to try to secure that his constituents do not suffer injustice at the hands of the Government. . . . We do not want to create any new institutions which would erode the functions of Members of Parliament . . . nor to replace remedies which the British Constitution already provides. Our proposal is to develop those remedies still further.
>
> Under our proposals, the Parliamentary Commissioner will be an independent officer, whose status and powers will be conferred by statute. He will be appointed by the Crown; his salary and pension will be a charge on the Consolidated Fund; and he will be secure from dismissal, except by parliamentary motion. He will report to Parliament each year and otherwise as occasion requires.

These general constitutional views were incorporated in the Act which eventually established the office. The most significant implication was that members of the public were not to have direct access to the Commissioner: they were required to address their complaints to Members of Parliament who would make use of him if they wished to do so. This is the policy which has been followed, for example, in France and West Germany.

The basic duty and the main jurisdiction of the British Parliamentary Commissioner is to investigate complaints by members of the public that they have been unjustly dealt with as a result of maladministration by a government department. The Commissioner has to apply his own interpretation to the words injustice and maladministration. Sometimes what is felt by a complainant to be an injustice may, in the eyes of the Commissioner, be only inconvenience. A long delay in processing an application for a vehicle licence number would probably be regarded by him as inconvenient rather than unjust.

The Commissioner always has to be satisfied that someone is potentially suffering a personal injustice. He refused, for example, to investigate a complaint against the Ministry of Agriculture whose officials were gassing badgers near the complainant's home as he was not convinced that this was causing him personal injustice. Similarly, he would probably reject a complaint against the culling of seals on the instructions of the Secretary of State for Scotland.

He also has to be satisfied that maladministration has occurred. For example, he received a complaint against the Department of Education and Science from a qualified teacher unable to find employment, on the grounds that the Department was not taking sufficiently effective action to reduce the number of teacher training places in colleges, and hence the potential supply of teachers. This could be construed as

218

misguided policy, but the Parliamentary Commissioner was unable to accept it as an example of maladministration.

The 1965 White Paper had this to say about maladministration: 'The Commissioner will be concerned with faults in administration. It will not be for him to criticize policy or to examine a decision on the exercise of discretionary powers unless it appears to him that the decision has been affected by a fault in administration'; and during the debate on the Bill establishing the Commissioner, the minister in charge, Richard Crossman, described maladministration as including 'bias, neglect, inattention, delay, incompetence, ineptitude, perversity, turpitude, arbitrariness'. This is as near a comprehensive definition as is likely to be found.

The Commissioner's powers of investigation are greater than those, rather tentatively, proposed in the Whyatt Report. Section 8 of the Parliamentary Commissioner Act 1967 gives him power to require: 'Any Minister, officer or member of the department or authority concerned or any person who . . . is able to furnish information or produce documents relevant to the investigation to furnish any such information or produce any such document.' His jurisdiction is confined to central government, except that since 1973 he has also been given the task of acting as Health Service Commissioner for England, Scotland, and Wales. Complaints against local authorities are the concern of different Commissioners and those against the nationalized industries are dealt with by a different kind of machinery.

One significant power the Parliamentary Commissioner lacks is that of being able to enforce his findings. He has to rely on publicity and moral persuasion. He is by no means unique in this; many ombudsmen in other parts of the world lack powers of enforcement. The British Parliamentary Commissioner is now assisted by a House of Commons select committee which can, at times, add additional weight to his views. On one occasion, for example, he found that a taxpayer had suffered an injustice at the hands of the Inland Revenue, and in his report recommended a financial remedy. The Member of Parliament to whom the Commissioner's report went took up the case in the House of Commons and the Treasury minister accepted there had been maladministration. The Treasury, he said, was prepared to apologize but not to provide a financial remedy. The Parliamentary Commissioner reported this to the Select Committee who issued their own report calling upon the Inland Revenue to compensate the complainant financially. This proved to be sufficient and the taxpayer received his compensation.

The first three people to hold office as a Parliamentary Commissioner for Administration in this country were all former senior civil servants. The first was Sir Edmund Compton (1966–71), the second Sir Alan Marré (1971–6) and the third Sir Idwal Pugh (1976–8). It is possible to argue that there is a considerable advantage in putting former civil servants in this office on the principle of 'setting a thief to catch a thief'. On the other hand, there is a danger that someone 'from the inside' will be too conscious of the practical constraints of administration and tend to have too much sympathy for his former colleagues.

From 3 January 1979 the first Ombudsman from outside the civil service took office. He is Sir Cecil Clothier, QC, a former judge of appeal in the Isle of Man and a Recorder since 1965. On taking up office, Sir Cecil said he wished to make his activities better known, particularly through the media. He brought a refreshing candour and enthusiasm to his task but whether he and his work are more understood and appreciated by the general public is questionable.

219

In 1981 the Parliamentary Commissioner received 1170 complaints, 929 of which were dealt with and 241 carried forward to the following year. His major investigations have, obviously, been very thorough, taking, on average, about six months. Of the 1170 complaints received in 1981, he was obliged to reject 694 because they were not within the scope of his jurisdiction, and of the cases which qualified for investigation about half warranted criticism of the department concerned.

At the beginning of 1984 Sir Cecil published two damning reports of instances of maladministration by the DHSS and the Home Office. The DHSS was forced to apologize for 'excessive and inexcusable delays' in handling a claim for supplementary benefit. The Department had taken nearly two years to pay the claim. A representative of the Civil and Public Services Association, expressing deep concern about the delay, blamed it entirely on staff shortages. The report on maladministration within the Home Office was even more condemnatory. It concerned a man, John Preece, convicted of murder in 1973 and sentenced to life imprisonment, who was freed in 1981 after the Scottish Court of Appeal decided that the evidence of the forensic scientist, on which his conviction had been based, was doubtful. The scientist, employed by the Home Office, had been suspended from duty in 1977 because of doubts about the quality of his evidence, and, although after his suspension an investigation into his work had been initiated, Home Office officials had made no attempt to discover how many of his previous cases, including that of Mr Preece, were still in existence.

Such courageous and forthright reports have done much to enhance the reputation of the current Parliamentary Commissioner, even though the disquiet about the limitation on his jurisdiction remains.

The local ombudsmen

The local ombudsmen, or **Commissioners for Local Administration**, to give them their full title, carry out a similar function in local government to that of the Parliamentary Commissioner in central government. There are separate commissioners for Scotland and Wales. England is divided into three areas, London and the South East, the North and East, and the West and Midlands, each with its own Commissioner. Their job is to deal with complaints of maladministration in local authorities above parish and community council level, water authorities, and police authorities. They were established by the Local Government Act 1974, several years later than the Parliamentary Commissioner, with whom they are clearly expected to work, as they are given powers to investigate certain complaints jointly.

It is evident that there is still widespread confusion over their role. They were given powers to examine and report on complaints of injustice through maladministration resulting from an administrative action or decision, in very much the same way as the Parliamentary Commissioner. In other words, maladministration can occur whenever the action of a local official has been seriously inadequate or improper. However, maladministration does not include actions or decisions where the local authority has some discretion. For example, an applicant who has been refused a housing grant cannot turn to the local ombudsman to investigate the decision merely because he is unhappy with the result. There has to be some evidence of maladministration in the procedure by which the decision was arrived at.

Local ombudsmen are limited in their powers and jurisdiction in the same way as the Parliamentary Commissioner. They are unable to put right an injustice themselves. They may only report on the matter, although they can make a further report if they are not satisfied that the local authority concerned has taken reasonable steps to correct an injustice they have found. There are also limits to the areas they may investigate. Any matters where the complainant has a right of appeal to another legal body, such as the courts, a tribunal, or a minister, are precluded, unless the local commissioner thinks it is unreasonable in the particular circumstances to expect the complainant to have taken advantage of these other remedies. Other areas outside their scope include decisions which might affect the public at large, such as a decision to increase the rates, legal proceedings, investigations of crime, certain commercial transactions, the appointment of staff, pay, discipline, and other personnel matters.

The ombudsmen's fairly closely defined powers are matched by carefully framed procedures for receiving and investigating complaints. They seem designed to allow local authorities time to put right any injustice before a full report is made, and there is evidence that these procedures tend to confuse and deter many people who might otherwise pursue a complaint.

Complaints can only be dealt with if they are referred to a commissioner by a councillor. The only occasion when a complaint may be accepted direct is if the commissioner is satisfied that a councillor has been asked to refer one to him and has not done so. After a complaint has been received, the local authority is given time to rectify the matter itself. If it takes no action, the ombudsman will investigate the complaint, usually by sending one of his inspectors to examine documents and conduct interviews, and then he will produce a report. Copies of the report will be sent to the complainant, the councillor, any person complained of, and to the local authority. It must also be made available to the public and the press, which is a useful means of encouraging the local authority to take action. It is then left to the local authority to tell the ombudsman what action it has taken. If it has done nothing, or the ombudsman is not satisfied with the action, he can make a further report and the process of publication is repeated.

In the year 1981–2 the local commissioners considered 2501 complaints, 389 of which were settled locally. The commissioners issued 279 formal investigation reports, finding no evidence of maladministration in 106 cases, minor failures in 15, but 'maladministration causing injustice' in 158. Housing was the most common area of complaint.

An evaluation of the British ombudsmen

In July 1975 Justice held a conference in London with its French counterpart, *Libre Justice*, in the course of which it was decided to ask the Administrative Law Committee of Justice to undertake an up-to-date study of the work of the British Parliamentary Commissioner so as to identify any reforms which might seem necessary. The Committee, under the chairmanship of David Widdicombe QC reported in 1977.[3] Although the study was directed primarily at the Parliamentary Commissioner many of the criticisms made are equally applicable to the local ombudsmen. The Report said that, despite his limited terms of reference, the Parliamentary Commissioner had done good work but he suffered from two main deficiencies. The first was that he is under-utilized, and the second that he is confined to acts of maladministration.

To substantiate its claim that the ombudsman is under-utilized, the Widdicombe Committee pointed out that in 1975 he received 928 complaints through MPs and, largely because they were outside his jurisdiction, felt obliged to reject 587, or 63 per cent, of them. In the same year he received 1068 complaints direct from members of the public, all of which he had to decline because they had not been submitted through Members of Parliament. Thus, in 1975 only 17 per cent of complaints made, directly or indirectly, were investigated. The Report pointed out that in 1974, while the British ombudsman investigated 252 cases, in a country with a population of 55 million, in Sweden, with a population of 8 million, 2368 cases were investigated. Arguing that the British Parliamentary Commissioner is too inaccessible, the Widdicombe Report pointed out that in Quebec the Public Protector, as the ombudsman there is called, can be approached by visiting his office in the central area of Quebec or Montreal.

The British Parliamentary Commissioner in this country has a staff of 55, who are either permanently appointed to him or civil servants on secondment. Although he personally, by the terms of his appointment, is assured of independence, the staffing of his office has to be approved by the Treasury, which has the final say on the size of his budget. He has no legal adviser of his own and is dependent for legal advice either on the Treasury Solicitor or on legal advisers from the departments he is called upon to investigate.

On the whole, the Widdicombe Report for Justice is an authoritative, well-argued document. Much of what it says has been endorsed by other observers who have made a study of this area of public administration.

The main points which have emerged from recent critical studies of the British approach to ombudsmen, including the Widdicombe Report, and which apply to both the central and local systems, may be summarized as:

1. Access should be easier and more uniform. There is direct access to the Northern Ireland Complaints Commissioner and to the Health Service Commissioner, who is, of course, the same person as the Parliamentary Commissioner. Local commissioners can accept direct complaints if a councillor has refused to forward them.
2. Their powers of investigation should be extended from merely 'maladministration' to 'unreasonable, unjust, or oppressive action'.
3. Their staffing should be more generous and more within the commissioners' own control. Better staffing might help to reduce the time taken to investigate complaints.
4. They should take much more positive and active steps to publicize their activities.

It is clear from reports they have issued that all the commissioners are aware of most of their shortcomings and would like to effect improvements.

Complaints against quasi-governmental bodies

As we have seen, the use of ombudsmen does not extend to the nationalized industries nor to other quasi-governmental bodies. There is accountability in matters of major policy but in their day-to-day running they are mostly exempt from public control.

The nationalized industries have a structure of consumer councils to which complaints can be addressed and which, on paper, looks very impressive. There

222

seems, however, to be more form than substance to them: studies of them reveal that they are little known and little used and their effectiveness is in doubt. The selection of members intended to represent the average consumer is arbitrary and secret and, although most have been in existence for a substantial time, they have made little impact.

The argument is often put forward that the nationalized industries should be given as much commercial freedom as their competitors in the private sector but the fact that they are all in some kind of monopolistic position, as well as supplying vital services, cannot be ignored. If you are dissatisfied with the service given by your local gas board to whom can you apply for an alternative supply of gas?

Outside the nationalized industries there is no special machinery for bringing an external view to bear on the work of quasi-governmental bodies, despite large sums of money many of them dispense and despite their considerable impact on the social, economic, and industrial life of the nation.

Legal aid and advice

There is an old adage that the law courts, like the Ritz Hotel, are open to everyone. Despite the growth in social service provision there is still a lot of relevance in the saying today. Magistrates and the county courts provide simple and inexpensive criminal and civil justice but at a higher level legal costs tend to be prohibitive. Even in the lower courts the ability to afford a solicitor or barrister can make the difference between a conviction or an acquittal.

Legal aid and advice was introduced in 1949 as a means of ensuring that people of lower incomes would receive at least minimal legal advice and representation. There are three kinds of services available under the Legal Aid Act: advice, representation in civil proceedings, and representation in criminal prosecutions. In all cases a means test is applied.

If no court proceedings are involved, a free or low-cost service is available from a solicitor who, in addition to providing advice, can draft letters or wills, or obtain an opinion from a barrister. In some urban areas law centres have been established for a similar purpose but operating through local authorities or on a voluntary basis. More numerous than the law centres are the citizens' advice bureaux which can provide, in addition to information and help about the social services, limited legal advice. The availability and quality of law centres and citizens' advice bureaux are very variable.

The Law Society, under the general control of the Lord Chancellor, operates the civil legal aid scheme which is intended to provide representation in civil cases for people below a low income level. Area committees determine eligibility for benefiting from the scheme. It is financed from a legal aid fund for which the Lord Chancellor is accountable to Parliament.

The criminal legal aid scheme is operated by the courts under the general supervision of the Home Secretary. If a court considers that the interests of justice will be served and a defendant's means are low enough, it has power to make an order for legal aid. In murder cases and appeals to the Court of Criminal Appeal a defendant has a right to be granted legal aid. In some magistrates' courts voluntary duty solicitor schemes operate whereby a solicitor, from a panel of volunteers, offers his services on behalf of a client. Although the legal aid and advice schemes are an improvement on what had preceded them, there are still grounds for criticism. The

223

first defect, as we have already noted, is that the distribution of legal aid is extremely haphazard. The second is that there is still a strong flavour of the old poor law approach surrounding them. Some progressive lawyers have urged the establishment of a 'national legal service', providing a comprehensive and uniform free service of advice and representation for all. There is, as yet, no evidence that such a service will be provided in the foreseeable future.

The President of the Law Society recently criticized the costly administrative practices concerned with legal aid. The DHSS employs about 500 people and spends about £5 million per year on the review of applications for aid. These reviews add, on average, over a month's delay to each case. Between 1980 and 1982 the cost of the criminal aid scheme rose from £60 million to £80 million. Are these delays and rising costs a reasonable price to pay for justice? Most people would probably answer this question in the affirmative.

Citizen versus state: the balance of advantage

We posed five questions earlier in this chapter, for most of which an answer has been attempted. Let us now try to draw the threads together.

In a conflict between the individual and the state it must be admitted that the advantages are not evenly balanced. The ordinary citizen lacks the resources and the knowledge available to the state. His ultimate weapon is what can best be described as the democratic process and this process involves, as we have seen, more than just the formal representative machinery. It includes the activities of pressure groups of all kinds.

Despite developments in the past twenty years or so gaps in 'grievance satisfaction' remain. The most obvious one is that identified by the Whyatt Report: an absence of adequate appeals machinery from discretionary decisions by ministers and civil servants. The system of ombudsmen is far from perfect and there are areas of quasi-governmental activity almost wholly exempt from formal public scrutiny.

If the ordinary citizen is to do something to redress the balance of advantage, or disadvantage, then he must be prepared to help himself more than he has done in the past. It is not enough to repeat the cliché that all organizations thrive on an active minority and a passive majority. Participation in the processes of government is the topic with which we will conclude our introduction to public administration.

References

1. *The Citizen and the Administration*, a Report by Justice, Stevens, 1961.
2. *A Parliamentary Commissioner for Administration*, Cmnd. 2767, HMSO, 1965.
3. *Our Fettered Ombudsman*, a Report by Justice, Stevens, 1977.

Assignments

33. 'We should either appoint more ombudsmen or abandon the system.' Do you agree. Give a reasoned answer.

Sources: Read the reports of the Parliamentary Commissioner and the local ombudsmen.

34. Test the effectiveness of your local citizens' advice bureau questioning a cross-section of people who have used it.

21
The participative process

Government by participation

It is possible to argue that a fully democratic system of government should involve more than just the establishment of representative institutions with ultimate responsibility of the executive, through the legislature, to the electorate. It should also include a high degree of participation, by as many electors as possible, in the governmental process. This is perhaps the ideal but, in a nation of more than 50 million people, how practicable is it?

In Chapter 3 we spent some time examining the role of interest groups and even formed some tentative conclusions about the degree of pluralism in our present-day society. We said that governments find it necessary to 'negotiate' with powerful interest groups before feeling confident enough to put policy proposals before Parliament, and that the democratic process includes not just elected representatives and members of political parties but also representatives of these powerful, organized interests. In other words, we have agreed that the substance of democracy is more important than the form. Democratic government demands democratic institutions but the institutions are, in themselves, not enough: they must allow people outside them to play some part as well. Participation can range from, at one extreme, voting in general elections, to holding high political office, at the other, as Fig. 21.1 attempts to depict. The percentages are based on average levels of participation in recent years and are not intended to be exactly accurate for any particular year.

Clearly, more than three-quarters of the electorate seem quite satisfied to leave active participation to the other quarter and view their own contributions as a right to put a cross on a ballot paper every five years or less. Even the activities of interest groups, as part of the total political process, are dominated by an active minority with the passive majority showing its support by payment of the appropriate membership fee.

In recent years 'participation' has become something of a political catchphrase and many people with a serious interest in politics have become suspicious of it. The scepticism which is often attached to it is perhaps best summed up in the words printed on a poster displayed by French students during the 1968 disturbances in Paris. Translated into English, it read:

I participate
Thou participatest
He participates
We participate
You participate
THEY PROFIT

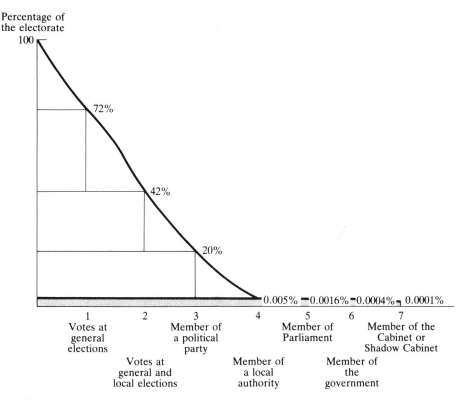

Fig. 21.1 The political participation curve

Participation in industry has also become a fashionable concept in recent years, although the Bullock Report on Industrial Democracy[1] has made it a divisive one.

Whether it is political or industrial participation, the one thing that sceptics ask is: how real is it? In other words, to participate effectively must mean to be able, as a consequence of the participation, to have some influence over any resultant decisions. Thus trade unionists often criticize managements for paying only lip-service to participation, arguing that to involve them in joint discussions *after* the board of directors has taken a policy decision is much too late. If the joint discussions are to be effective then they must start before the policy has been formulated. Critics of 'cosmetic' participation by government make exactly the same point. Discussion *after* a White Paper has been published is much too late.

As part of the popularization process of participation in recent years, politicians of all parties have spoken about 'open government'. Edward Heath became Prime Minister on the basis of an election manifesto which promised, among other things, a more open government. Other Prime Ministers and ministers have preached the same gospel: none, so far, has been particularly successful at practising it.

The concept of open government

An open system of government is usually interpreted as one in which there is a positive obligation on the government, either in a written constitution or a specific piece of legislation, to disclose and make available all official documents which have progressed beyond a certain stage and have become what are known in government circles as 'working papers'.

In an earlier chapter we discussed policy formulation and said that at a certain stage of discussion a tentative idea, or set of ideas, crystallizes into something more definite and future policy begins to emerge. It is at about this stage that a policy proposal would acquire the status of a working paper. It is sufficiently well defined to be unambiguous but not so firm as to be unalterable. A 'closed' system of government, on the other hand, is one in which there is no requirement to disclose and make available working documents. Whether or not it does so is entirely at the discretion of the government. Most governments in the world today operate closed systems of varying degrees. The two which may be said to be open are in Sweden and the United States of America. In Sweden the general right of public access to official documents is enshrined in the Freedom of the Press Act of 1949, which is part of the Swedish Constitution. In the United States a guarantee of open access is contained in the Freedom of Information Act of 1967, as amended in 1974.

In Britain it is certain that most politicians think of open government in a much less precise way. It is probably fair to say that to them openness means an extension of the practice of issuing consultative documents, or Green Papers as some of them are called, before making a firm policy announcement in the form of a White Paper. National security is usually put forward as a reason for not allowing publication of a wide range of documents. In the United Kingdom the perennial doctrine of ministerial responsibility gives added weight to the argument against unrestricted disclosure.

To be fair, it must be admitted that both Sweden and the United States have written constitutions and in each country there is a clear separation of powers between the executive and the legislature. Indeed, the Franks Committee on the Official Secrets Act, which reported in 1972,[2] pointed out strongly that political and constitutional factors were more important to the concept of openness than legal considerations. Incidentally, this Franks Committee, which we shall look at more closely shortly, must not be confused with the earlier Committee on Tribunals and Enquiries; the only thing the two had in common was the chairman.

The Official Secrets Acts

There are actually several Official Secrets Acts since the principal one has been amended more than once, but the significant Act is that of 1911: Section 1 deals with spying and Section 2 with wider matters. It is Section 2 to which many people, and particularly the press, take exception. It is couched in very wide and unqualified terms. It says, in effect, that if someone discloses official information in an 'unauthorized' way he is guilty of a criminal offence. Every civil servant, at the start of his career and on retirement, signs a declaration, written in forbidding language, that his attention has been drawn to the Act.

In theory, Section 2 of the Act means that a civil servant could be guilty of a criminal offence if, when he returns home at night, he discusses any aspect of the day's work with his wife. In reality, most civil servants have a fairly clear idea of what is authorized and what is unauthorized, and in their day-to-day work the Act causes them few problems. Its existence, however, does tend to make a naturally cautious breed of men and women even more so, and the public are likely to suffer as a result.

The number of frivolous prosecutions under Section 2 of the Act have been rare and, in any case, each has to be personally authorized by the Attorney-General. The press, however, find it objectionable because they have no clear and consistent idea of what information is acceptable for publication since they are not able to read the Attorney-General's mind. They also see Section 2 as a device available to the government to silence information on a specific subject more or less at will, on the grounds that it is 'prejudicial to the safety or interests of the state'.

Probably the most exceptional, and objectionable, aspect of the Official Secrets Act of 1911, and particularly of Section 2, is the manner in which it was passed. It replaced an earlier Act of 1889 and was introduced at a time when there was widespread disquiet about German espionage activities in this country. In 1911 newspapers were full of stories of German spies allegedly taking photographs or drawing plans of strategic defence establishments. The Bill was introduced in the House of Lords in July 1911 and was passed almost immediately to the House of Commons, which was on the point of rising for the summer recess. On 2 August 1911 it passed through all its stages in one day and Section 2 was not mentioned at all. One explanation for this quick passage is that it was thought to be needed to meet a national emergency. Another view, supported by the Franks Committee, is that the government spokesman deliberately adopted a low key approach which fitted well into the atmosphere of the House as members were preparing to take their summer holidays. Whatever the explanation, the manner of its birth is not particularly creditable.

The effects of Section 2 of the Act are subtle and insidious. They have, in the long run, tended to make a formally closed system of government much less open than it might be if this shadowy, indefinite threat of potential illegality did not hang, like a sword of Damocles, over the publication of all official information.

The British approach to open government

Despite the daunting presence of the Official Secrets Act, from the early 1960s onwards there has been a steady, if at times reluctant, movement by politicians and public servants towards a more open form of government in this country.

You were warned earlier not to confuse the two Franks Committees' reports, with the advice that the only thing they had in common was their chairman. This is not strictly true. One of the recommendations of the Franks Committee on Administrative Tribunals and Enquiries was that the reasons behind the recommendations of inspectors at public inquiries should be published. Despite strong opposition from civil servants in the Ministry of Housing and Local Government, as the Department of the Environment then was, this eventually came about and was the first practical move towards a form of open government. This was in 1958.

In 1965 that ever-vigilant body Justice published a report[3] by a working party consisting of lawyers and newspaper editors under the chairmanship of Sir Hartley Shawcross, as he then was, which had looked at the relationship between the law and the press. Among its conclusions, it thought that a distinction should be more clearly made between information which was prejudicial to the security of the state and to the

229

precisely defined national interest, and information which related solely to the efficiency or integrity of a government department or public authority. The Justice working party accepted that the first categories of information should remain within the scope of the Official Secrets Acts and argued that information in the latter category should not.

In 1967 the arrival of the Parliamentary Commissioner for Administration meant that, in the course of an investigation of a complaint alleging maladministration, departmental files and records now had to be made available. This represents a further significant development.

In the same year, the government of Harold Wilson introduced the first Green Paper (the name given to a pre-White Paper consultative document). Although the quality and importance of Green Papers have varied enormously, they too constitute an important movement in the direction of open government. Two Green Papers published in 1976 are of particular significance: *Transport Policy*,[4] which looked at the balance of advantages and disadvantages between rail and road transport; and *Priorities for Health and Personal Social Services in England*,[5] which positively sought public participation in establishing priorities in this vital area of government activity.

The Fulton Report on the Civil Service, published in 1968, added its voice to the calls for more open government, saying, in one passage: 'In our view, therefore, the concept of anonymity should be modified and civil servants, as professional administrators, should be able to go further than now in explaining what their departments are doing.'

In 1969 the government published a White Paper, *Information and the Public Interest*,[6] which was the report of an inquiry instituted inside the civil service in response to the recommendation by the Fulton Committee. The White Paper argued that up to a certain stage in the policy formulation process secrecy was necessary if ministers and civil servants were not to be greatly inhibited, but agreed that once any possible ambiguities had been resolved more openness was useful. The Paper then went on to say that the Official Secrets Acts were 'not in any way a barrier to greater openness of government' since they dealt only with 'unauthorized' disclosures of information. To some critics this sounded very much like begging the question, since only ministers and civil servants themselves were in a position to rule on what should be authorized and what should be unauthorized.

The 1969 White Paper had been produced by the government of Harold Wilson. In June 1970 the Conservatives, under Edward Heath, returned to power with a declared commitment to their own brand of open government. While not necessarily differing from its predecessor's views about the general effects of the Official Secrets Acts on openness of government, the new administration thought it timely to examine the precise effects of Section 2 of the 1911 Act, which had always caused, and continued to cause, most public concern. It appointed a Home Office departmental committee, under the chairmanship of Lord Franks, as he now was, to investigate the operation of Section 2. The Committee reported in September 1972.

The main conclusion in the Report was that 'the present law is unsatisfactory and that it should be changed so that criminal sanctions are retained only to protect what is of real importance'. It recommended that something should replace Section 2 which would be 'more limited' and 'more certain in operation'. The replacement it suggested was a new statute called the Official Information Act which would restrict criminal liability to six closely defined categories of information:

1. defence and internal security;
2. foreign relations;
3. currency and the reserves;
4. maintenance of law and order;
5. cabinet documents; and
6. information given confidentially to the government by private individuals or concerns.

Most fair-minded observers would say that the report of the Franks Committee was sound as far as it went, or, to be more precise, as far as it was allowed to go, because its terms of reference were very narrowly phrased and clearly inhibiting. The Fulton Committee had said: '. . . the Government should set up an enquiry to make recommendations for getting rid of unnecessary secrecy in this country. Clearly the Official Secrets Acts would need to be included in such a review. . . .' The Franks Committee's task had been fined down to just one Section of the 1911 Act, and it was precluded from examining the wider aspects of official secrecy and openness of government.

The Report was debated in the House of Commons in June 1973, at a time when industrial relations and incomes policy were higher in the Conservative government's order of priorities than openness of government. During the debate the Home Secretary, while accepting that Section 2 needed to be replaced, urged caution. The resignation of Edward Heath in March 1974 meant that a new government, under Harold Wilson, would have to state the official view on the implementation of the Franks Report.

Before it did so, in November 1976, other developments had taken place. It was announced in 1975 that *The Sunday Times* was proposing to serialize, and Jonathan Cape to publish in book form, the posthumous diaries of Richard Crossman, against the wishes of the Secretary of the Cabinet. A convention, supporting the principle of the collective responsibility of the Cabinet, has been in operation for many years which has restricted the publication by scholars and civil servants of Cabinet documents for a period of 50 years after their original date of writing. In 1970 the 50 years was reduced to 30 and the head of the civil service said that sympathetic consideration would be given to a relaxation of the rule where papers were needed for research to assist in the training of public administrators. Politicians, including former ministers, seemed to be able to break the rule more easily by getting material they wished to publish cleared by the Secretary of the Cabinet. In the case of the *Crossman Diaries*, the Secretary gave clearance and when *The Sunday Times* and Jonathan Cape declared their intentions of going ahead with the publication, the Attorney-General, on behalf of the government, obtained an injunction to prevent it. The newspaper and the publishers appealed to the Appeal Court, which upheld their case, saying that it had to consider whether the 'public interest' would be adversely affected by publication, particularly as 10 years had elapsed since the events referred to in the diaries had taken place. The court concluded that the public interest would not suffer and that even 'today's Cabinet would not be inhibited, even though some are the same people'. Much of what Richard Crossman had to say proved to be gossip rather than potential state secrets. Nevertheless, the Appeal Court's decision represents one further step towards more open government.

On 22 November 1975 the Home Secretary made a 'statement of intent' in the

House of Commons which indicated that the government would introduce legislation broadly in line with the recommendations of the Franks Report.

In the same year the government had been embarrassed by the publication in *New Society* of alleged discussions within the Cabinet on social security benefits. Following these disclosures, a Committee of Privy Councillors, under the chairmanship of Lord Houghton, was appointed 'to examine the procedures for handling Cabinet and Cabinet committee papers inside the government'. The Houghton Committee reported[7] within a week of the Home Secretary's statement of intent and recommended a set of procedures which Cabinet ministers should follow to maintain and improve Cabinet secrecy.

In July 1978 the government, now headed by James Callaghan, published a White Paper, *Reform of Section 2 of the Official Secrets Acts, 1911*,[8] setting out its firm proposals for implementing the recommendations of the Franks Report. When he introduced the White Paper in the House of Commons, the Home Secretary received a particularly hostile reception from his own backbenchers, to the left of the Labour Party. He said that an Official Information Bill would eventually be introduced, based on the Franks Report, which would define much more clearly the kind of information which would be subject to criminal sanctions. In a leading article commenting on the White Paper, *The Times* expressed considerable scepticism about the genuineness of the government's intentions to make government more open. The article identified the hand of No. 10 Downing Street, and the Prime Minister himself, behind the document, saying: 'In maintaining the ramparts of Whitehall's forbidden city, Mr Callaghan, is, as in so many other ways, a Prime Minister in the traditional mould.' To underline its point, *The Times* revealed that formal requests made to the Home Office and the Civil Service Department for background papers, used to brief the Cabinet committee which had drafted the White Paper, had been refused.

By any objective standards, the British government's approach to open government has deteriorated and hardened in recent years, despite the advocacy of a more open system by senior civil servants. The First Division Association, which represents top civil servants from Under-Secretary rank upwards, in 1983 circulated to its members a discussion paper outlining ways in which more openness might be achieved. The paper argued that too many official documents were unnecessarily classified as secret, and suggested that all unclassified papers should be made available to the public as a matter of routine. This would help to stem the numerous 'leaks' of which the Cabinet Secretary, Sir Robert Armstrong, was highly critical.

There has been little evidence of the government being willing to accept this advice. Indeed, the doors of Whitehall seem to have been shut more tightly than ever before. The prosecution of a junior civil service clerk, Sarah Tisdall, and her conviction and sentence to six months' imprisonment in March 1984, reflected this growing addiction to secrecy. Miss Tisdall was clearly in technical breach of Section 2 of the Official Secrets Act when she provided *The Guardian* newspaper with a copy of a minute from the Secretary of State for Defence to the Prime Minister, relating to the arrival of cruise missiles at the Greenham Common airbase in Berkshire. The minute was subsequently published by *The Guardian*. Its publication was, obviously, highly embarrassing to the government but whether it posed even a potential threat to national security was in doubt. This case was, perhaps, the most vivid example of the iniquities of this much criticized piece of legislation. Commenting on the case, *The Guardian* reported that several senior Civil Servants, who asked not to be named, believed that a prosecution should not have been brought under the Official Secrets Act. A curious aspect of the episode is that the newspaper could also have been prosecuted for publishing the minute, and so contravening the Act, but it was not. In announcing sentence on Miss Tisdall, Mr Justice Cantley made it clear that her severe sentence was intended as a warning and example to other civil servants.

Open government and the press

In an earlier chapter we looked at some aspects of the role of the press within the field of politics and at the activities of lobby correspondents. We said that the press, in conjunction with the other mass media, performed a vital function in informing the public of current political events and opinions. We also saw that the relationship between the government and the lobby correspondents was, as with organized interests, a two-way one, with each, to some extent, dependent on the other.

As part of this relationship a form of voluntary censorship operates through a body representing the press and broadcasting organizations on the one hand and the government and the armed forces on the other. It is called the **Services, Press, and Broadcasting Committee**. Its main function is to advise the media when it would be against the national interest to publish certain information and to secure their agreement not to do so. This advice takes the form of 'D-notices'; they have no legal force and are not part of the Official Secrets Acts, but if an editor or programme presenter ignores them he might automatically find himself in conflict with Section 2 of the 1911 Act.

In the 1960s the media began to suspect that the 'D-notice' system was being abused and that the government was using it not to protect information for security reasons but to avoid embarrassment to itself. Evidence of this was the publication in foreign newspapers of matters which had been included in 'D-notices'. A striking example was the attempt to place an embargo on information about the Foreign Office defectors, Philby, Burgess, and Maclean, although information about them was freely available abroad. Although the 'D-notice' arrangements continue, the media have not lost any of their suspicions, and generally would prefer a much more open and straightforward method of protecting vital national information.

The way in which the Ministry of Defence obviously 'managed' the news from the South Atlantic during the Falklands conflict was resented by many sections of the press as well as the general public, and the Ministry's announcement, in October 1983, of new rules for the reporting of military operations caused concern in Fleet Street. As *The Times* defence correspondent has pointed out, under these rules his distinguished predecessor would not have been able to report the Charge of the Light Brigade.

An evaluation of the participative process

On balance, governments have more to lose than to gain if, because of over-cautious and introspective attitudes, they fail to raise the level of political participation in this country. Ministers and public servants cannot be right all the time: some sceptics would say, much of the time. Their chances of being right, or at least justifying their mistakes, would be greater if they involved ordinary men and women in their policy deliberations at a much earlier stage than they have generally been willing to do so far.

Many people see that a significant improvement in industrial relations is most likely to come about through greater participation in decision making by supervisory and shop-floor workers with management, although not necessarily in the manner proposed by the Bullock Report. A corresponding view can be taken of central and local government.

As we have seen, there have been signs that there is a genuine movement in this country towards more open government but it is also evident that there are still strong reactionary forces in political and administrative circles. One of the last major tasks performed by Sir Douglas Allen, now Lord Croham, as head of the civil service, was to write to all Permanent Secretaries asking them to take steps to produce 'background papers', providing information about the stages leading up to a government statement of firm policy, so that they could be made available for publication. Following news of this letter, *The Times* made a determined attempt to obtain the background papers behind several White Papers which were subsequently published. It met with very little success.

Participation implies sharing. In the past political participation has been weak because the average man-in-the-street has not been prepared to take an active interest in current affairs unless they had a very direct impact on him. If this attitude is to change the government must be prepared to participate itself, by much more fully sharing its own views and information.

A campaign to combat excessive secrecy in government was launched in January 1984 by the Leaders of the Labour, Liberal, and Social Democratic parties, backed by 150 backbench MPs from all parties. The campaign had the intention of promoting the case for a Freedom of Information Act, similar to that which we have already discussed. The Chairman of the 1984 Committee for Freedom of Information is Des Wilson, who, as Chairman of Shelter, proved himself to be one of the most powerful publicists and interest group leaders in this country. The campaign has received support from a variety of quarters, including Sir Patrick Nairne, a former Cabinet Office adviser on defence. Mrs Thatcher's immediate reaction to the campaign's launch was to say that it was unnecessary. She said: 'We already have a clear policy to make more information available and the necessary machinery to do so.' Despite the united front for more open government by the opposition parties, a student of politics cannot avoid a measure of scepticism. Virtually every party in recent years has professed a wish and an intention to remove secrecy and make information more accessible to the press and the public, but none so far has translated words into deeds.

Perhaps the most savage criticism of Section 2 of the Official Secrets Act, which is at the core of closed government in this country, was made, in evidence to the Franks Committee, by the, then, Professor of English Law at Oxford University, Henry Wade. He said: '(it was) a blot on the statute book which needs to be removed. . . . The law as it now stands shows a complete failure to understand that accessibility of information about the government of the country is of vital importance in a democracy.'

References

1. *Report of the Departmental Committee on Industrial Democracy*, Cmnd. 6706, HMSO, 1977.
2. *Report of the Departmental Committee on Section 2 of the Official Secrets Act, 1911.* Cmnd. 5104, HMSO, 1972.
3. *The Law and the Press*, Stevens, 1965.
4. *Transport Policy: a consultative document*, HMSO, 1976.
5. *Priorities for Health and Personal Social Services in England: a consultative document*, HMSO, 1976.
6. *Information and the Public Interest*, Cmnd. 4809, 1969.
7. *Report of the Committee of Privy Councillors on Ministerial Memoirs*, Cmnd. 6386, HMSO, 1976.
8. *Reform of Section 2 of the Official Secrets Act, 1911*, Cmnd. 7285, HMSO, 1978.

Assignments

35. Argue the case for and against the introduction of a Freedom of Information Act. This assignment can also be used as the basis for a class debate on the motion: 'This House believes that a Freedom of Information Act would be beneficial to both the public and the government.'

36. Take a specific issue which has political significance and compare its coverage on television for one week by BBC1, BBC2, your local ITV channel, and Channel 4.

22

Current issues

The purpose of this chapter

Any book about politics is bound to be out of date within months, even weeks, of its being written. That is why it is essential that any serious student of government should be a regular follower of current events. Fortunately, there are excellent radio and television programmes which not only inform and enlighten but also entertain. ITV's *Weekend World*, *World in Action*, and *A Week in Politics* are some examples, as are BBC's *Panorama* and *Newsnight*, and even the lighter *Question Time*. There are, and will be, others, of course, and on radio, in addition to *Yesterday in Parliament* and *The Week in Westminster*, there are numerous single or small series programmes which can prove invaluable. In 1983, for example, the BBC Reith Lectures by Sir Douglas Wass were well worth listening to.

The Listener reproduces most of the radio talks and discussions and should be read from time to time, if not weekly. Regrettably, the coverage of politics by the popular press is highly selective and generally superficial, but *The Times*, *The Sunday Times*, *The Guardian*, *The Observer*, and *The Daily Telegraph* are all, in their different ways, reliable. People fortunate enough to have a major regional newspaper, such as *The Scotsman*, *Birmingham Post*, *Western Mail*, *Yorkshire Post*, and others, should find their coverage of political events and issues satisfactory.

The purpose of this final chapter is not to attempt to keep this book up to date in terms of current events: that would be impossible. In any case, the most significant political issues are, at their hearts, perennial: they merely change their form from time to time.

These final pages, rather, seek to highlight some of these issues as a reminder to you, the reader, that although you are studying a living, rapidly changing, scene, at its core there are fundamental, permanent, or recurring features which must be understood and appreciated if your studies are to be worth while.

A final point. As far as possible the author has tried to subordinate his own political views so as to treat each topic and issue honestly and objectively. This has proved to be a virtually impossible task, so if any bias or particular emphasis is discernible it stems from two fundamental beliefs, for which no apology is offered: a belief in the importance of free and open discussion, whatever the issue, and a belief that governments are established for the benefit of the people they are intended to serve, and not for the benefit of the people who govern. The issues which follow are selective, but important.

The governments of Mrs Thatcher

More than at any time in recent years it is possible to speak about government in personalized terms and refer to the Conservative administrations since 1979 as the governments of Mrs Thatcher. This is an indication of the degree and extent to which she has dominated the political stage in this period.

Her 1984 Cabinet contained only 9 of the original 22 1979 members, and only 8 of the Cabinet of her Conservative predecessor, Edward Heath. Fortuitously, she has been able to appoint 23 of the 27 permanent secretaries in the civil service during her terms of office, simply because so many of them were reaching the age of retirement as she came into power. The Civil Service Department, established by Harold Wilson, has been disbanded, as has Edward Heath's CPRS. The PAR system of the Heath regime has been replaced by the MINIS of Michael Heseltine. The NEB no longer exists, nor do several other quangos deemed to be unnecessary. The size of the civil service has been significantly reduced and the process continues. The abolition of the metropolitan councils is being undertaken and a progressive programme of privatization is planned.

All this has occurred during a space of five years and, in the same period, the nation has fought and won a war in circumstances so logistically difficult as to be thought virtually impossible. By any standards, this is an impressive catalogue of events, resulting in Mrs Thatcher making an apparently indelible mark on the history of politics and government in this country. But how indelible will that mark be seen in decades to come?

One thing is reasonably certain. The governments of Margaret Thatcher are so distinctive that their like may never be seen again. That is why it is so difficult to draw long-term conclusions from developments over the past five years or so.

Mrs Thatcher has readily and openly accepted her description as a 'conviction politician', with all the strengths and weaknesses this implies. As a conviction politician, she has demonstrated the admirable qualities of dedication, industry, forthrightness, and determination, to the point of ruthlessness. From the start of her period of office she turned her back on 'consensus politics', believing that compromise implied fudging and weakness. All these attributes came to the fore during the war in the Falklands.

But politics in peacetime is, as we have so strenuously argued, essentially concerned with compromise and consensus: only an autocrat can afford the arrogance of believing he is always right and so ignore the views of others. Herein lies the weakness of 'conviction politics'. Mrs Thatcher obviously has a vision of the kind of Britain she would like to create: a Britain of 'go getters', to quote one expression she has used. But it is *her* vision, and not necessarily that of the majority of her fellow countrymen and women. Furthermore, it is a vision rather than a carefully prepared plan.

It is the pursuit of a vision which has led her governments into a number of short-term policies, some ending as culs-de-sac: the long-term future of the Falklands; the permanent relationship between central and local government; Britain's future role in Europe; a long-term defence policy; the future of the welfare state; the successful operation of a mixed economy. All these are long-term issues which need to be thought through and worked out in a climate of compromise and consensus. They are not really the stuff of 'conviction politics'.

These comments are intended merely to inject a note of caution, in that it would be unwise to read too much into the experience of the past few years and assume that profound political and constitutional changes have occurred.

The British Constitution, is, as we argued in the early chapters, extremely adaptable. It can accommodate almost any kind of political leader or regime. It evolves, but this is a slow process when seen in historical perspective, however dramatic the changes may seem in the short term.

The views of the former mandarins

During the past few years there has been, as we have already noted, a significant movement of top civil servants, of permanent secretary rank, from the public administration scene into retirement or some more active occupation. This movement has been essentially fortuitous and should not be seen as having any political undertones.

Some of these former mandarins have felt themselves sufficiently freed to be able to express themselves publicly on aspects of their previous work. We will examine the views of three of them, although one, Sir John Hoskyns, was not really a mandarin, but a temporary adviser to Mrs Thatcher. Of the other two, Sir Douglas Wass was joint head of the civil service and Sir Leo Pliatzky was permanent secretary at the Department of Industry and second permanent secretary at the Treasury.

Sir Douglas Wass: the 1983 BBC Reith Lectures

Sir Douglas began by defining what he saw as the essentials of 'good government', namely efficiency and responsiveness. He devoted the first three lectures mainly to the question of efficiency and the last three mainly to responsiveness.

He thought our system of parliamentary and cabinet government was not particularly efficient. The Cabinet, in particular, was an imperfect device for developing and pursuing coordinated policies. Each case presented to it was by an interested party, the responsible minister, who was bound to be biased. No other member of the Cabinet, including the Prime Minister, had sufficient information to challenge his case and hence he usually won. The Cabinet was seldom, if ever, able to establish policy priorities and so could be easily 'railroaded'. It was also unable to undertake a continual review of the general thrust of the government's policies. Edward Heath established the CPRS to perform this task but Mrs Thatcher preferred her own No. 10 Policy Unit.

Sir Douglas considered several ways of making the Cabinet more effective but eventually rejected them. One would have been to strengthen the number of non-departmental ministers and the other to provide it with its own high-powered think tank.

Another possible solution would be to improve the Cabinet committee system or to make the Prime Minister more like a US President, with the equivalent of the White House Office in support. These two ideas were discarded because of their constitutional implications.

In his third lecture he discussed the politician–permanent secretary relationship and considered that the Sir Humphrey Appleby–Jim Hacker partnership, depicted in the excellent television series *Yes, Minister*, contained more than an element of truth, although greatly exaggerated.

Discussing the responsiveness of government, he felt that the Opposition in Parliament was at a considerable disadvantage when compared with the government of the day, supported by the civil service machine. Question Time in the House of Commons was largely ineffectual but the new select committees showed promise, provided more backbenchers were prepared to work seriously in them. On balance,

239

the House of Lords committees were more effective. He discussed the possibility of creating a Department of the Opposition, staffed by civil servants, even though there might be difficulties when governments changed. The possibility of seconding a few civil servants to assist the Opposition could be tried.

Sir Douglas felt that government in Britain could be much more open without any detriment to its operation. All policy background documents should be open to the public unless a minister explicitly banned them. To ensure that a minister did not abuse this right of veto, either an independent auditor, with access to all the files, could be appointed or the procedure could be controlled through a Freedom of Information Act. He said he was opposed to leaks and felt that open government should be achieved by amending the rules, not breaking them.

In his concluding lecture he floated the idea of a permanent royal commission which could look at major policy issues in an objective, non-partisan way. Three issues he identified were electoral reform, the disestablishment of the Church of England, and the reform of the jury system.

Understandably, perhaps, the views of a former head of the civil service contained little that had not been discussed before by students of politics. It is interesting, however, to find that someone so close to the heart of political power for so many years should corroborate several of the misgivings about the working of government that others have expressed from a much more distant standpoint.

Sir Douglas's lectures have been published in *The Listener*.[1]

Sir John Hoskyns: conservatism is not enough

Sir John Hoskyns was head of Mrs Thatcher's Policy Unit until 1982. In the annual lecture to the Institute of Directors, in September 1983, he took the opportunity of giving his views on the operation of central government based on his own first-hand experience. The lecture was subsequently printed in *Political Quarterly*.[2]

Sir John was obviously somewhat disillusioned by what he had found in Whitehall and Downing Street and felt that neither the Cabinet nor the civil service machine was equipped to govern in the way he would have liked. Both lacked a positive, forward-looking approach and he thought that the dismantlement of the CPRS, which had, to some extent, been able to play a strategic role, had left a vacuum in the centre of government.

In some respects Sir John was reiterating the earlier call by Sir Richard Clarke for a strong 'centre', but Sir John looked for something nearer to an approach which private sector businesses would adopt. In comparison with their counterparts in the private sector, he saw top civil servants playing games with ministers whom they were evaluating mainly on their ability to master a brief.

Sir John argued that, whereas in business the radical approach to problem solving was the norm, in the civil service it was the exception. He also criticized the governmental machine for not understanding strategy, by which he meant the step-by-step removal of constraints so that apparently insoluble problems could be solved. He instanced the case of public spending where civil servants and politicians, instead of asking *why* they found it impossible to reduce it, were asking *how* they could reduce it.

He identified what he called three rules which conditioned conventional politics:

1. that voters would never tolerate a cut in their peacetime living standards;
2. that ministers should never openly admit they did not have solutions to certain problems; and

3. that the average voter could only understand things which could be explained in childlike terms.

Sir John was sharply critical of what he described as the small club of three or four thousand people who made up the political establishment. Although it contained intelligent people, its thinking was mediocre and it was conformist and unnecessarily secretive. MPs lacked formal training for their work in Parliament and the transition from the backbenches to ministerial rank inevitably found many of them out of their depth. He said he found it extraordinary that a nation of 55 million people had to rely on a reservoir of political talent no greater than that available to a single multinational company.

Concluding his lecture, Sir John Hoskyns listed four essential changes that were needed:

1. The Prime Minister should be able to form a government from a wider range of people than the small pool of career politicians currently available.
2. Whitehall should be organized for strategy and innovation as well as day-to-day survival.
3. Top-quality outsiders should be brought into the civil service.
4. Ministers' workloads should be reduced.

Sir John's comments, like those of Sir Douglas Wass, were not, in their essentials, very new. They have been expressed frequently in the past by businessmen. In the 1950s and 1960s, for example, Lord Beeching and Lord Robens suggested that the country should be run as if it were Great Britain Limited.

The frustration of people who come into government from business is, perhaps, understandable, but the evidence of businessmen achieving success in politics is not encouraging. A notable example was John Davies who, after making a name for himself in business and becoming Director-General of the CBI, was brought into government by Edward Heath and spent an apparently unhappy and largely unsuccessful few years as a Cabinet minister. On the other hand, there are numerous examples of ex-politicians and ex-civil servants flourishing in the world of business.

Perhaps the French approach should be considered, whereby civil servants receive very good training, sufficient to equip them for top posts in either the public or the private sector, at their national college of administration. They can subsequently move easily in and out of government and business for the rest of their careers.

A former leading mandarin, Sir Leo Pliatzky, was invited to respond to Sir John Hoskyns's strictures and his views were also published in *Political Quarterly*.[3]

Sir Leo Pliatzky: Mandarins, Ministers, and the Management of Britain

Sir Leo considered that Sir John Hoskyns had misunderstood the problem and simplified the solution. He claimed that the British civil service was not very different from that of career services in other countries, with the exceptions of Japan, Germany, and France, where there was much more movement between public and private sectors. He thought there were probably too many Oxbridge people at the top, but how did you attract people of equal talent from elsewhere?

Sir Leo argued that the Whitehall machine operated more smoothly than Sir John alleged and that bringing in 'outsiders' could well undermine the integrity of the service and revert to the kind of political patronage which was criticized in some other countries.

Sir Leo's suggestions for improving British government included: electoral reform, to get away from 'pendulum politics'; reform of the House of Lords, by increasing the non-hereditary element; and a reduction in ministers' workloads. His views were, again, in no way novel, but none the less interesting.

The message coming through all these ruminations by people who have worked at the very centre of political power in this country seems to repeat many of the criticisms that students of politics have been voicing in recent years: that confrontation and excessive secrecy, which seem to dominate British politics at the present time, are not only not what the average voter wants, but also not helpful to the smooth and effective operation of government.

Efficiency versus accountability

Efficiency versus accountability has long been the subject of debate in the field of public administration. The debaters have usually been the civil servants and local government officers, representing the inside view, and the politicians and businessmen as the 'outsiders'. We have already seen how ex-mandarins and a political adviser have viewed this topic and there seems little prospect of one side of the argument being fully reconciled with the other.

The obvious first temptation for any minister wishing to improve the efficiency of his department is to look for a proven and established technique or system, usually successfully applied in the private sector, which can be translated to Whitehall. The most notable recent example of this was the creation of a management information system in the Department of the Environment by Michael Heseltine.

Management information systems (MISs) are widely used in the private sector to provide managements with up-to-date and relevant data on which to take decisions. A properly constructed system for a large organization would identify key areas and activities and ensure that data were collected on a regular basis and made available to managers in specific functions and to general management. Sales figures, stock levels, accounting ratios, cash flows, staff turnovers and the activities of cost and profit centres are all examples of the sort of information needed to manage a business successfully.

The Department of the Environment, even in its earlier form of Housing and Local Government and Regional Planning, in the Wilson administrations, had, mainly because of its size, felt it necessary to develop a more sophisticated system of coordination and control than many of its counterparts. In the Heath administration, Peter Walker, and later Geoffrey Rippon, attempted to achieve corporate unity through a management board of the top civil servants in all the various wings of the big department. This board was eventually called the **policy management group (PMG)**.

In November 1980 Michael Heseltine announced the introduction of what he called the MINIS system, management information system for ministers, containing many of the features he had experienced in the private sector. The purpose of MINIS was, essentially, to assist a minister who sought to attempt to manage his department. It was very much a personal innovation of Mr Heseltine and how far it will spread beyond the confines of the Department of the Environment, and possibly Defence, is debatable. There seems no obvious enthusiasm for it in the civil service generally and it would only spread if pushed hard at a political level.

We have already referred to the attempt at corporate planning introduced by Edward Heath, the PAR system. It has now disappeared and has been succeeded, in a very different way, by the so-called Rayner scrutinies. The Rayner approach is much less corporate and much more specific. It attempts to identify areas of waste and inefficiency by asking the awkward question *why*, when civil servants and politicians are usually asking *how*. In one form or another the Rayner approach will probably continue, if only because it can be applied without ruffling too many feathers in the top echelons of policy making.

Whichever system of achieving efficiency is attempted, it has to be balanced against the need for accountability. A simple example may, perhaps, help to illustrate this. Many years ago, Marks and Spencer, from whom Lord Rayner was, of course, seconded, decided to dispense with tight, time consuming, departmental stock control in its stores. It came to the conclusion that, if it recruited its staff well and trusted them, any significant stock losses arising from the ending of stock control would be more than offset by the economies achieved in staff time: and it was proved right. In other words, it scrapped accountability in favour of efficiency.

If this kind of approach were to be generally applied in central or local government then it would be necessary to rethink the whole concept of responsible and accountable government. As things stand, some inefficiency would seem to be the price we inevitably pay for public accountability.

The police and the public

The United Kingdom has always prided itself on the quality of its police service, comparing it favourably with those of other countries. Particular features which are cited as the envy of the rest of the world include: the fact that policemen do not normally carry firearms; the concept of individual forces, locally based and locally controlled; the knowledge that there is only one kind of policeman, the 'bobby', with no para-military units; and the feeling that the police, like the judiciary, are non-political and subject ultimately only to the rule of law.

These features reflect, perhaps, a rather 'romantic' view of the modern policeman who must, of course, be equipped and organized to combat the criminal of today and not of the past. Up to the late 1950s police forces *were* essentially locally based, locally controlled, and locally accountable and could be numbered in their hundreds. Today they are essentially regional, subject to loose, almost vague, local control and accountability, and, by a series of amalgamations, have been reduced to less than 50.

The last major inquiry into the police service was by the Willink royal commission, which reported in 1962. Although it received, in evidence, quite a number of radical recommendations, including the centralization of the police, the eventual report was bland, safe, and 'establishment minded'. It was followed by the Police Act, 1964, which allowed local forces to amalgamate, increased the Home Secretary's powers of supervision and control, and, correspondingly, reduced those of local authorities. As a result, police forces outside Greater London are responsible to police committees, comprising two-thirds councillors and one-third magistrates, and the duties of the committees are restricted to maintaining a police force and appointing a chief constable, but even this appointment, as well as those of his deputy and assistants, are

243

subject to the Home Secretary's approval. In Greater London the police service is directly controlled by and responsible to the Home Secretary.

What we have seen in recent years, therefore, has been the establishment of large police forces, covering the area of several local authorities who are responsible for maintaining them but able to exercise very little control.

With improvements in the speed and ease of communication it seems sensible that police forces should not be confined in their operations to artificially small communities, but police accountability is an issue which has disturbed a number of people in recent years. Chief constables of some of the metropolitan forces, such as Kenneth Oxford of Merseyside and James Anderton of Greater Manchester, have become powerful and controversial figures, sometimes seeming almost contemptuous of their police committees.

The Conservative government of Mrs Thatcher, with its strong commitment to 'law and order', has strengthened the position of the police and sought to improve morale by adopting a more generous pay policy to that of other public sector workers. The police forces themselves seem to have moved discernibly to the right. The Police Federation, representing the majority of police officers, replaced James Callaghan as their spokesman in Parliament with Conservative MP Eldon Griffiths and the Superintendents' Association, representing senior officers, chose another Conservative MP Bernard Braine. During the 1979 general election the chairman of the Federation openly canvassed for the return of the death penalty.

These developments have taken place at a time when the police forces, without any obvious wish on their part, have become involved in politically sensitive issues. Social unrest in areas of high unemployment and social deprivation have put them under the social microscope as they have never been before: in Toxteth on Merseyside, in Moss Side in Lancashire, in Bristol, and in Brixton. The Brixton riots resulted in a penetrating inquiry by Lord Scarman who, in his report, while praising the police for avoiding a total collapse of law and order, said that he believed that a major cause of the riots was the young blacks' hostility to and loss of confidence in the police. In particular, he criticized 'hard' policing, lack of consultation, inadequate complaints procedures, and racist attitudes of some policemen. Evidence of racist attitudes was revealed in a later inquiry instigated by Sir David McNee, when he was Commissioner for the London metropolitan police. It is to the considerable credit of his successor, Sir Kenneth Newman, that he published the inquiry's critical report in its entirety and immediately started to take steps to improve the situation.

It is probably true to say that, over the whole country, the great majority of police officers behave fairly, honestly, and with commendable restraint but there will always be public disquiet, and it will grow if their accountability and position within the machinery of government is not better clarified. The obvious coordination of police activity during the miners' strike, in the first half of 1984, created a popular impression that it was under the direct control of the Home Secretary, even though this was denied. Their increasing use of firearms and their use as 'riot police' also creates concern, despite the liberal stance of Sir Kenneth Newman and people like John Alderson, the former chief constable of Devon and Cornwall.

There is no evidence of our becoming a 'police state', as is the case in some countries, but the police must hold and retain the confidence of the public, in all areas, in all stations in life, and at all ages. They constitute, in total, no more than about a five-hundredth of the population but they are an essential part.

What should be done? The police service must be clearly and openly 'depoliticized', on the premise that not only must justice be done but it must be seen to be done. There must be genuine 'community policing' everywhere: lessons might be learnt from the experience of police forces in some of the cities in the United States. It may be that the most satisfactory approach would be to appoint another royal commission, better selected and better briefed than was the Willink commission, and with a request that it be as expeditious as possible in its operation.

The future of local government

'Nowhere has democracy ever worked well without a great measure of local self-government. . . . Where the scope of the political measures become so large that the necessary knowledge is almost exclusively possessed by the bureaucracy, the creative impulses of the private person must flag.' This is a quotation from a book by a man who has, reputedly, had a great influence on the political attitude of Margaret Thatcher, Frederick Hayek.[4] She, presumably, would endorse his views and yet her administrations have witnessed a greater curtailment of the independence of local authorities than at any time in recent years.

Tighter control from the centre is evidenced by the following: borrowing ceilings for capital projects; restrictions on the use of direct labour organizations; tighter grant controls; the creation of urban development corporations with powers to take over planning and housing functions from local authorities in certain areas; increased planning powers for the Secretary of State for the Environment; restrictions on the levying of supplementary rates; rates capping; and legislation to abolish the Greater London Council and the other metropolitan counties. This increasing intervention in local affairs seems to stem from two sources: an almost obsessive concern to reduce public spending and borrowing, and a sense of frustration that the 'big spenders' are almost all Labour-controlled.

It was decades, rather than centuries, ago that many local councillors were genuine independents in politics and had sought election because of their desire to benefit their local communities. Today, local politics is often used as an anteroom to the national stage and views have become sharply polarized. Despite this growth in local party politics, the apathy of the ordinary man-in-the-street, as shown by the way he votes, or rather does not vote, grows rather than diminishes.

The services currently provided by local authorities cannot be centralized except at considerable expense and inconvenience. Local government is, therefore, likely to be a permanent feature of our society, but if it is to operate effectively, and if its members and officers are to continue to have pride in what they do, its independence must be restored, and even strengthened.

Is there a simple solution? No, of course not, but two actions could be taken which could do much to start the process of restoring local independence. Rates could be replaced by a more buoyant and fairer source of revenue, as the Layfield Committee recommended, and proportional representation, which now operates in local elections in Northern Ireland, could be extended to the rest of the United Kingdom. Will our politicians have the courage to grasp the nettle of local government reform and introduce such changes?

Final thoughts

Plus ça change, plus c'est la même chose, which is a Frenchman's way of saying that the more you change the more you return to where you started. This is particularly true of politics and government and there must have been many occasions when a world-weary permanent secretary has felt it necessary to defuse the enthusiasm of his minister for a scheme which was tried and found wanting many years before.

Because of the cyclical nature of public affairs, it is easy to become cynical about politics and politicians, yet most of them entered Parliament or the local council because they genuinely wished to reform and believed that they could. In case they happen to read these pages, these final words are addressed to them.

However complex or difficult the process of government becomes, we should not lose sight of basic principles. The public can be fooled for some of the time but the average person recognizes honesty and fairness when he sees it and is willing to extend a considerable amount of latitude if he believes the ultimate intentions are sound. The ordinary voter is more intelligent than many politicians allow and could well be trusted much more. To govern in a democratic society is to serve and not to prescribe: to administer is to provide and not to decree.

References

1. *The 1983 Reith Lectures, The Listener*, 10 November–15 December 1983.
2. Hoskyns, J. *Conservatism is not Enough, Political Quarterly*, January–March 1984.
3. Pliatzky, L. *Mandarins, Ministers and the Management of Britain, Political Quarterly*, January–March 1984.
4. Hayek, F. *The Road to Serfdom*, Routledge, 1976.

Select bibliography: a guide to further reading

The political framework

Blondel, J., *Political Parties*, Wildwood House, 1977.
— —, *Voters, Parties and Leaders: Social Fabric of British Politics*, Penguin, 1974.
Crick, B., *In Defence of Politics*, Penguin, 1973.
Richardson, J.J. and A.G. Jordan, *Governing under Pressure*, Martin Robertson, 1979.
Rose, R., *Politics in England: An Interpretation for the 1980's*, Faber, 1980.
Sampson, A., *The Changing Anatomy of Britain*, Hodder, 1982.
Sedgemore, B., *The Secret Constitution*, Hodder, 1980.

The institutional framework

Alexander, A., *Local Government in Britain since Reorganization*, Allen and Unwin, 1982.
Barker, A. (ed.), *Quangos in Britain: Government and the Networks of Public Policy Making*, Macmillan, 1982.
Bogdanor, V. *Devolution*, Oxford University Press, 1979.
Brown, R.G.S. and D.R. Steel, *The Administrative Process in Britain*, Methuen, 1971.
Byrne, T. *Local Government in Britain*, Penguin, 1981.
Clarke, R., *New Trends in Government I*, HMSO, 1971.
Elcock, H., *Politicians, Professionals and the Public in Local Authorities*, Methuen, 1982.
Jones, G. and J. Stewart, *The Case for Local Government*, Allen and Unwin, 1983.
King, A. (ed.), *The British Prime Minister: A Reader*, Macmillan, 1969.
Mackintosh, J.P., *The British Cabinet*, Stevens, 1977.
— —, *Government and Politics in Britain* (revised by P.G. Richards), Hutchinson, 1977.
Plowden, W. (ed.), *Policy and Practice: The Experience of Government*, RIPA, 1980.

People in public administration

Beaumont, P.B., *Government as Employer: Setting an Example?*, RIPA, 1981.
Fowler, A., *Personnel Management in Local Government*, Institute of Personnel Management, 1975.
Garrett, J., *Managing the Civil Service*, Heinemann, 1980.
Hawker, G., *Who's Master, Who's Servant?: Reforming Bureaucracy*, Allen and Unwin, 1981.

Kellner, P. and N. Crowther-Hunt, *The Civil Servants: An Inquiry into Britain's Ruling Class*, Futura, 1981.

Parris, H., *Staff Relations in the Civil Service: 50 Years of Whitleyism*, RIPA, 1973.

Poole, K.P., *The Local Government Service in England and Wales*, Allen and Unwin, 1978.

Thomson, A.W.J. and P.B. Beaumont, *Public Sector Bargaining: A Study of Relative Gain*, Saxon House, 1978.

The state and the economy

Burch, M. and B. Wood, *Public Policy in Britain*, Martin Robertson, 1983.

Coombes, D., *Representative Government and Economic Power*, Heinemann, 1982.

Grant, W., *The Political Economy of Industrial Policy*, Butterworth, 1982.

Levitt, R., *Implementing Public Policy*, Croom Helm, 1980.

Pliatzky, L., *Getting and Spending: Public Expenditure, Employment and Inflation*, Blackwell, 1982.

Pryke, R., *The Nationalized Industries: Policies and Performance since 1968*, Martin Robertson, 1981.

The public interest and the private interest

Boaden, N., M. Goldsmith and P. Stringer, *Public Participation in Local Services*, Longman, 1982.

Darke, R. and R. Walker, *Local Government and the Public*, Hill, 1977.

Delbridge, R. and M. Smith (eds), *Consuming Secrets: How Official Security Affects Everyday Life in Britain*, Hutchinson, 1982.

Hill, M., *The State, Administration and the Individual*, Fontana, 1976.

James, M., *The Politics of Secrecy: Confidential Government and the Public Right to Know*, Penguin, 1982.

Justice, *The Citizen and the Administration*, Stevens, 1973.

——, *The Local Ombudsmen: A Review of the First Five Years*, Stevens, 1980.

——, *Our Fettered Ombudsman*, Stevens, 1977.

RIPA, *Parliament and the Executive*, RIPA, 1982.

Robertson, K.G., *Public Secrets: A Study in the Development of Government Secrecy*, Macmillan, 1982.

Stacey, F., *Ombudsmen Compared*, Oxford University Press, 1978.

Wheare, K.C., *Maladministration and its Remedies*, Stevens, 1974.

Wraith, R. E., *Open Government: The British Interpretation*, RIPA, 1977.

Index